GOTHAM CITY GARAGE

VOLUME 2

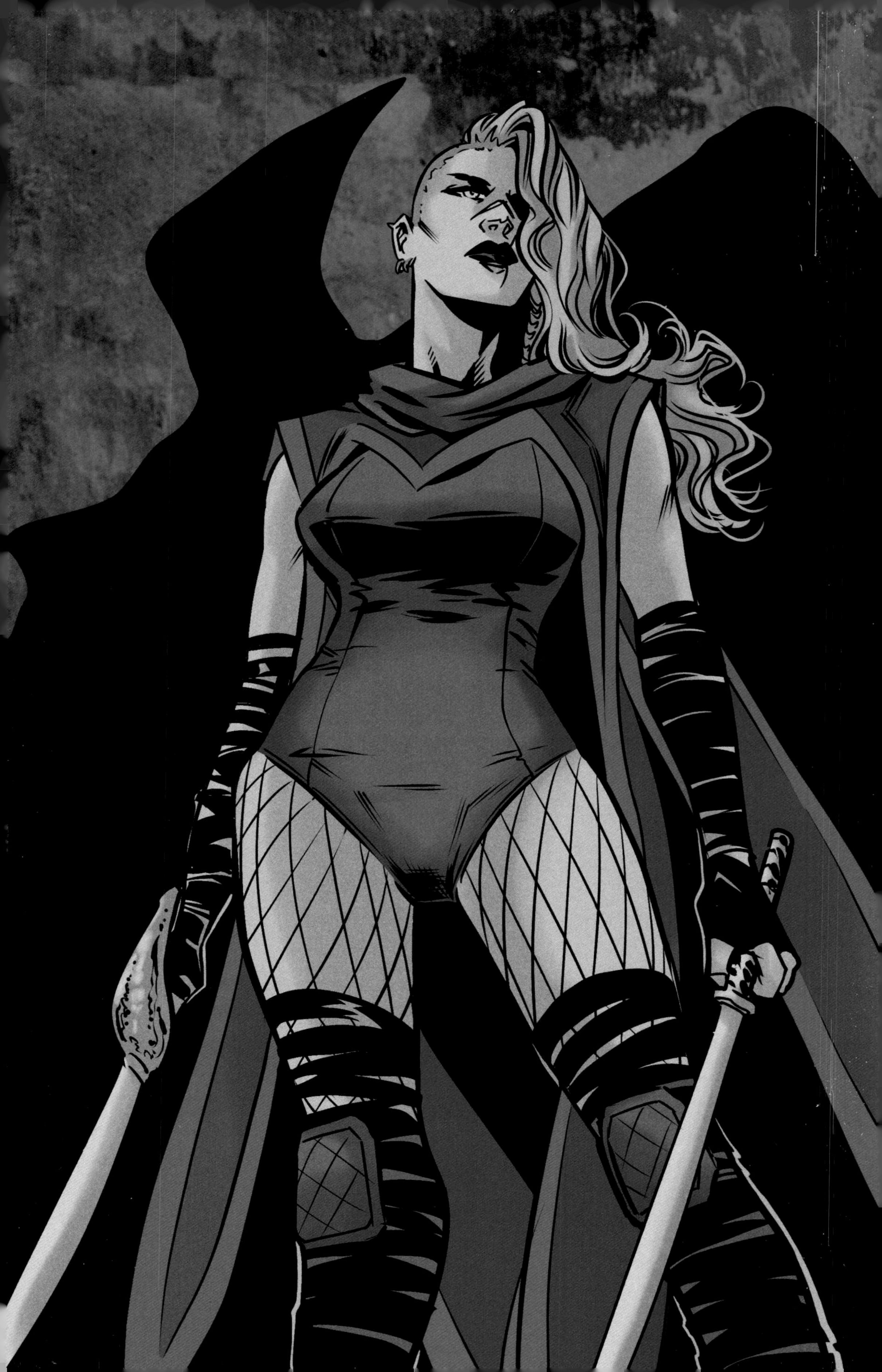

GOTHAM CITY GARAGE

VOLUME 2

COLLIN KELLY • JACKSON LANZING
writers

**BRIAN CHING • MING DOYLE • ANEKE
LYNNE YOSHII • NEIL GOOGE • ERYK DONOVAN
DARICK ROBERTSON • COLLEEN DORAN**
artists

**KELLY FITZPATRICK • TONY AVIÑA
TRISH MULVIHILL • COLLEEN DORAN**
colorists

WES ABBOTT
letterer

DOUG MAHNKE and WIL QUINTANA
collection cover artists

SUPERGIRL based on characters created by JERRY SIEGEL and JOE SHUSTER
By special arrangement with the Jerry Siegel family

KRISTY QUINN Editor - Original Series • **JEB WOODARD** Group Editor - Collected Editions • **ERIKA ROTHBERG** Editor - Collected Edition
STEVE COOK Design Director - Books • **SHANNON STEWART** Publication Design

BOB HARRAS Senior VP - Editor-in-Chief, DC Comics • **PAT McCALLUM** Executive Editor, DC Comics

DAN DiDIO Publisher • **JIM LEE** Publisher & Chief Creative Officer
AMIT DESAI Executive VP - Business & Marketing Strategy, Direct to Consumer & Global Franchise Management
BOBBIE CHASE VP & Executive Editor, Young Reader & Talent Development
MARK CHIARELLO Senior VP - Art, Design & Collected Editions • **JOHN CUNNINGHAM** Senior VP - Sales & Trade Marketing
BRIAR DARDEN VP - Business Affairs • **ANNE DePIES** Senior VP - Business Strategy, Finance & Administration
DON FALLETTI VP - Manufacturing Operations • **LAWRENCE GANEM** VP - Editorial Administration & Talent Relations
ALISON GILL Senior VP - Manufacturing & Operations • **JASON GREENBERG** VP - Business Strategy & Finance
HANK KANALZ Senior VP - Editorial Strategy & Administration • **JAY KOGAN** Senior VP - Legal Affairs
NICK J. NAPOLITANO VP - Manufacturing Administration • **LISETTE OSTERLOH** VP - Digital Marketing & Events
EDDIE SCANNELL VP - Consumer Marketing • **COURTNEY SIMMONS** Senior VP - Publicity & Communications
JIM (SKI) SOKOLOWSKI VP - Comic Book Specialty Sales & Trade Marketing
NANCY SPEARS VP - Mass, Book, Digital Sales & Trade Marketing • **MICHELE R. WELLS** VP - Content Strategy

GOTHAM CITY GARAGE VOL. 2

DC Comics, 2900 West Alameda Ave., Burbank, CA 91505
Printed by Times Printing, LLC, Random Lake, WI, USA. 10/5/18. First Printing.
ISBN: 978-1-4012-8498-5

Library of Congress Cataloging-in-Publication Data is available.

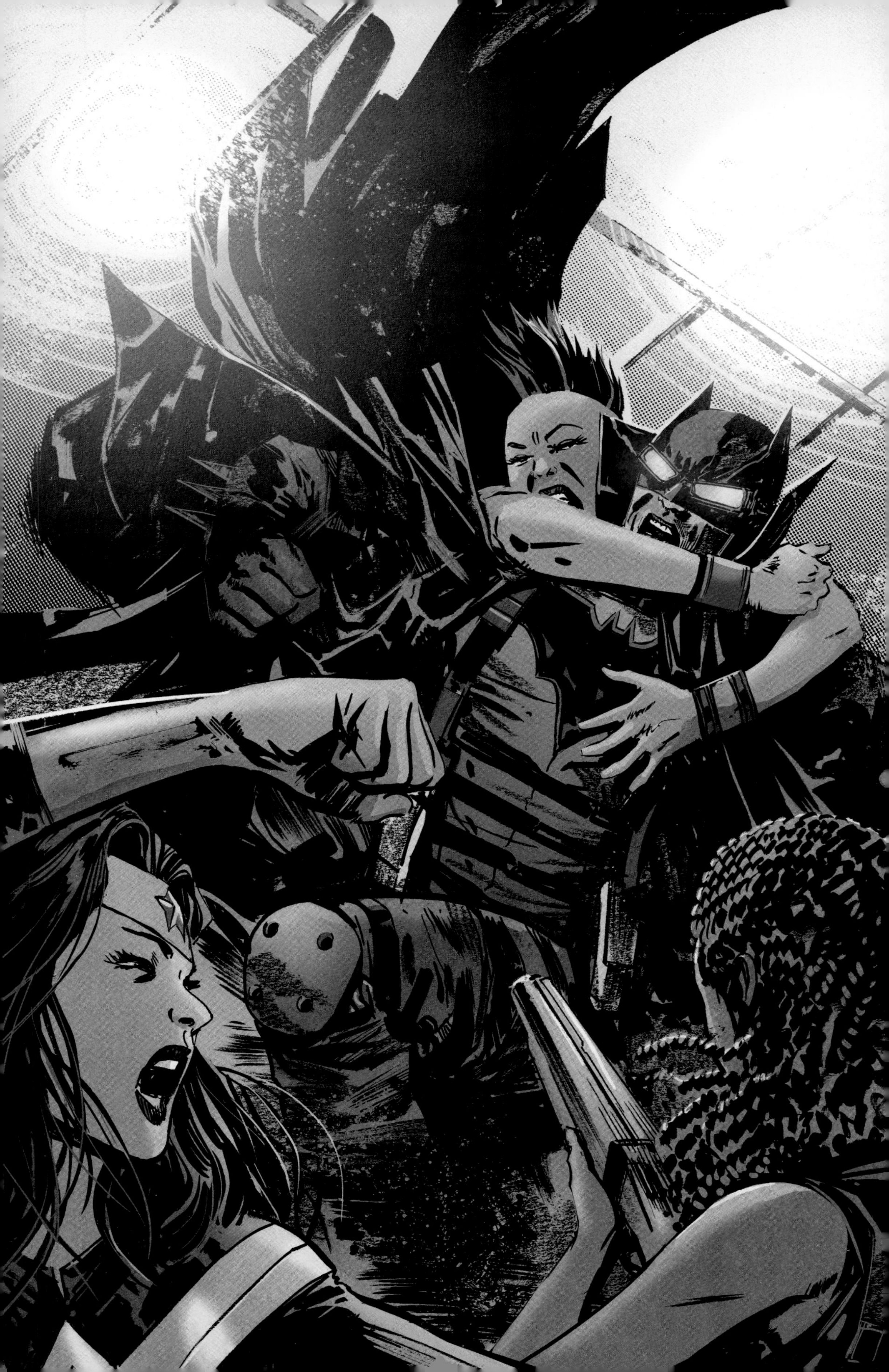

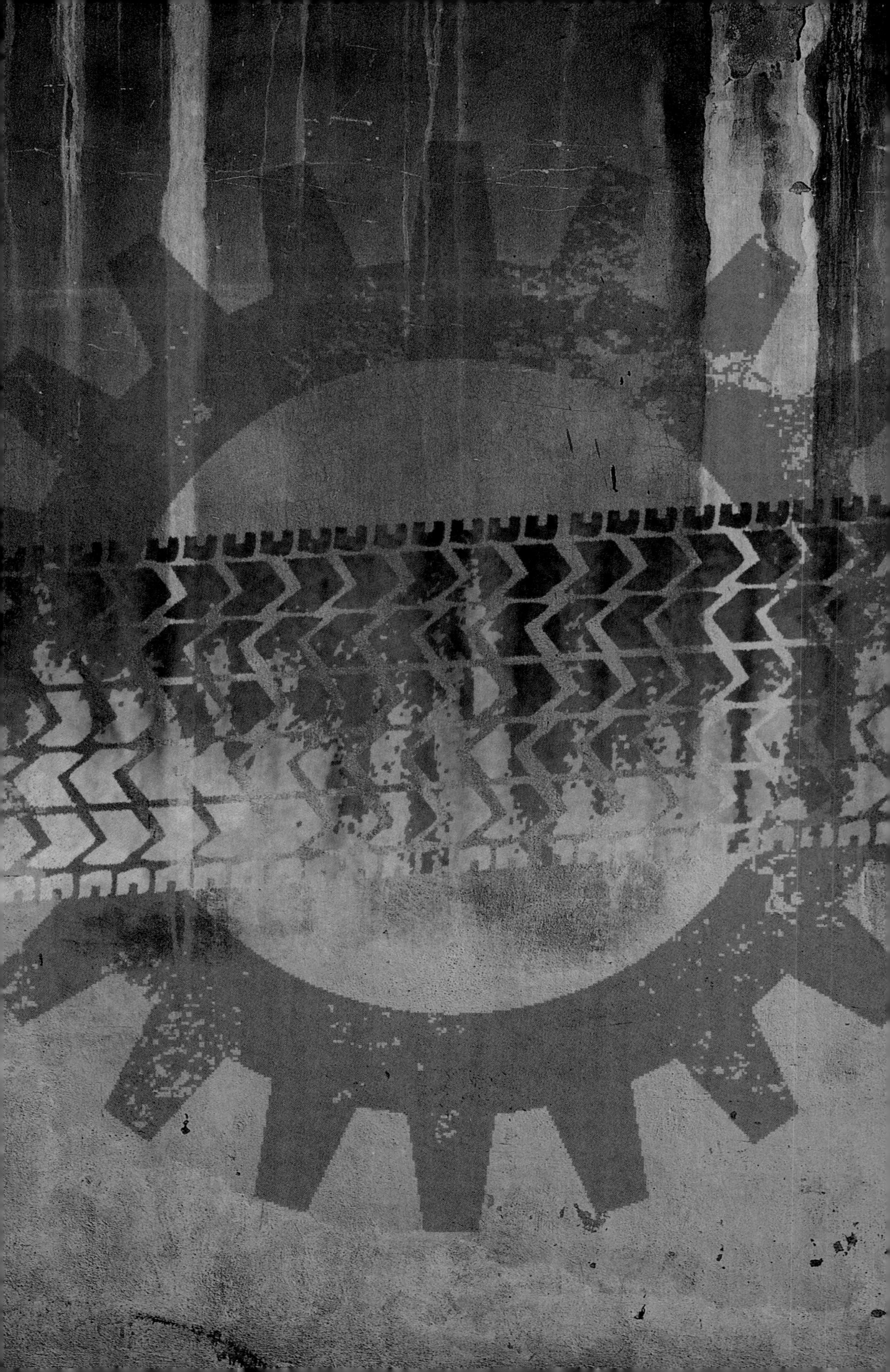

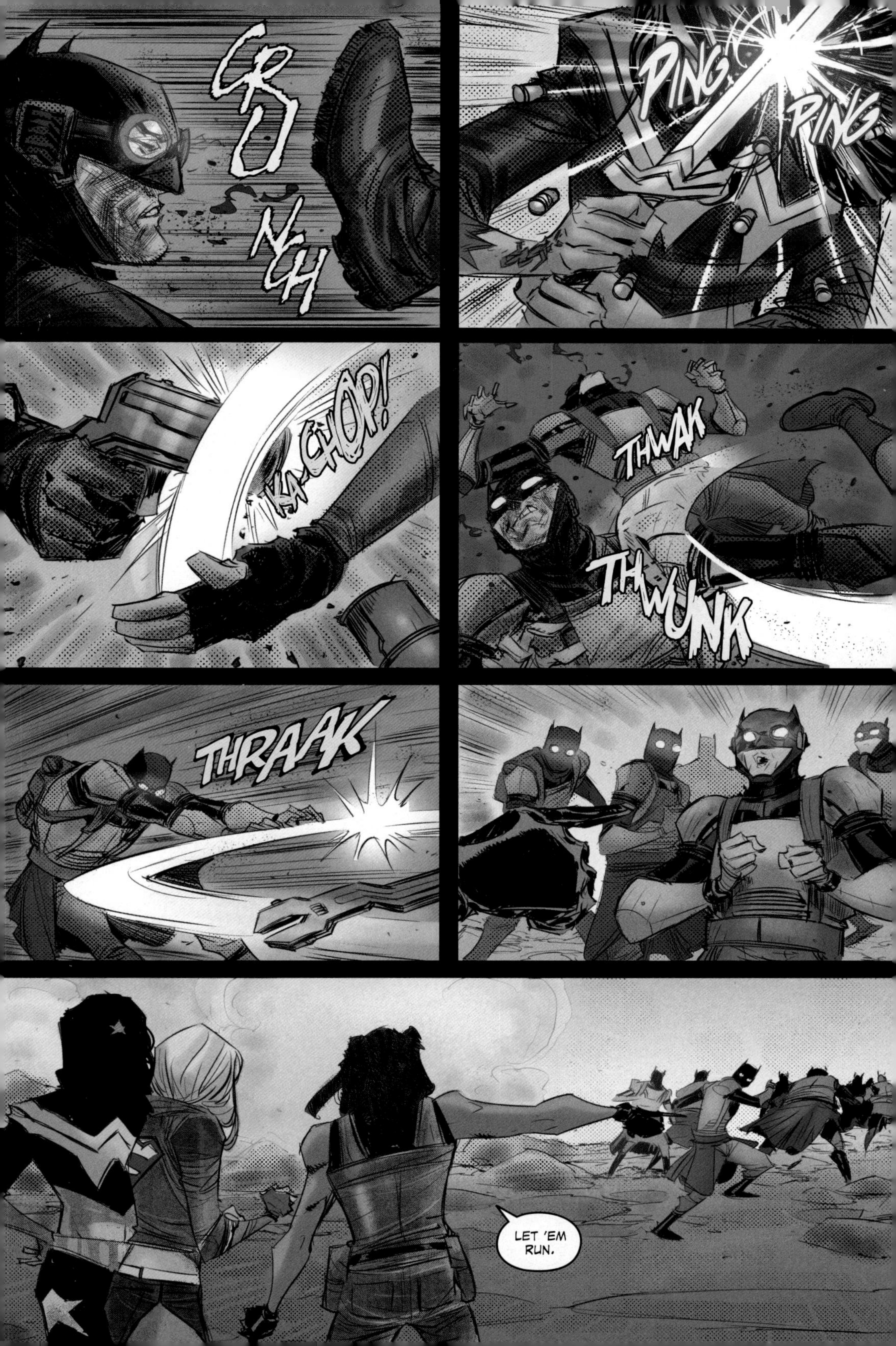

CRUNCH
PING
PING
KA-CHOP!
THWAK
THWUNK
THRAAK
LET 'EM RUN.

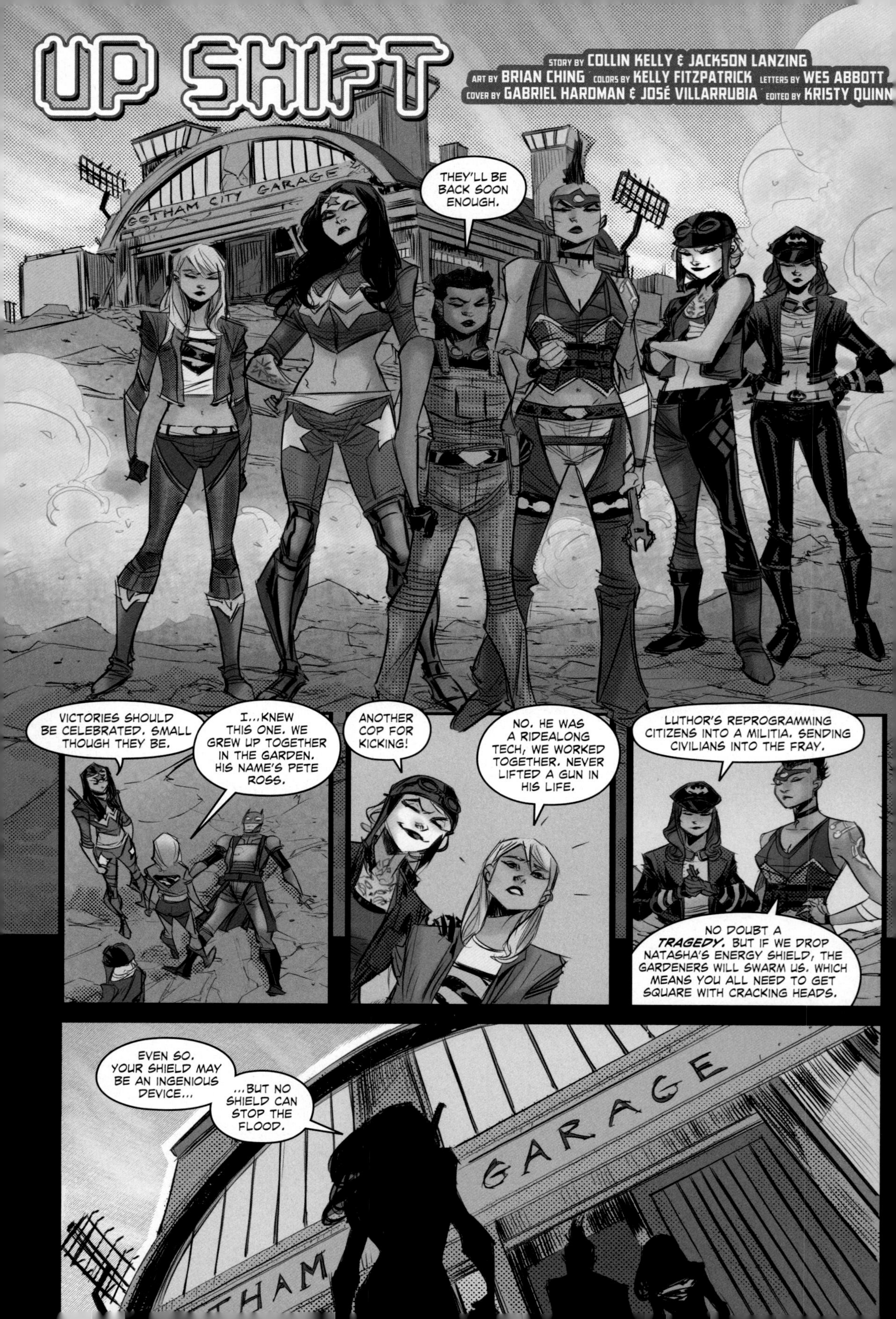
UP SHIFT
STORY BY COLLIN KELLY & JACKSON LANZING
ART BY BRIAN CHING COLORS BY KELLY FITZPATRICK LETTERS BY WES ABBOTT
COVER BY GABRIEL HARDMAN & JOSÉ VILLARRUBIA EDITED BY KRISTY QUINN
GOTHAM CITY GARAGE
THEY'LL BE BACK SOON ENOUGH.
VICTORIES SHOULD BE CELEBRATED. SMALL THOUGH THEY BE.
I...KNEW THIS ONE. WE GREW UP TOGETHER IN THE GARDEN. HIS NAME'S PETE ROSS.
ANOTHER COP FOR KICKING!
NO. HE WAS A RIDEALONG TECH, WE WORKED TOGETHER. NEVER LIFTED A GUN IN HIS LIFE.
LUTHOR'S REPROGRAMMING CITIZENS INTO A MILITIA. SENDING CIVILIANS INTO THE FRAY.
NO DOUBT A *TRAGEDY*. BUT IF WE DROP NATASHA'S ENERGY SHIELD, THE GARDENERS WILL SWARM US. WHICH MEANS YOU ALL NEED TO GET SQUARE WITH CRACKING HEADS.
EVEN SO. YOUR SHIELD MAY BE AN INGENIOUS DEVICE...
...BUT NO SHIELD CAN STOP THE FLOOD.
GARAGE
THAM

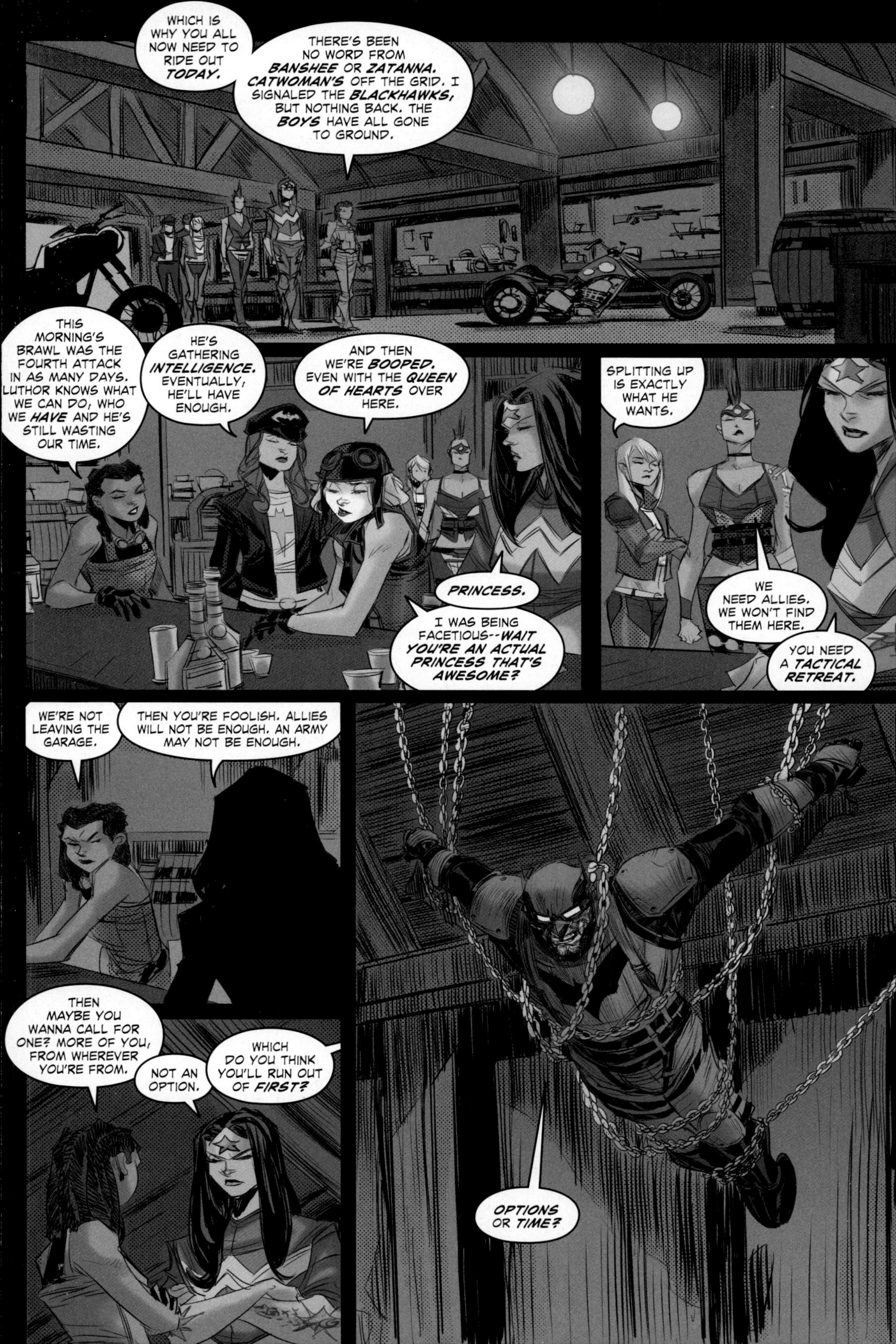
WHICH IS WHY YOU ALL NOW NEED TO RIDE OUT TODAY.
THERE'S BEEN NO WORD FROM BANSHEE OR ZATANNA. CATWOMAN'S OFF THE GRID. I SIGNALED THE BLACKHAWKS, BUT NOTHING BACK. THE BOYS HAVE ALL GONE TO GROUND.
THIS MORNING'S BRAWL WAS THE FOURTH ATTACK IN AS MANY DAYS. LUTHOR KNOWS WHAT WE CAN DO, WHO WE HAVE AND HE'S STILL WASTING OUR TIME.
HE'S GATHERING INTELLIGENCE. EVENTUALLY, HE'LL HAVE ENOUGH.
AND THEN WE'RE BOOPED. EVEN WITH THE QUEEN OF HEARTS OVER HERE.
PRINCESS.
I WAS BEING FACETIOUS--WAIT YOU'RE AN ACTUAL PRINCESS THAT'S AWESOME?
SPLITTING UP IS EXACTLY WHAT HE WANTS.
WE NEED ALLIES. WE WON'T FIND THEM HERE.
YOU NEED A TACTICAL RETREAT.
WE'RE NOT LEAVING THE GARAGE.
THEN YOU'RE FOOLISH. ALLIES WILL NOT BE ENOUGH. AN ARMY MAY NOT BE ENOUGH.
THEN MAYBE YOU WANNA CALL FOR ONE? MORE OF YOU, FROM WHEREVER YOU'RE FROM.
NOT AN OPTION.
WHICH DO YOU THINK YOU'LL RUN OUT OF FIRST?
OPTIONS OR TIME?

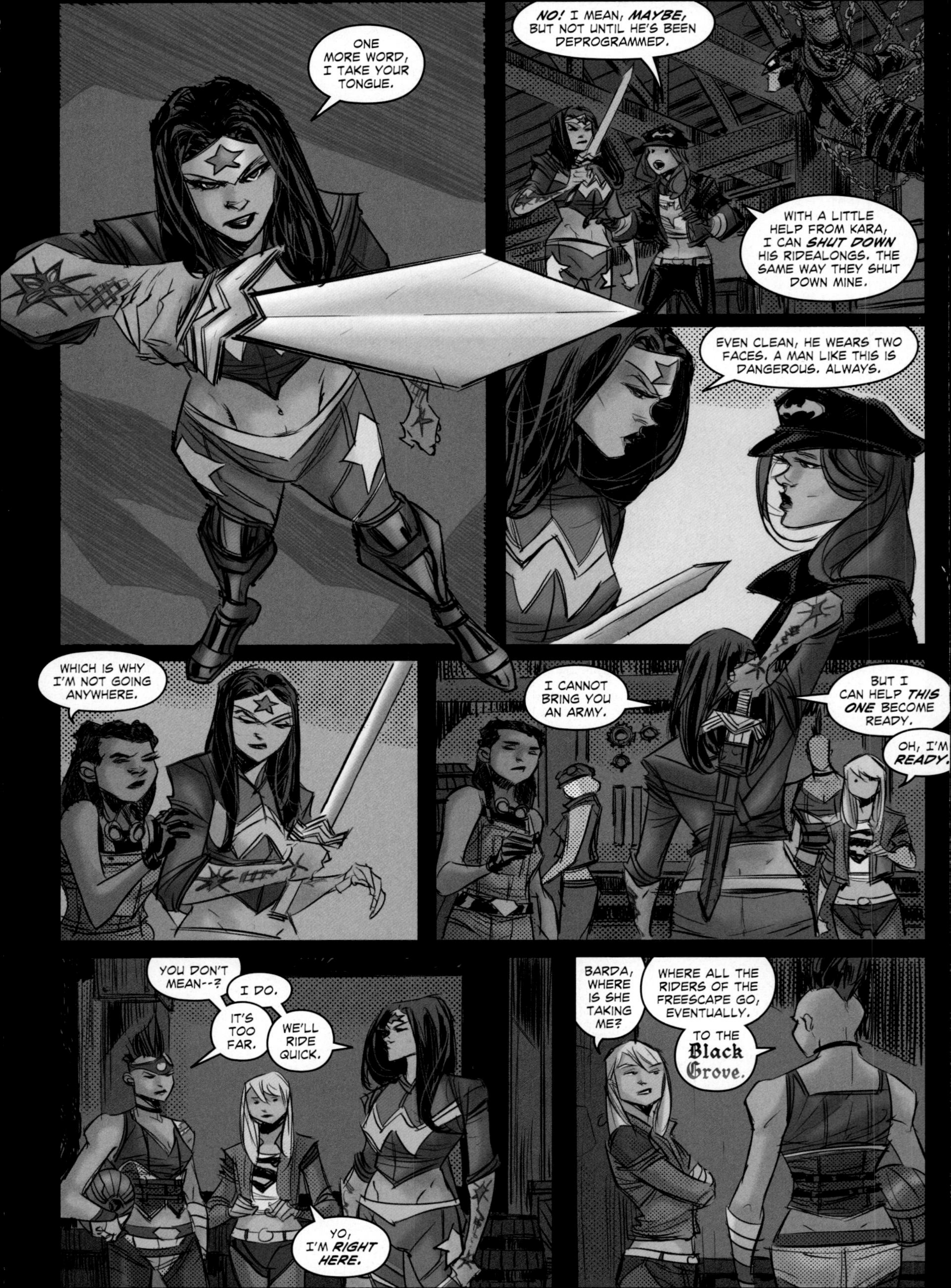
ONE MORE WORD, I TAKE YOUR TONGUE.
NO! I MEAN, MAYBE, BUT NOT UNTIL HE'S BEEN DEPROGRAMMED.
WITH A LITTLE HELP FROM KARA, I CAN SHUT DOWN HIS RIDEALONGS. THE SAME WAY THEY SHUT DOWN MINE.
EVEN CLEAN, HE WEARS TWO FACES. A MAN LIKE THIS IS DANGEROUS. ALWAYS.
WHICH IS WHY I'M NOT GOING ANYWHERE.
I CANNOT BRING YOU AN ARMY.
BUT I CAN HELP THIS ONE BECOME READY.
OH, I'M READY.
YOU DON'T MEAN--?
I DO.
IT'S TOO FAR.
WE'LL RIDE QUICK.
YO, I'M RIGHT HERE.
BARDA, WHERE IS SHE TAKING ME?
WHERE ALL THE RIDERS OF THE FREESCAPE GO, EVENTUALLY.
TO THE Black Grove.

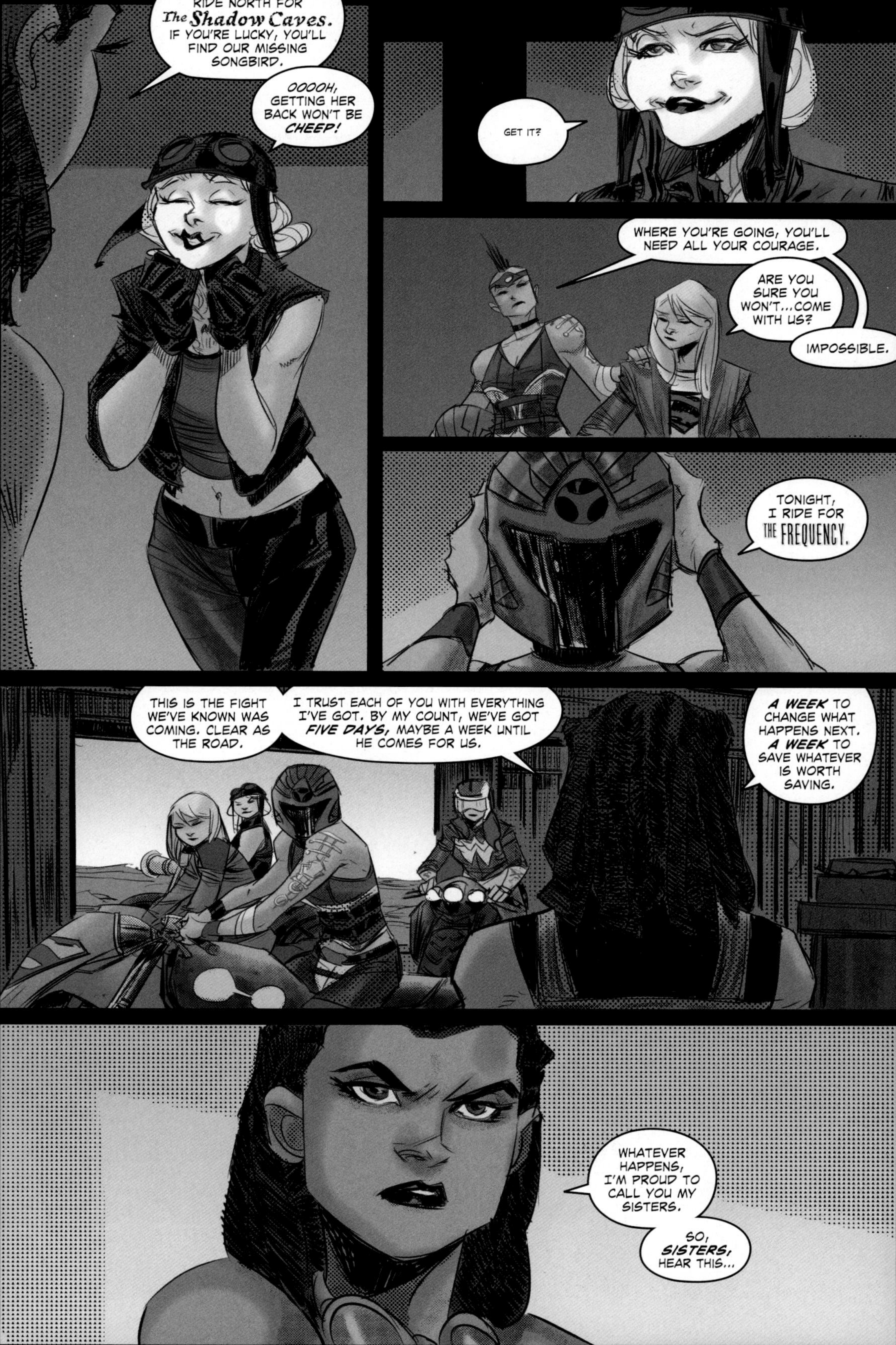
HARLEY, YOU'LL RIDE NORTH FOR The Shadow Caves. IF YOU'RE LUCKY, YOU'LL FIND OUR MISSING SONGBIRD.
OOOOH, GETTING HER BACK WON'T BE CHEEP!
GET IT?
WHERE YOU'RE GOING, YOU'LL NEED ALL YOUR COURAGE.
ARE YOU SURE YOU WON'T...COME WITH US?
IMPOSSIBLE.
TONIGHT, I RIDE FOR THE FREQUENCY.
THIS IS THE FIGHT WE'VE KNOWN WAS COMING. CLEAR AS THE ROAD.
I TRUST EACH OF YOU WITH EVERYTHING I'VE GOT. BY MY COUNT, WE'VE GOT FIVE DAYS, MAYBE A WEEK UNTIL HE COMES FOR US.
A WEEK TO CHANGE WHAT HAPPENS NEXT. A WEEK TO SAVE WHATEVER IS WORTH SAVING.
WHATEVER HAPPENS, I'M PROUD TO CALL YOU MY SISTERS.
SO, SISTERS, HEAR THIS...

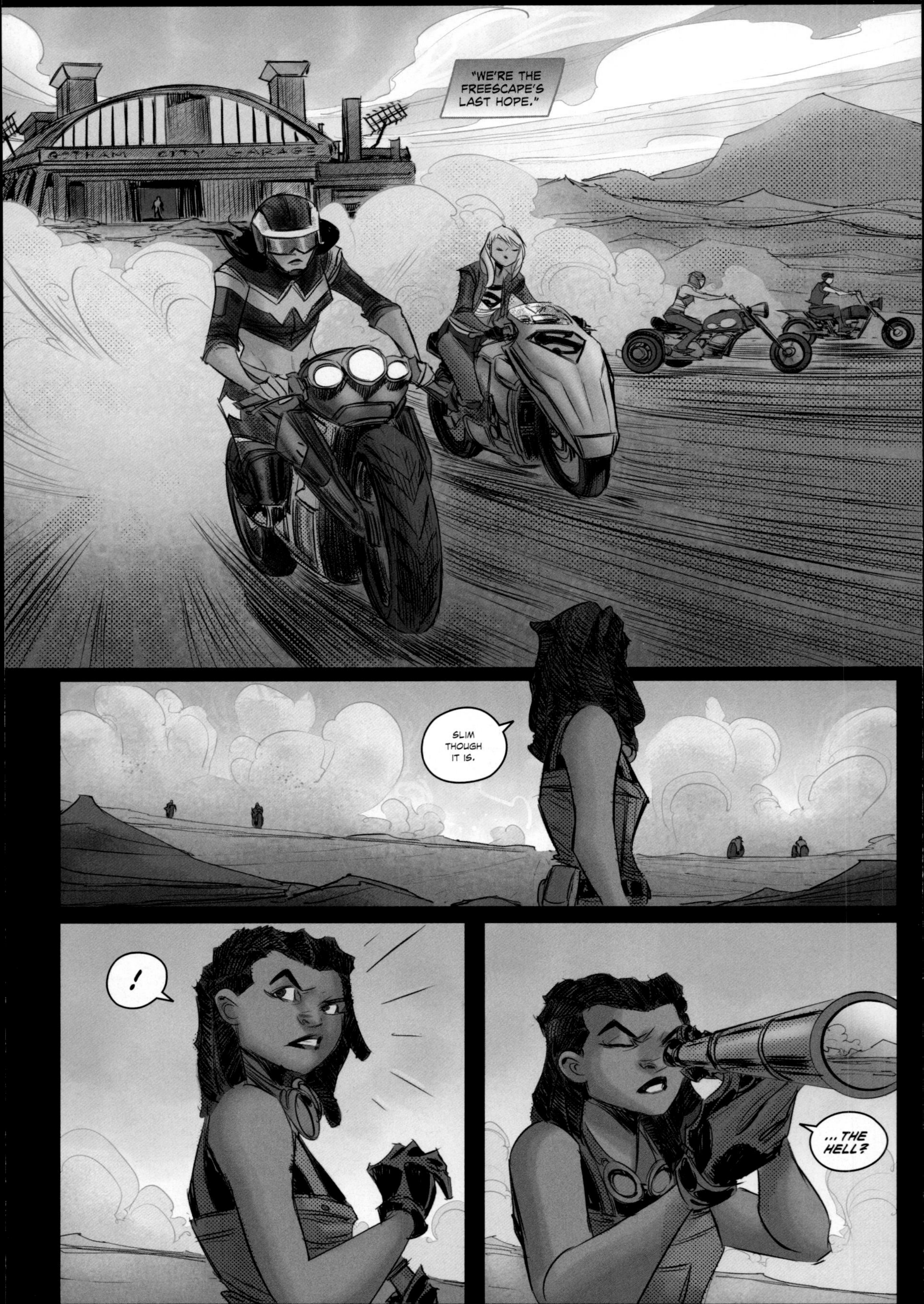
"WE'RE THE FREESCAPE'S LAST HOPE."
GOTHAM CITY GARAGE
SLIM THOUGH IT IS.
!
...THE HELL?

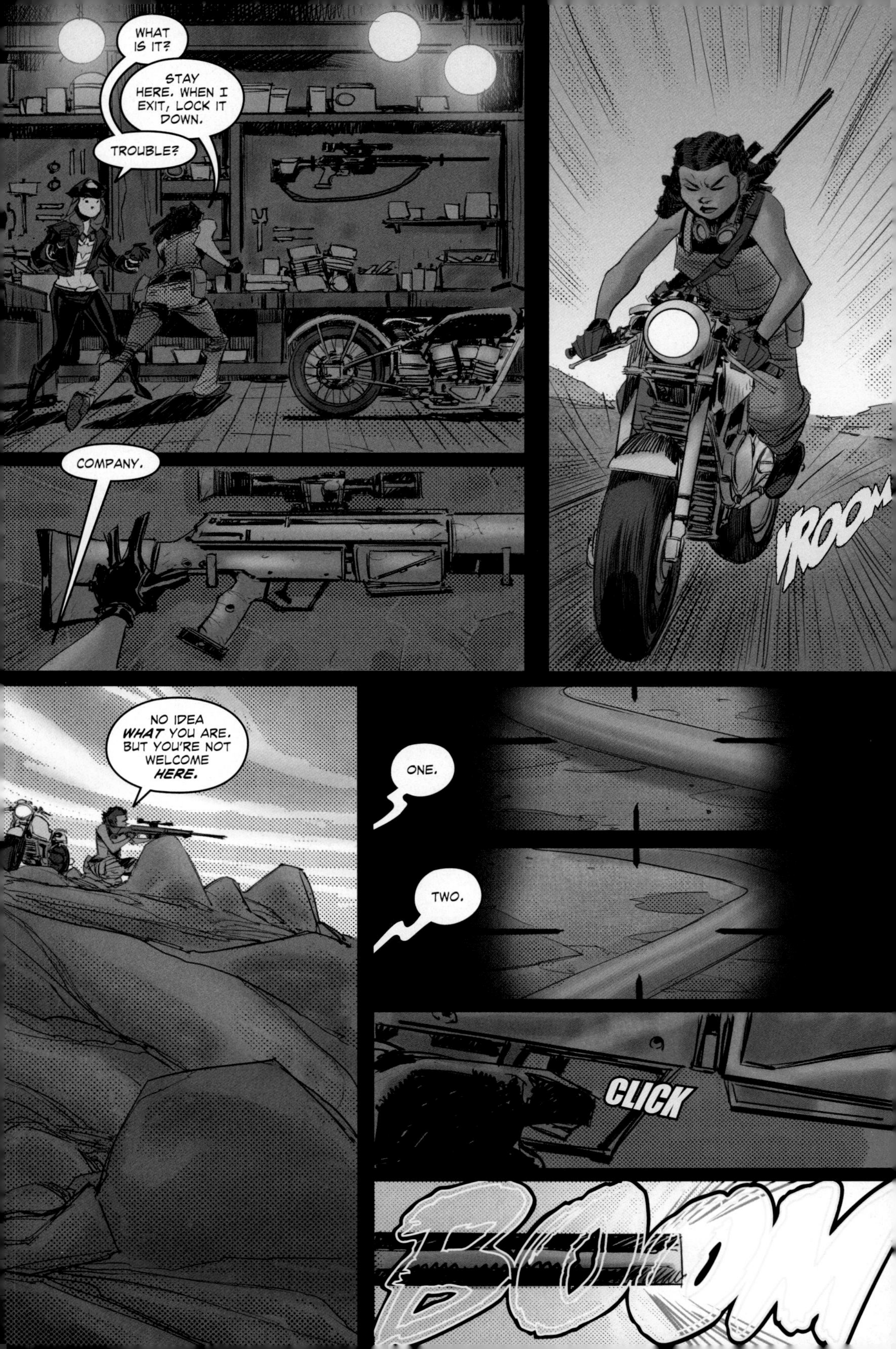
WHAT IS IT?
STAY HERE. WHEN I EXIT, LOCK IT DOWN.
TROUBLE?
COMPANY.
VROOM
NO IDEA *WHAT* YOU ARE. BUT YOU'RE NOT WELCOME *HERE.*
ONE.
TWO.
CLICK
BOOM

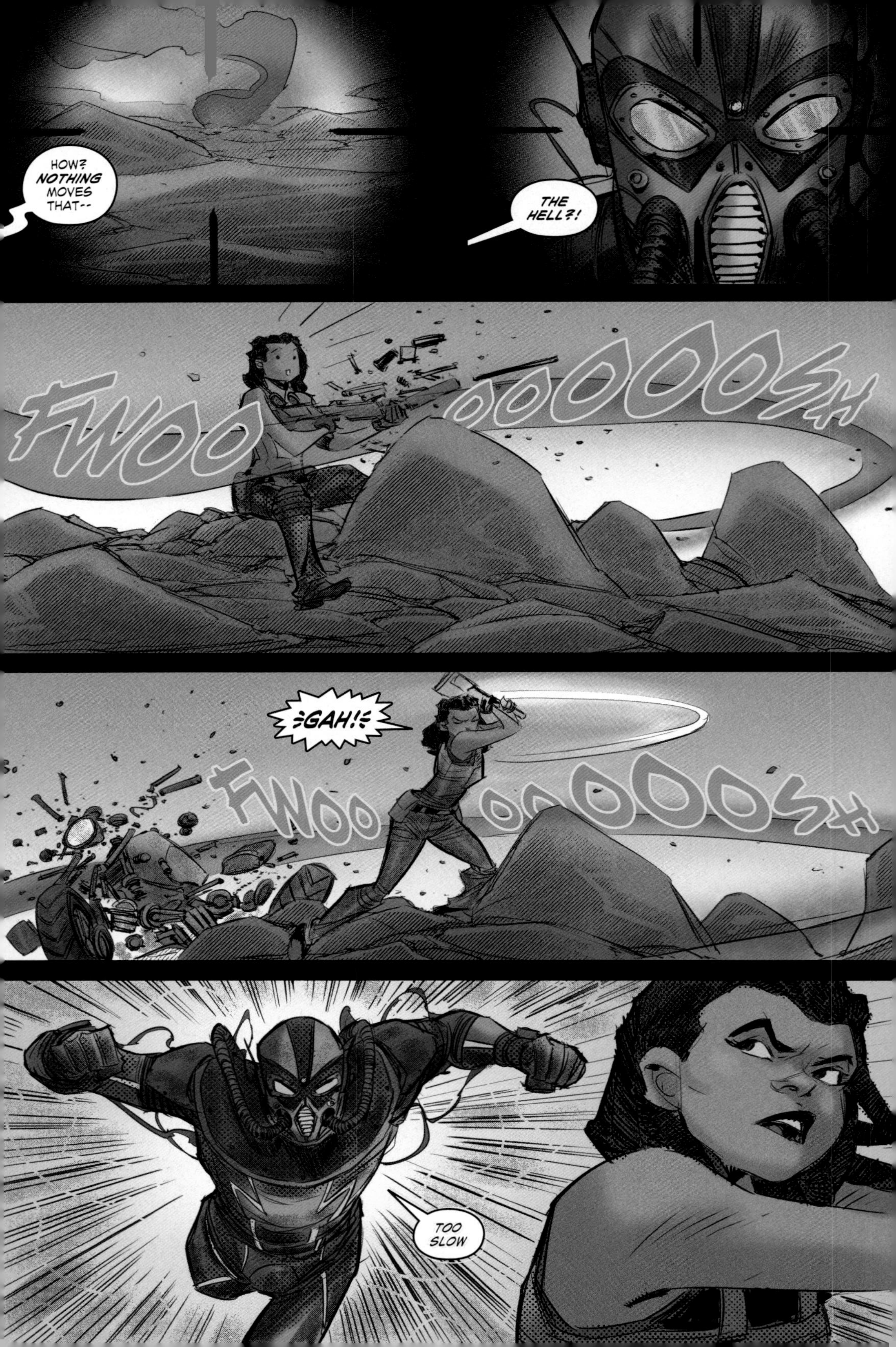

HOW? NOTHING MOVES THAT--
THE HELL?!
FWOOOOOOOOSH
GAH!
FWOOOOOOOOSH
TOO SLOW

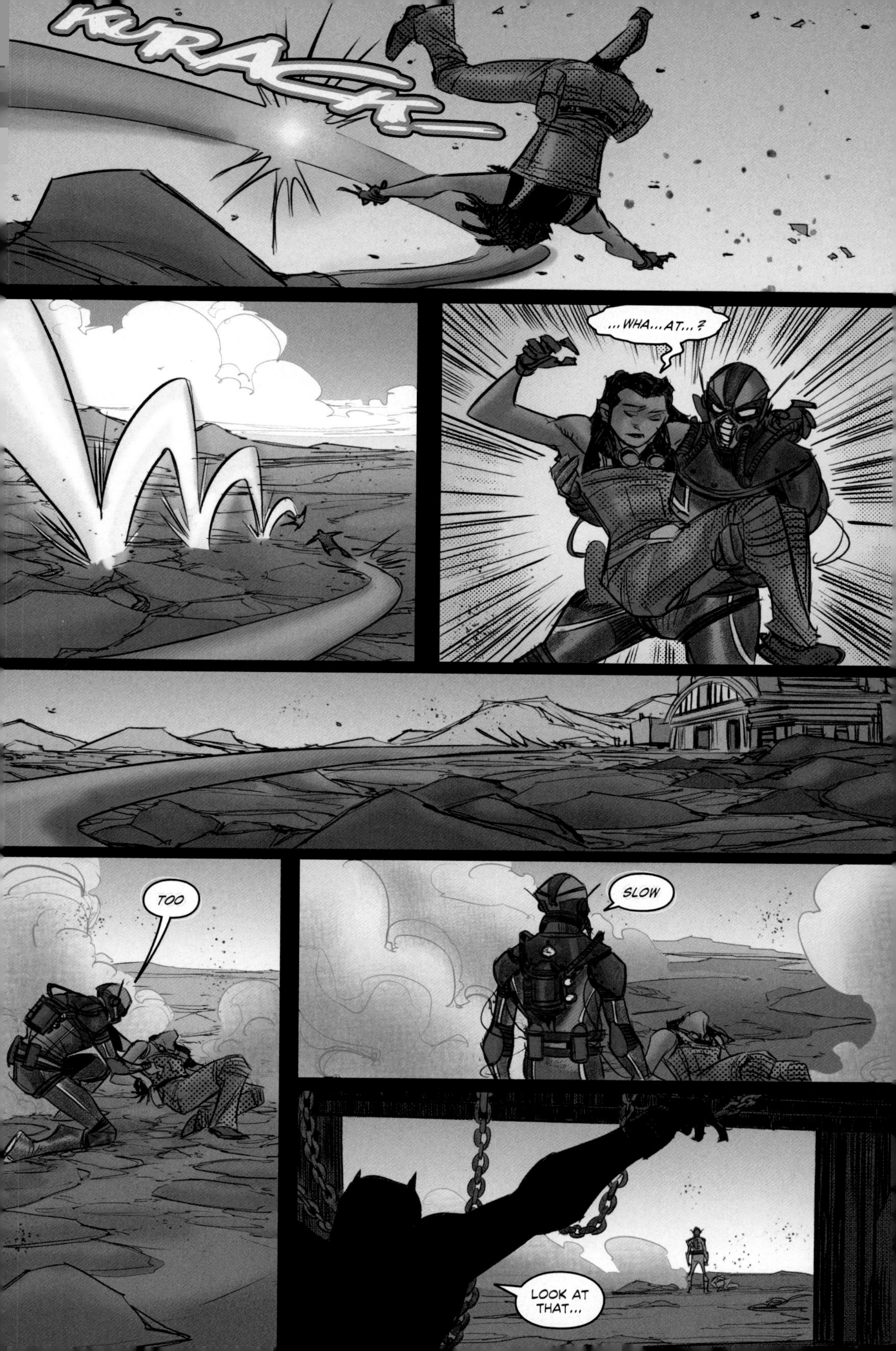
KKRAAK!!
...WHA...AT...?
TOO
SLOW
LOOK AT THAT...

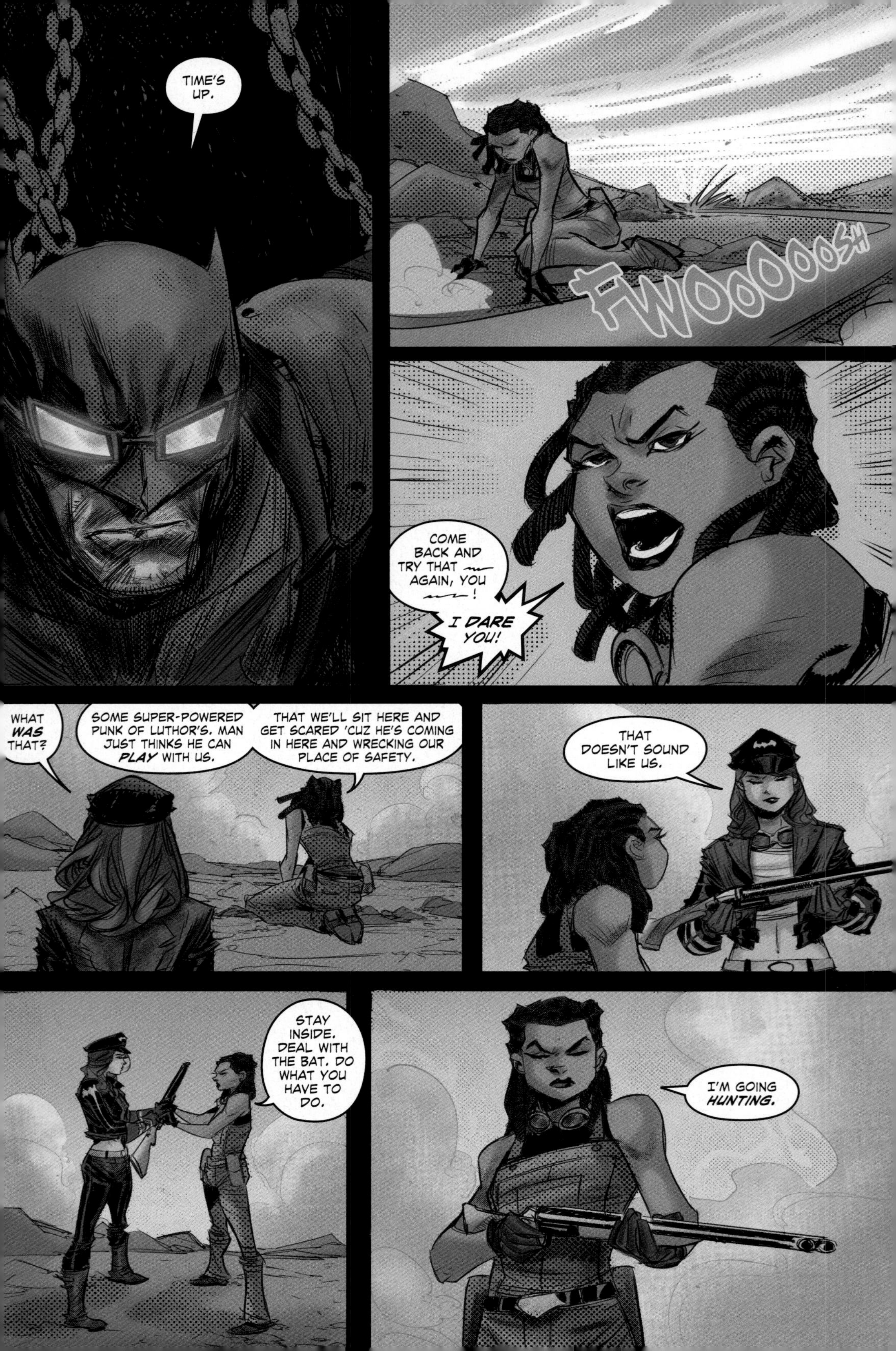
TIME'S UP.
FWOOOOOSH
COME BACK AND TRY THAT ~~ AGAIN, YOU ~~!
I DARE YOU!
WHAT WAS THAT?
SOME SUPER-POWERED PUNK OF LUTHOR'S. MAN JUST THINKS HE CAN PLAY WITH US.
THAT WE'LL SIT HERE AND GET SCARED 'CUZ HE'S COMING IN HERE AND WRECKING OUR PLACE OF SAFETY.
THAT DOESN'T SOUND LIKE US.
STAY INSIDE. DEAL WITH THE BAT. DO WHAT YOU HAVE TO DO.
I'M GOING HUNTING.

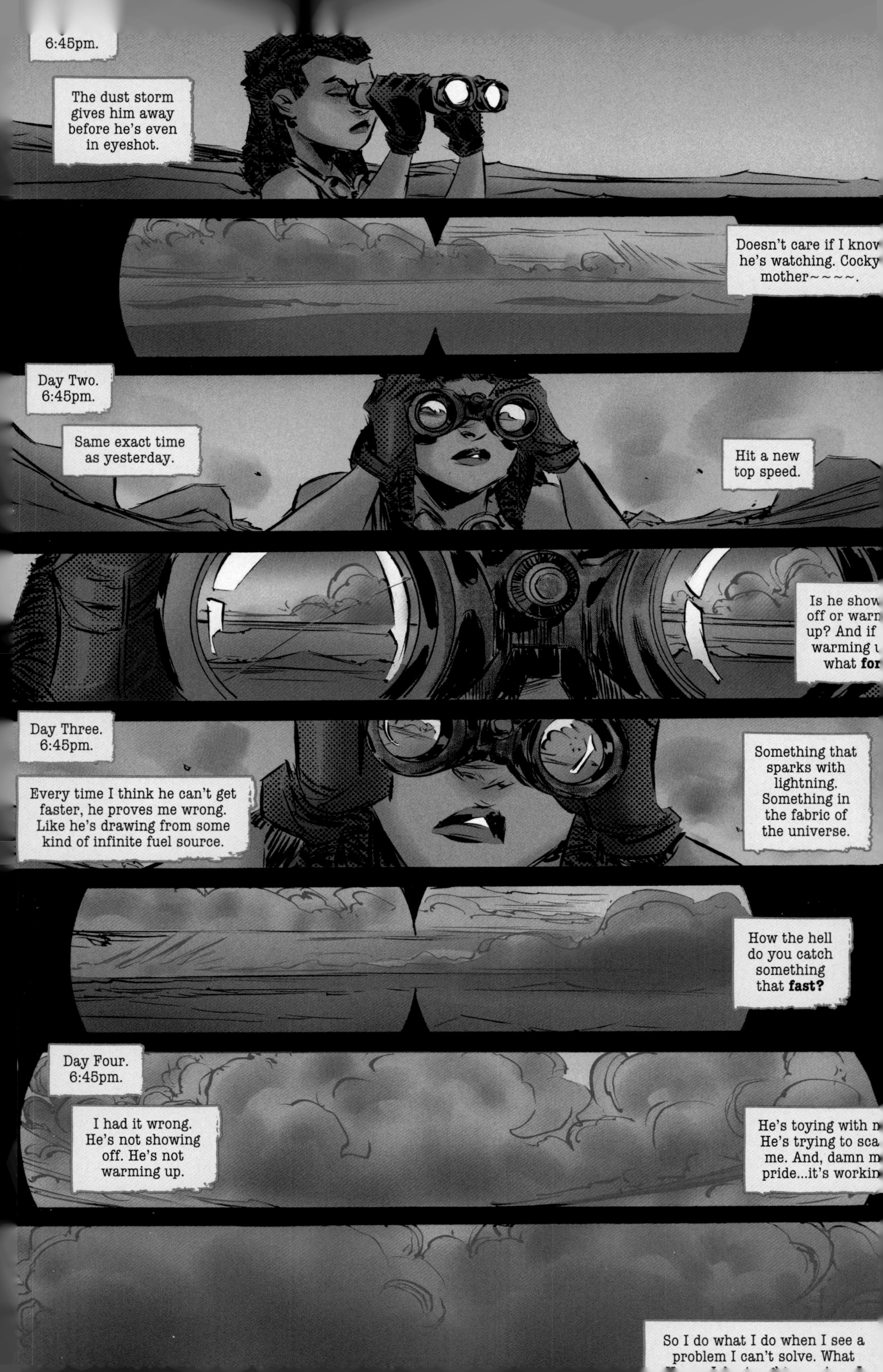
6:45pm.
The dust storm gives him away before he's even in eyeshot.
Doesn't care if I knov he's watching. Cocky mother~~~~.
Day Two. 6:45pm.
Same exact time as yesterday.
Hit a new top speed.
Is he show off or warn up? And if warming u what for
Day Three. 6:45pm.
Every time I think he can't get faster, he proves me wrong. Like he's drawing from some kind of infinite fuel source.
Something that sparks with lightning. Something in the fabric of the universe.
How the hell do you catch something that **fast?**
Day Four. 6:45pm.
I had it wrong. He's not showing off. He's not warming up.
He's toying with n He's trying to sca me. And, damn m pride...it's workin
So I do what I do when I see a problem I can't solve. What

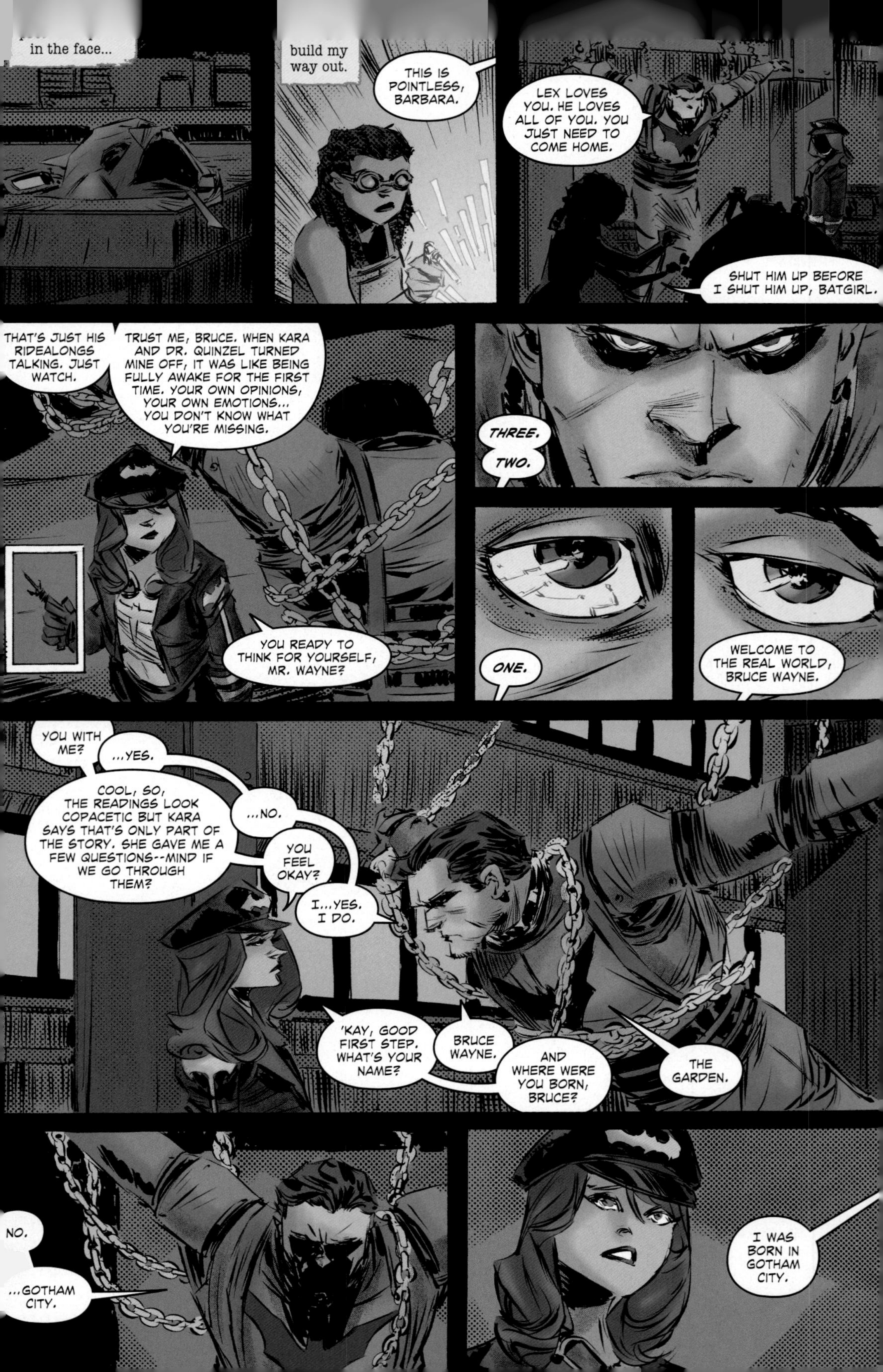
in the face...
build my way out.
THIS IS POINTLESS, BARBARA.
LEX LOVES YOU. HE LOVES ALL OF YOU. YOU JUST NEED TO COME HOME.
SHUT HIM UP BEFORE I SHUT HIM UP, BATGIRL.
THAT'S JUST HIS RIDEALONGS TALKING. JUST WATCH.
TRUST ME, BRUCE. WHEN KARA AND DR. QUINZEL TURNED MINE OFF, IT WAS LIKE BEING FULLY AWAKE FOR THE FIRST TIME. YOUR OWN OPINIONS, YOUR OWN EMOTIONS... YOU DON'T KNOW WHAT YOU'RE MISSING.
YOU READY TO THINK FOR YOURSELF, MR. WAYNE?
THREE.
TWO.
ONE.
WELCOME TO THE REAL WORLD, BRUCE WAYNE.
YOU WITH ME?
...YES.
COOL, SO, THE READINGS LOOK COPACETIC BUT KARA SAYS THAT'S ONLY PART OF THE STORY. SHE GAVE ME A FEW QUESTIONS--MIND IF WE GO THROUGH THEM?
...NO.
YOU FEEL OKAY?
I...YES. I DO.
'KAY, GOOD FIRST STEP. WHAT'S YOUR NAME?
BRUCE WAYNE.
AND WHERE WERE YOU BORN, BRUCE?
THE GARDEN.
NO.
...GOTHAM CITY.
I WAS BORN IN GOTHAM CITY.

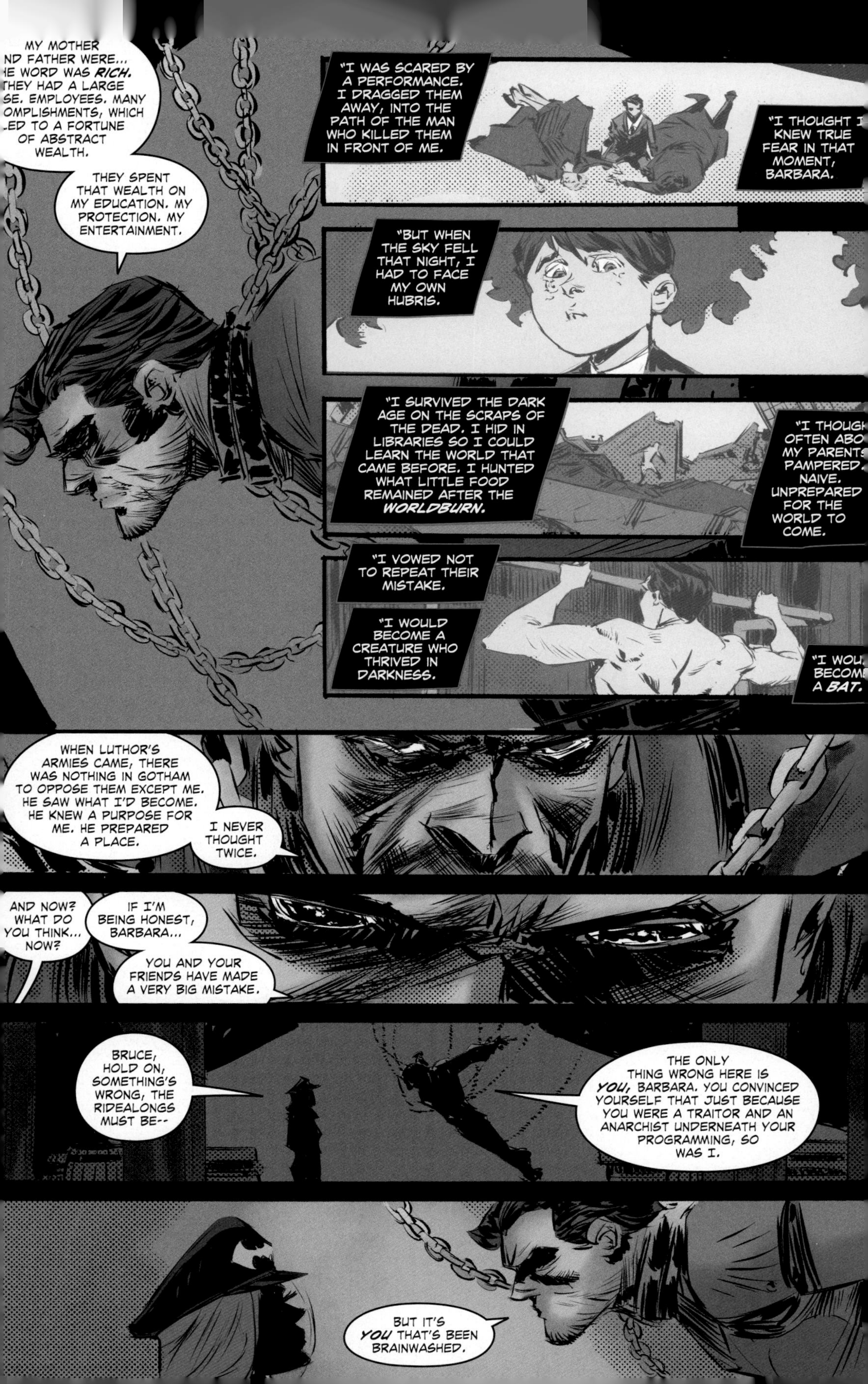
MY MOTHER
ND FATHER WERE... HE WORD WAS *RICH.* THEY HAD A LARGE SE. EMPLOYEES. MANY OMPLISHMENTS, WHICH ED TO A FORTUNE OF ABSTRACT WEALTH.
THEY SPENT THAT WEALTH ON MY EDUCATION. MY PROTECTION. MY ENTERTAINMENT.
"I WAS SCARED BY A PERFORMANCE. I DRAGGED THEM AWAY, INTO THE PATH OF THE MAN WHO KILLED THEM IN FRONT OF ME.
"I THOUGHT I KNEW TRUE FEAR IN THAT MOMENT, BARBARA.
"BUT WHEN THE SKY FELL THAT NIGHT, I HAD TO FACE MY OWN HUBRIS.
"I SURVIVED THE DARK AGE ON THE SCRAPS OF THE DEAD. I HID IN LIBRARIES SO I COULD LEARN THE WORLD THAT CAME BEFORE. I HUNTED WHAT LITTLE FOOD REMAINED AFTER THE *WORLDBURN.*
"I THOUG OFTEN ABO MY PARENTS PAMPERED. NAIVE. UNPREPARED FOR THE WORLD TO COME.
"I VOWED NOT TO REPEAT THEIR MISTAKE.
"I WOULD BECOME A CREATURE WHO THRIVED IN DARKNESS.
"I WOU BECOM A *BAT.*
WHEN LUTHOR'S ARMIES CAME, THERE WAS NOTHING IN GOTHAM TO OPPOSE THEM EXCEPT ME. HE SAW WHAT I'D BECOME. HE KNEW A PURPOSE FOR ME. HE PREPARED A PLACE.
I NEVER THOUGHT TWICE.
AND NOW? WHAT DO YOU THINK... NOW?
IF I'M BEING HONEST, BARBARA...
YOU AND YOUR FRIENDS HAVE MADE A VERY BIG MISTAKE.
BRUCE, HOLD ON, SOMETHING'S WRONG, THE RIDEALONGS MUST BE--
THE ONLY THING WRONG HERE IS *YOU,* BARBARA. YOU CONVINCED YOURSELF THAT JUST BECAUSE YOU WERE A TRAITOR AND AN ANARCHIST UNDERNEATH YOUR PROGRAMMING, SO WAS I.
BUT IT'S *YOU* THAT'S BEEN BRAINWASHED.

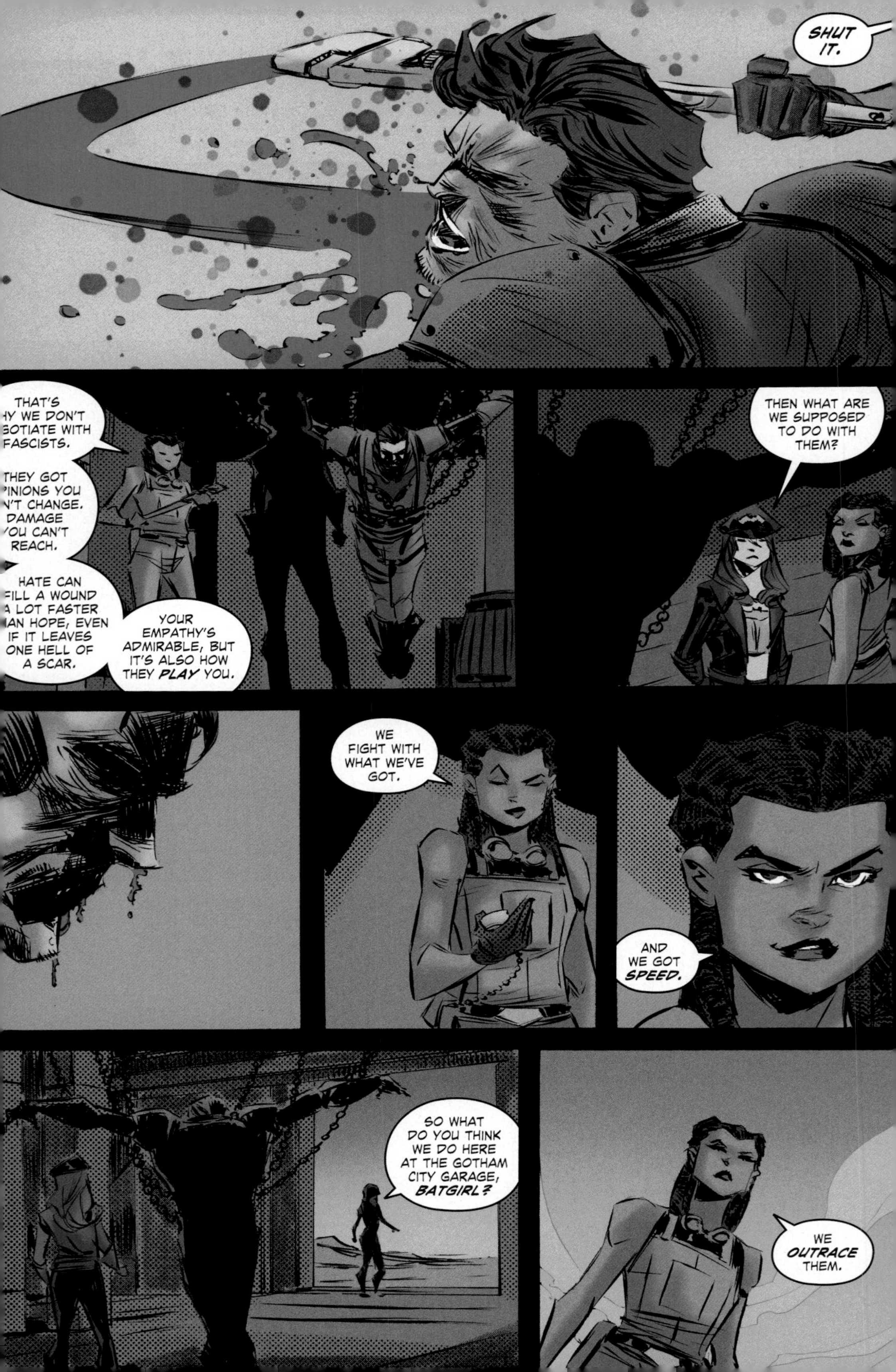
SHUT IT.
THAT'S
HY WE DON'T
GOTIATE WITH
FASCISTS.
THEY GOT
PINIONS YOU
N'T CHANGE.
DAMAGE
YOU CAN'T
REACH.
HATE CAN
FILL A WOUND
A LOT FASTER
AN HOPE, EVEN
IF IT LEAVES
ONE HELL OF
A SCAR.
YOUR EMPATHY'S ADMIRABLE, BUT IT'S ALSO HOW THEY PLAY YOU.
THEN WHAT ARE WE SUPPOSED TO DO WITH THEM?
WE FIGHT WITH WHAT WE'VE GOT.
AND WE GOT SPEED.
SO WHAT DO YOU THINK WE DO HERE AT THE GOTHAM CITY GARAGE, BATGIRL?
WE OUTRACE THEM.

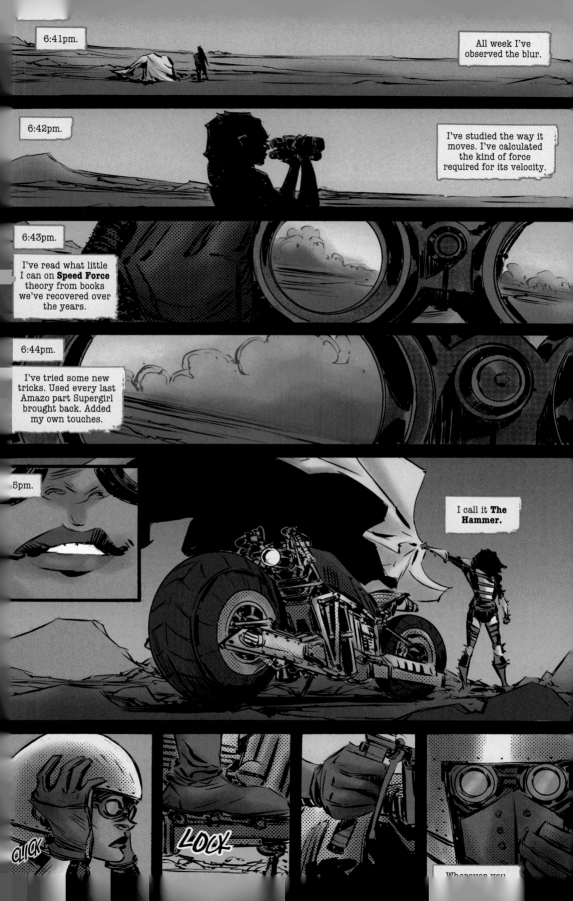

6:41pm.

All week I've observed the blur.

6:42pm.

I've studied the way it moves. I've calculated the kind of force required for its velocity.

6:43pm.

I've read what little I can on **Speed Force** theory from books we've recovered over the years.

6:44pm.

I've tried some new tricks. Used every last Amazo part Supergirl brought back. Added my own touches.

5pm.

I call it **The Hammer.**

CLICK

LOCX

Whenever you

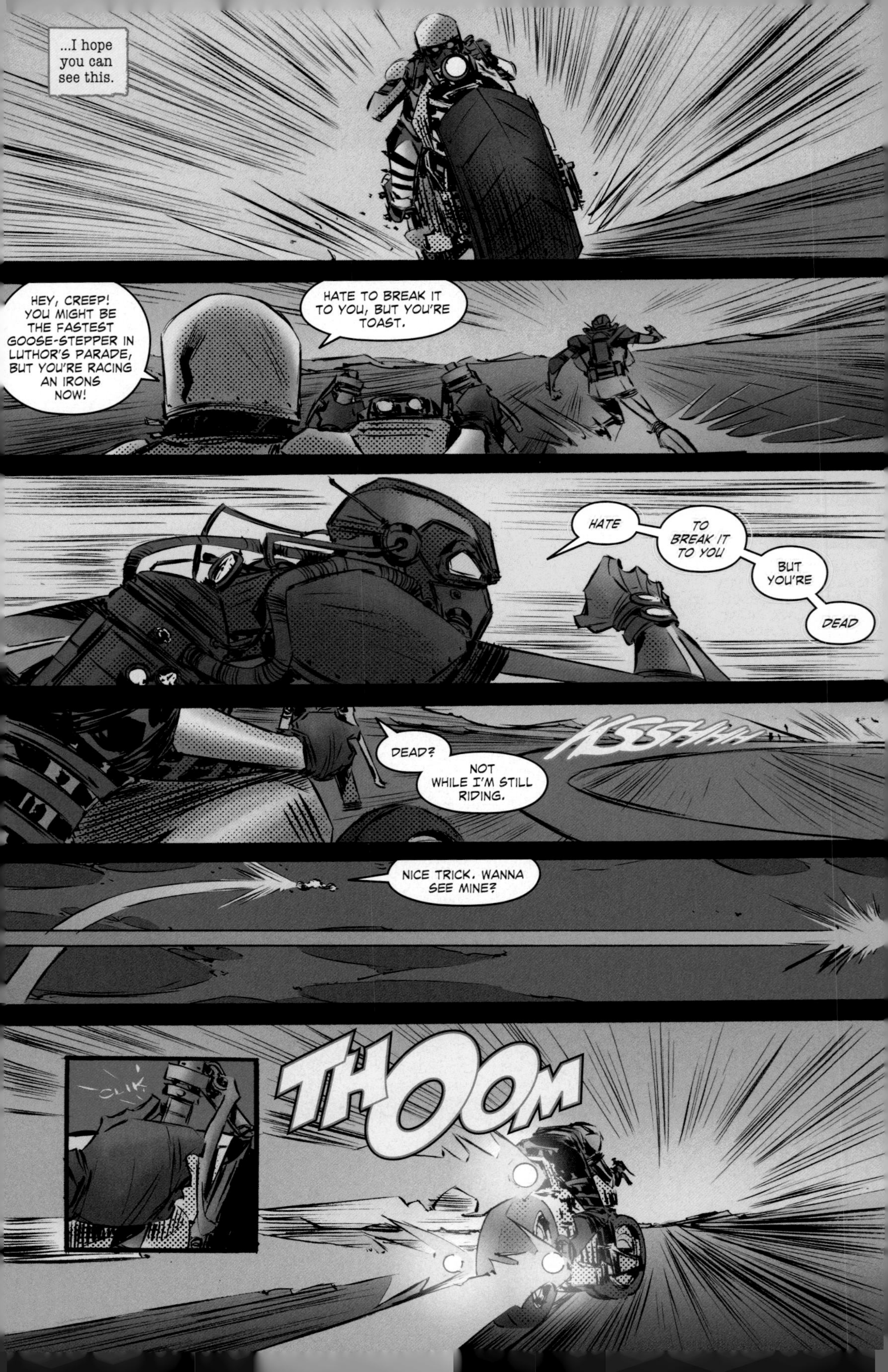
...I hope you can see this.
HEY, CREEP! YOU MIGHT BE THE FASTEST GOOSE-STEPPER IN LUTHOR'S PARADE, BUT YOU'RE RACING AN IRONS NOW!
HATE TO BREAK IT TO YOU, BUT YOU'RE TOAST.
HATE
TO BREAK IT TO YOU
BUT YOU'RE
DEAD
KSSSHHH
DEAD?
NOT WHILE I'M STILL RIDING.
NICE TRICK. WANNA SEE MINE?
CLIK
THOOM

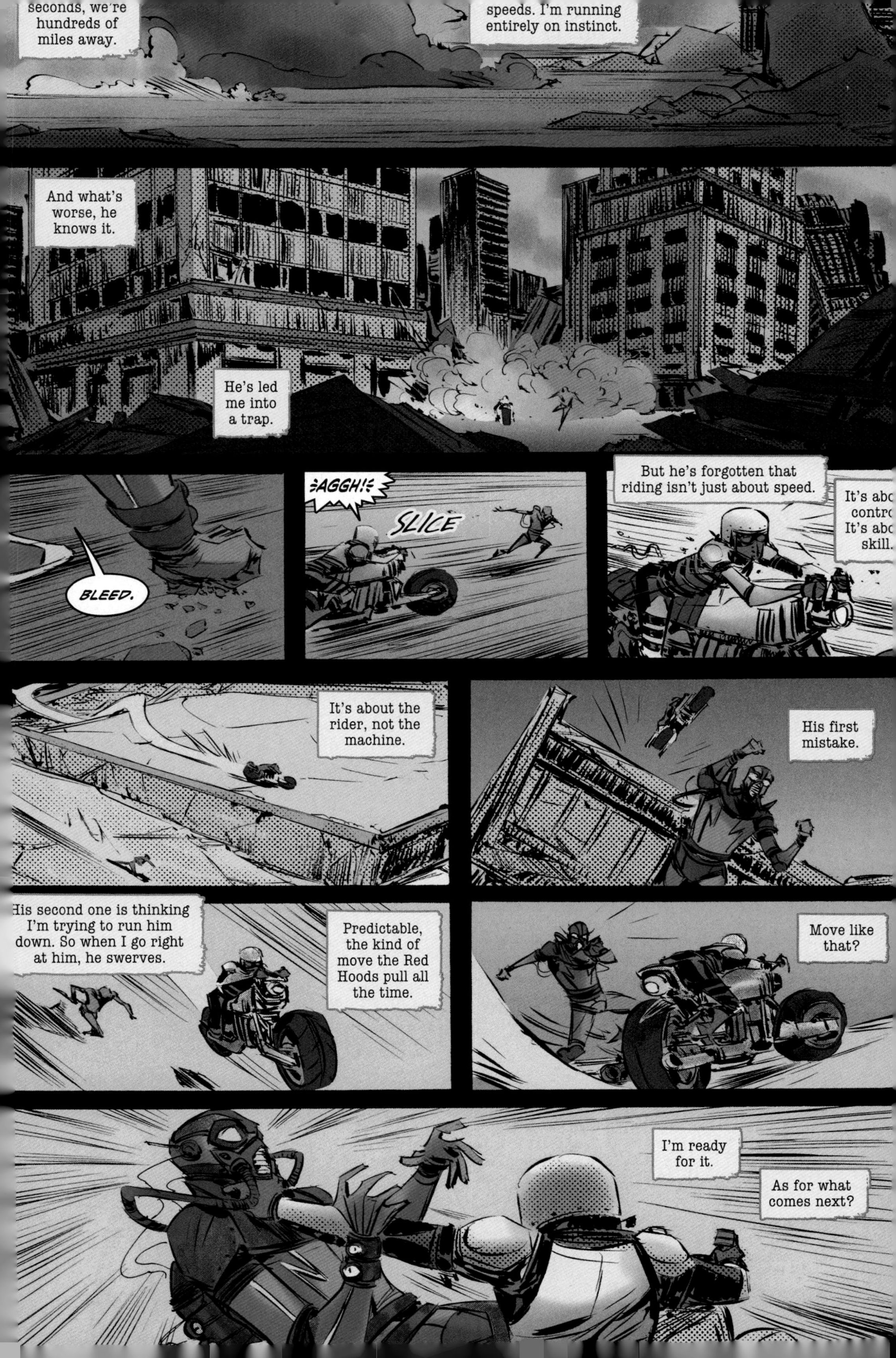
seconds, we're hundreds of miles away.
speeds. I'm running entirely on instinct.
And what's worse, he knows it.
He's led me into a trap.
BLEED.
AGGH!
SLICE
But he's forgotten that riding isn't just about speed.
It's abo contro It's abo skill.
It's about the rider, not the machine.
His first mistake.
His second one is thinking I'm trying to run him down. So when I go right at him, he swerves.
Predictable, the kind of move the Red Hoods pull all the time.
Move like that?
I'm ready for it.
As for what comes next?

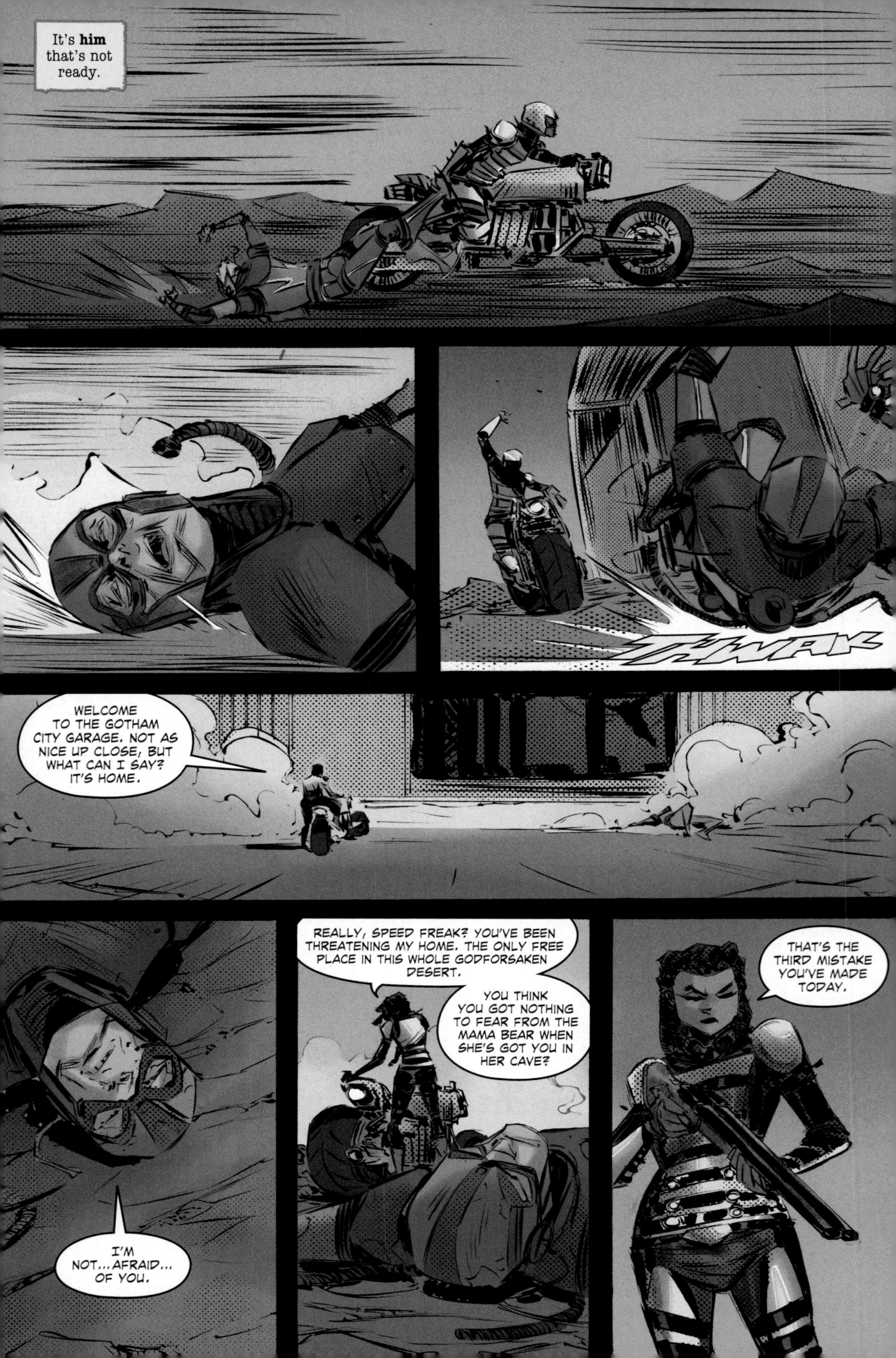
It's **him** that's not ready.
THWAK
WELCOME TO THE GOTHAM CITY GARAGE. NOT AS NICE UP CLOSE, BUT WHAT CAN I SAY? IT'S HOME.
I'M NOT...AFRAID... OF YOU.
REALLY, SPEED FREAK? YOU'VE BEEN THREATENING MY HOME. THE ONLY FREE PLACE IN THIS WHOLE GODFORSAKEN DESERT.
YOU THINK YOU GOT NOTHING TO FEAR FROM THE MAMA BEAR WHEN SHE'S GOT YOU IN HER CAVE?
THAT'S THE THIRD MISTAKE YOU'VE MADE TODAY.

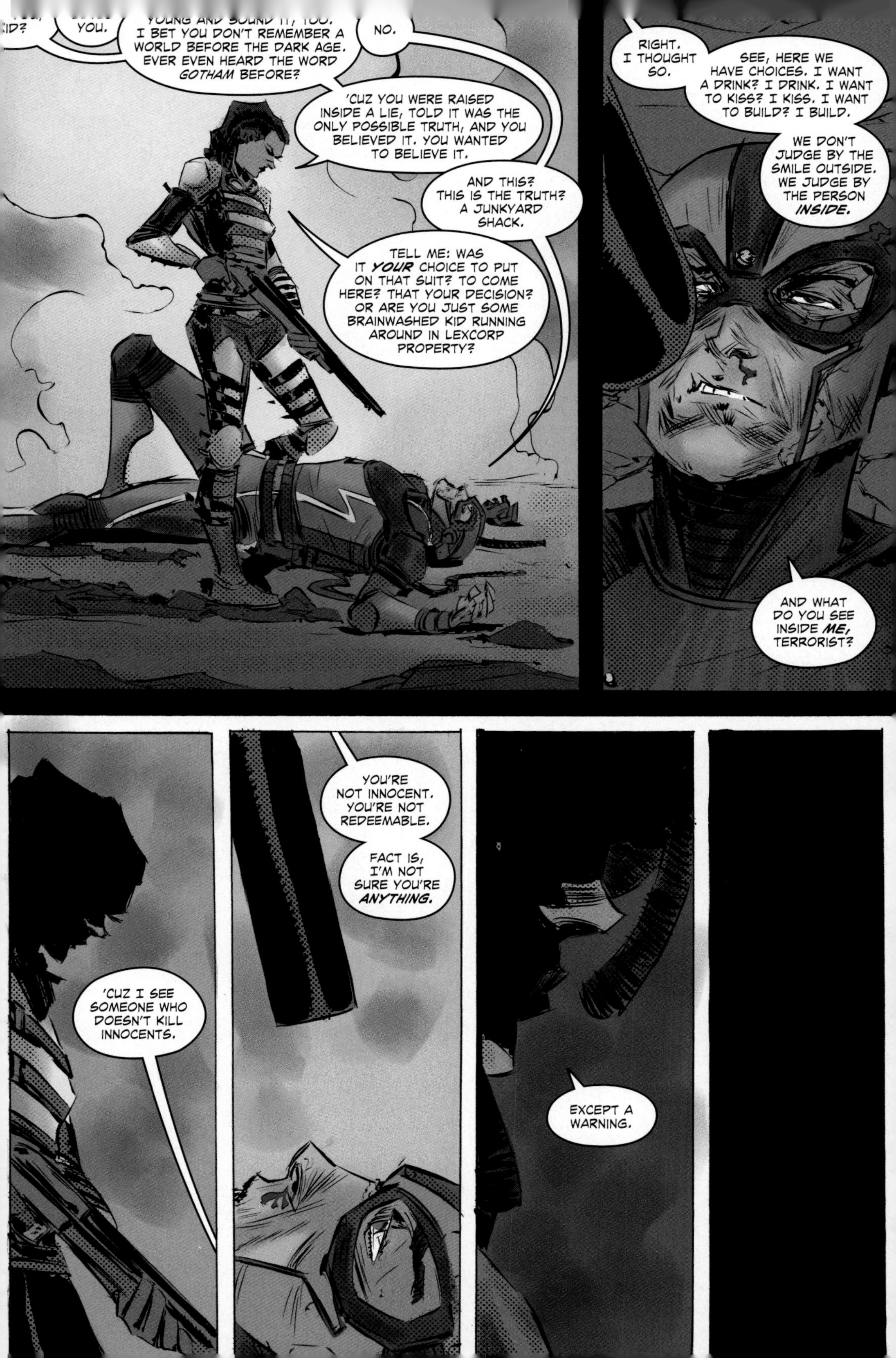

YOU.
I BET YOU DON'T REMEMBER A WORLD BEFORE THE DARK AGE. EVER EVEN HEARD THE WORD *GOTHAM* BEFORE?
NO.
'CUZ YOU WERE RAISED INSIDE A LIE, TOLD IT WAS THE ONLY POSSIBLE TRUTH, AND YOU BELIEVED IT. YOU WANTED TO BELIEVE IT.
AND THIS? THIS IS THE TRUTH? A JUNKYARD SHACK.
TELL ME: WAS IT ***YOUR*** CHOICE TO PUT ON THAT SUIT? TO COME HERE? THAT YOUR DECISION? OR ARE YOU JUST SOME BRAINWASHED KID RUNNING AROUND IN LEXCORP PROPERTY?
RIGHT. I THOUGHT SO.
SEE, HERE WE HAVE CHOICES. I WANT A DRINK? I DRINK. I WANT TO KISS? I KISS. I WANT TO BUILD? I BUILD.
WE DON'T JUDGE BY THE SMILE OUTSIDE. WE JUDGE BY THE PERSON ***INSIDE.***
AND WHAT DO YOU SEE INSIDE ***ME,*** TERRORIST?
'CUZ I SEE SOMEONE WHO DOESN'T KILL INNOCENTS.
YOU'RE NOT INNOCENT. YOU'RE NOT REDEEMABLE.
FACT IS, I'M NOT SURE YOU'RE ***ANYTHING.***
EXCEPT A WARNING.

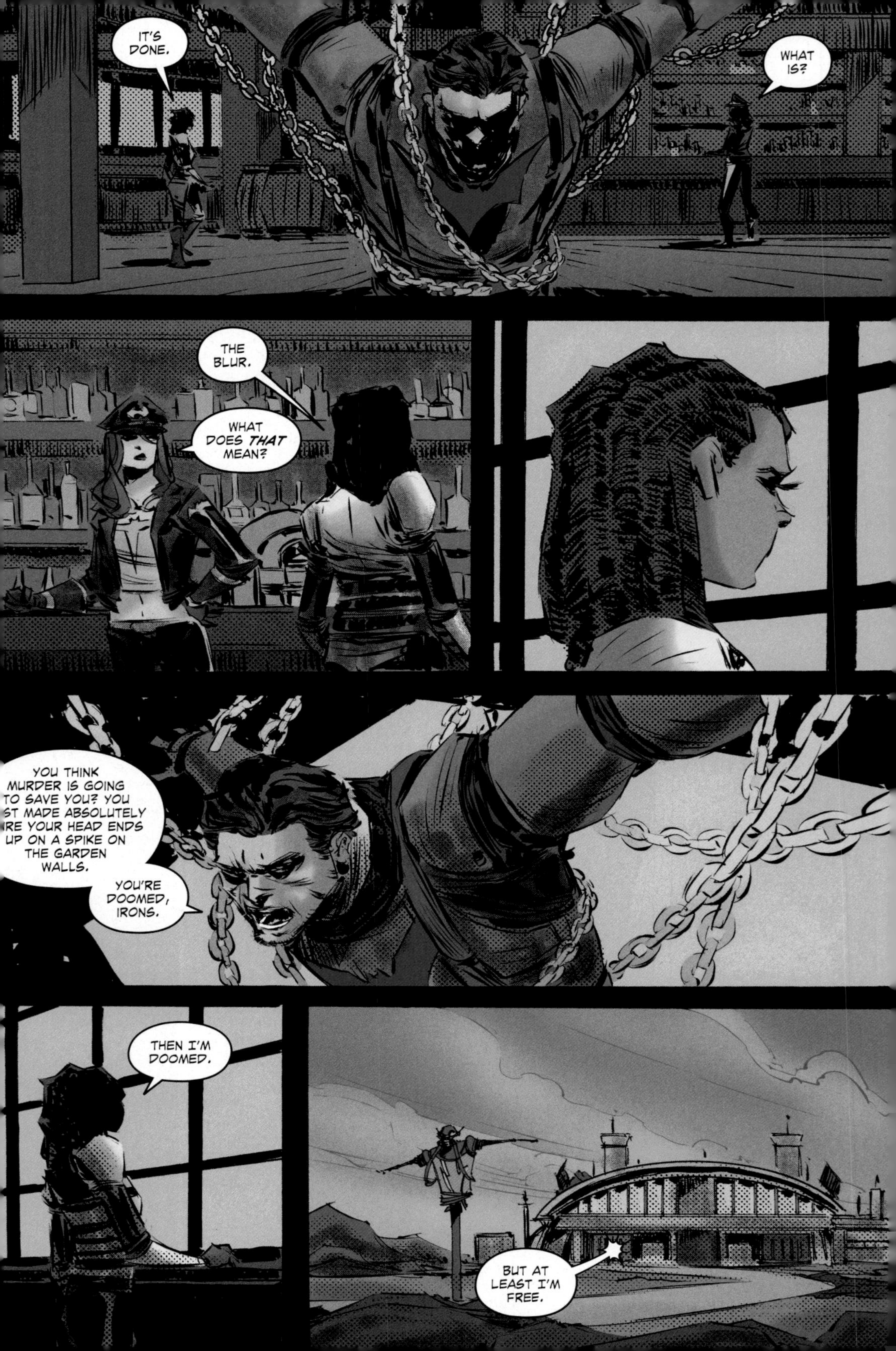
IT'S DONE.
WHAT IS?
THE BLUR.
WHAT DOES *THAT* MEAN?
YOU THINK MURDER IS GOING TO SAVE YOU? YOU ST MADE ABSOLUTELY RE YOUR HEAD ENDS UP ON A SPIKE ON THE GARDEN WALLS.
YOU'RE DOOMED, IRONS.
THEN I'M DOOMED.
BUT AT LEAST I'M FREE.

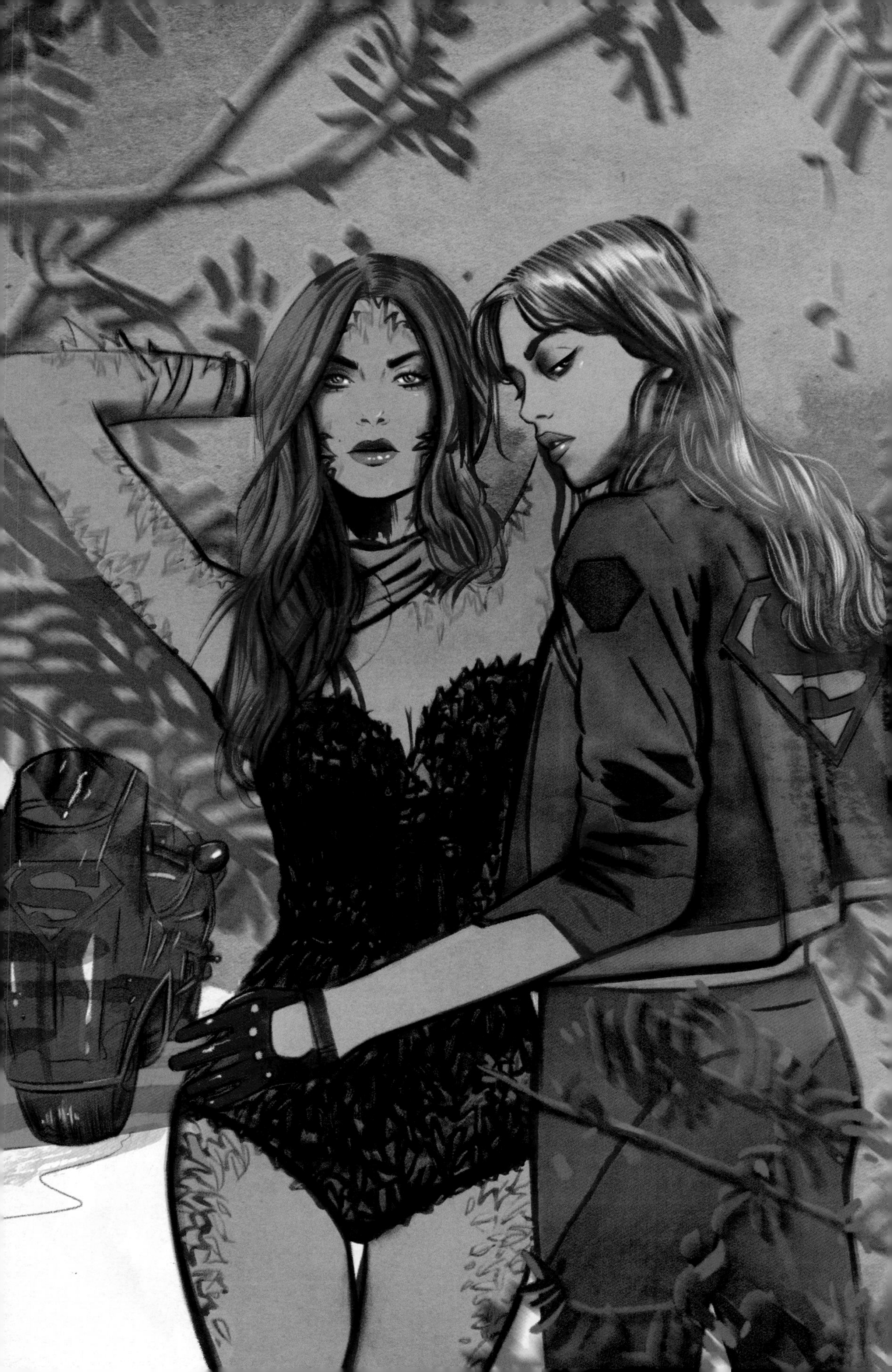

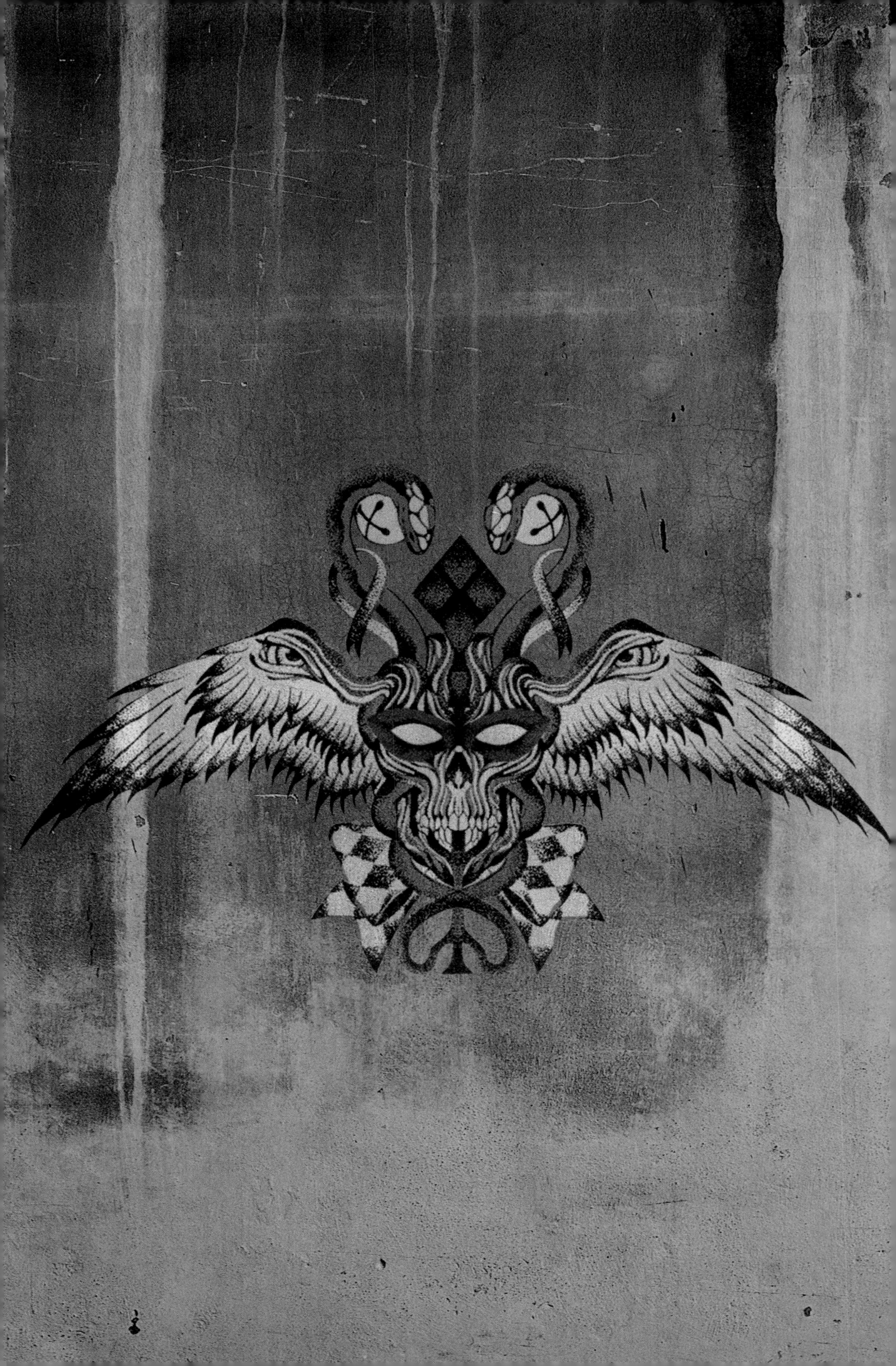

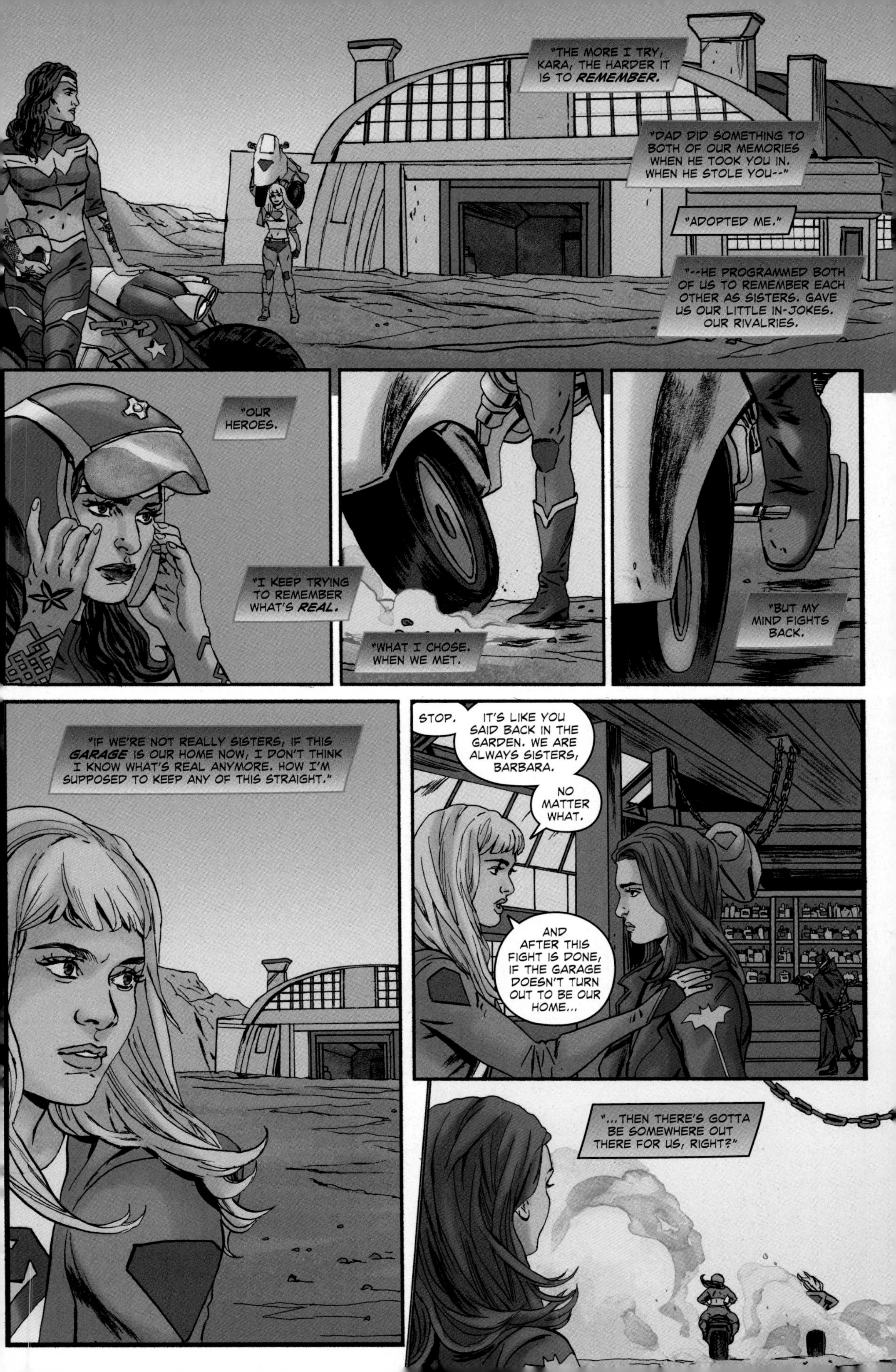
"THE MORE I TRY, KARA, THE HARDER IT IS TO *REMEMBER.*
"DAD DID SOMETHING TO BOTH OF OUR MEMORIES WHEN HE TOOK YOU IN. WHEN HE STOLE YOU--"
"ADOPTED ME."
"--HE PROGRAMMED BOTH OF US TO REMEMBER EACH OTHER AS SISTERS. GAVE US OUR LITTLE IN-JOKES. OUR RIVALRIES.
"OUR HEROES.
"I KEEP TRYING TO REMEMBER WHAT'S *REAL.*
"WHAT I CHOSE. WHEN WE MET.
"BUT MY MIND FIGHTS BACK.
"IF WE'RE NOT REALLY SISTERS, IF THIS *GARAGE* IS OUR HOME NOW, I DON'T THINK I KNOW WHAT'S REAL ANYMORE. HOW I'M SUPPOSED TO KEEP ANY OF THIS STRAIGHT."
STOP.
IT'S LIKE YOU SAID BACK IN THE GARDEN. WE ARE ALWAYS SISTERS, BARBARA.
NO MATTER WHAT.
AND AFTER THIS FIGHT IS DONE, IF THE GARAGE DOESN'T TURN OUT TO BE OUR HOME...
"...THEN THERE'S GOTTA BE SOMEWHERE OUT THERE FOR US, RIGHT?"

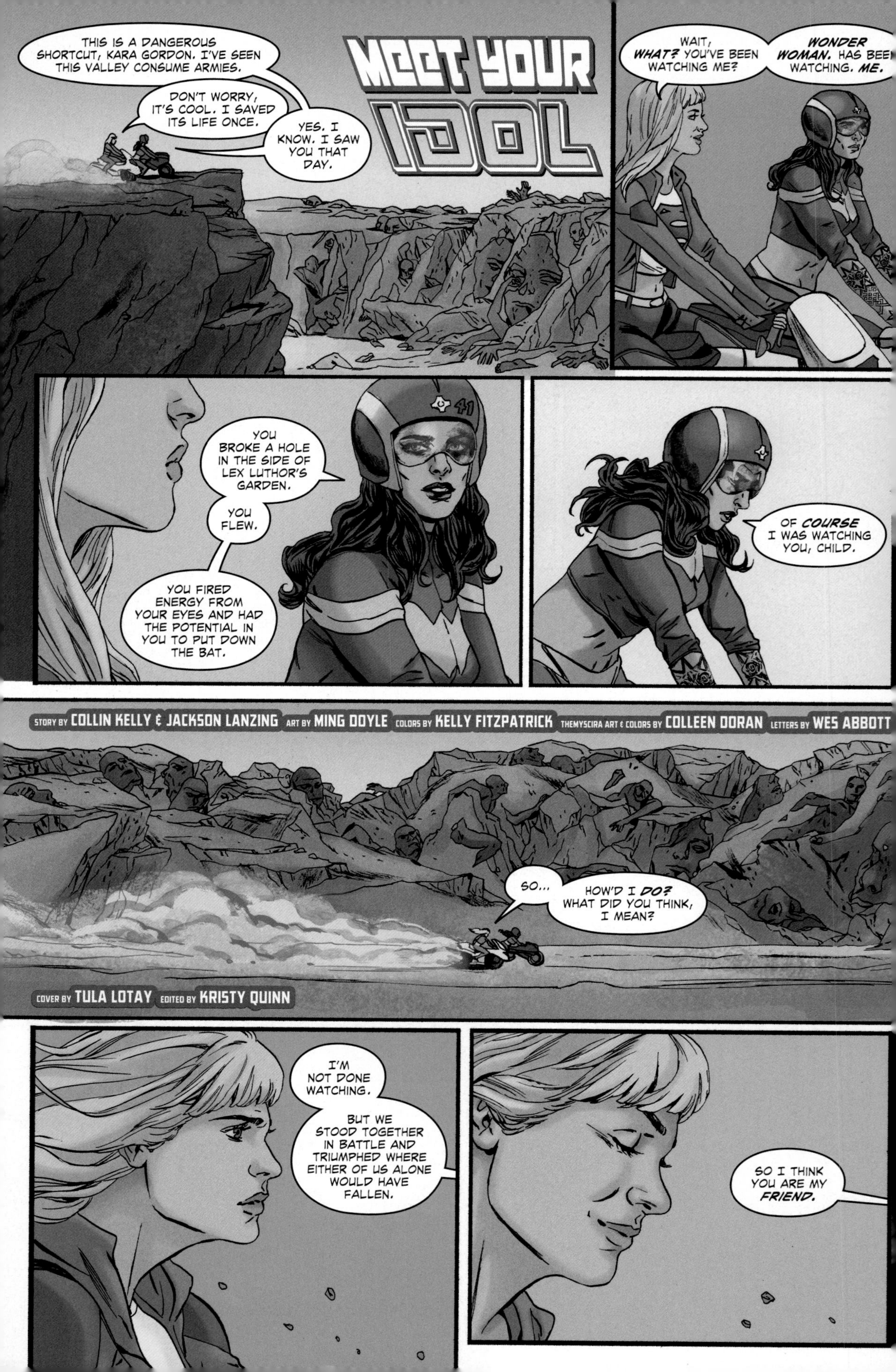
MEET YOUR IDOL
THIS IS A DANGEROUS SHORTCUT, KARA GORDON. I'VE SEEN THIS VALLEY CONSUME ARMIES.
DON'T WORRY, IT'S COOL. I SAVED ITS LIFE ONCE.
YES. I KNOW. I SAW YOU THAT DAY.
WAIT, WHAT? YOU'VE BEEN WATCHING ME?
WONDER WOMAN. HAS BEEN WATCHING. ME.
YOU BROKE A HOLE IN THE SIDE OF LEX LUTHOR'S GARDEN.
YOU FLEW.
YOU FIRED ENERGY FROM YOUR EYES AND HAD THE POTENTIAL IN YOU TO PUT DOWN THE BAT.
OF COURSE I WAS WATCHING YOU, CHILD.
STORY BY COLLIN KELLY & JACKSON LANZING ART BY MING DOYLE COLORS BY KELLY FITZPATRICK THEMYSCIRA ART & COLORS BY COLLEEN DORAN LETTERS BY WES ABBOTT
SO...
HOW'D I DO? WHAT DID YOU THINK, I MEAN?
COVER BY TULA LOTAY EDITED BY KRISTY QUINN
I'M NOT DONE WATCHING.
BUT WE STOOD TOGETHER IN BATTLE AND TRIUMPHED WHERE EITHER OF US ALONE WOULD HAVE FALLEN.
SO I THINK YOU ARE MY FRIEND.

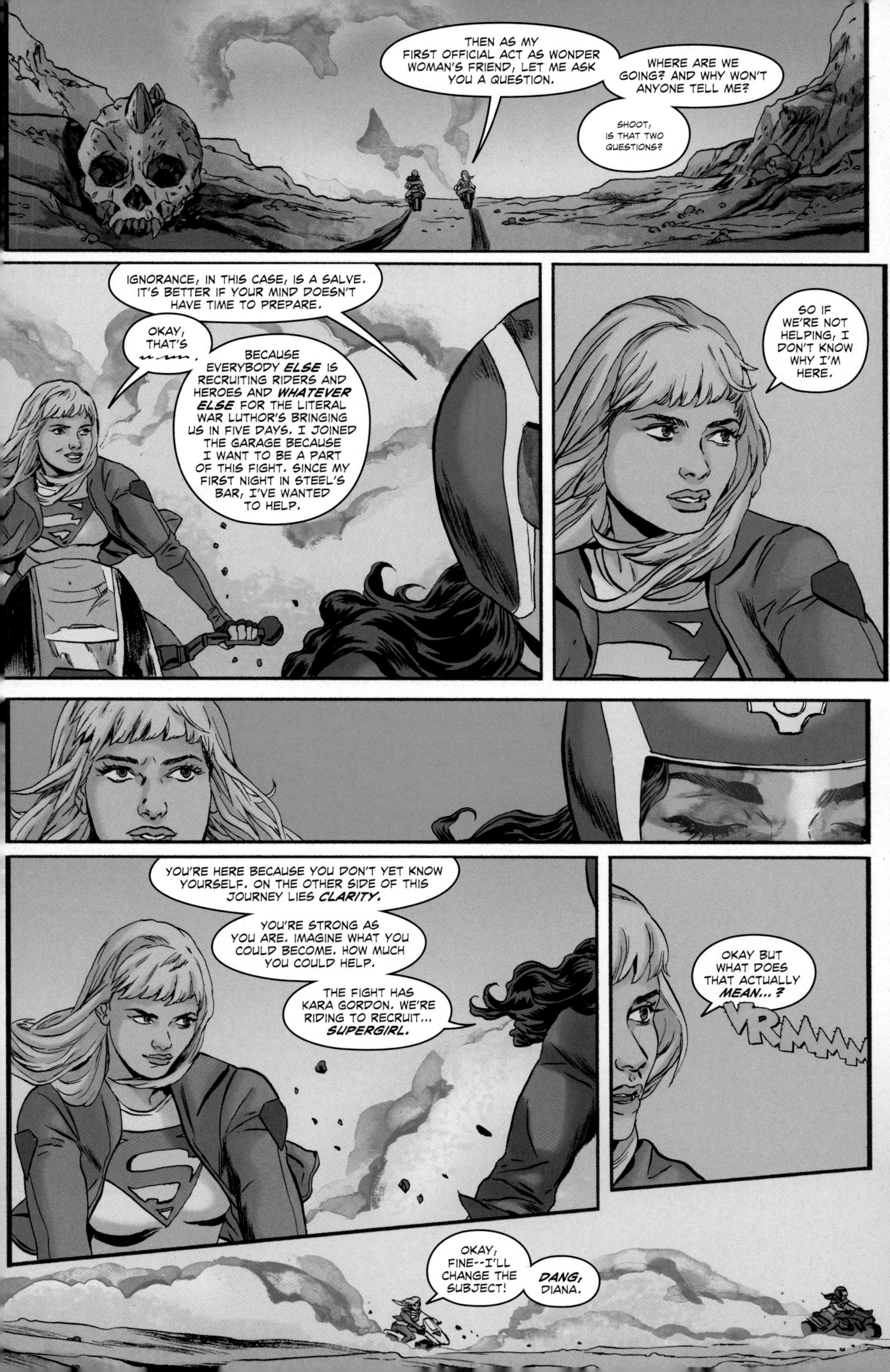
THEN AS MY FIRST OFFICIAL ACT AS WONDER WOMAN'S FRIEND, LET ME ASK YOU A QUESTION.
WHERE ARE WE GOING? AND WHY WON'T ANYONE TELL ME?
SHOOT, IS THAT TWO QUESTIONS?
IGNORANCE, IN THIS CASE, IS A SALVE. IT'S BETTER IF YOUR MIND DOESN'T HAVE TIME TO PREPARE.
OKAY, THAT'S
BECAUSE EVERYBODY ***ELSE*** IS RECRUITING RIDERS AND HEROES AND ***WHATEVER ELSE*** FOR THE LITERAL WAR LUTHOR'S BRINGING US IN FIVE DAYS. I JOINED THE GARAGE BECAUSE I WANT TO BE A PART OF THIS FIGHT. SINCE MY FIRST NIGHT IN STEEL'S BAR, I'VE WANTED TO HELP.
SO IF WE'RE NOT HELPING, I DON'T KNOW WHY I'M HERE.
YOU'RE HERE BECAUSE YOU DON'T YET KNOW YOURSELF. ON THE OTHER SIDE OF THIS JOURNEY LIES ***CLARITY.***
YOU'RE STRONG AS YOU ARE. IMAGINE WHAT YOU COULD BECOME. HOW MUCH YOU COULD HELP.
THE FIGHT HAS KARA GORDON. WE'RE RIDING TO RECRUIT... ***SUPERGIRL.***
OKAY BUT WHAT DOES THAT ACTUALLY ***MEAN...?***
VRMMMM
OKAY, FINE--I'LL CHANGE THE SUBJECT!
DANG, DIANA.

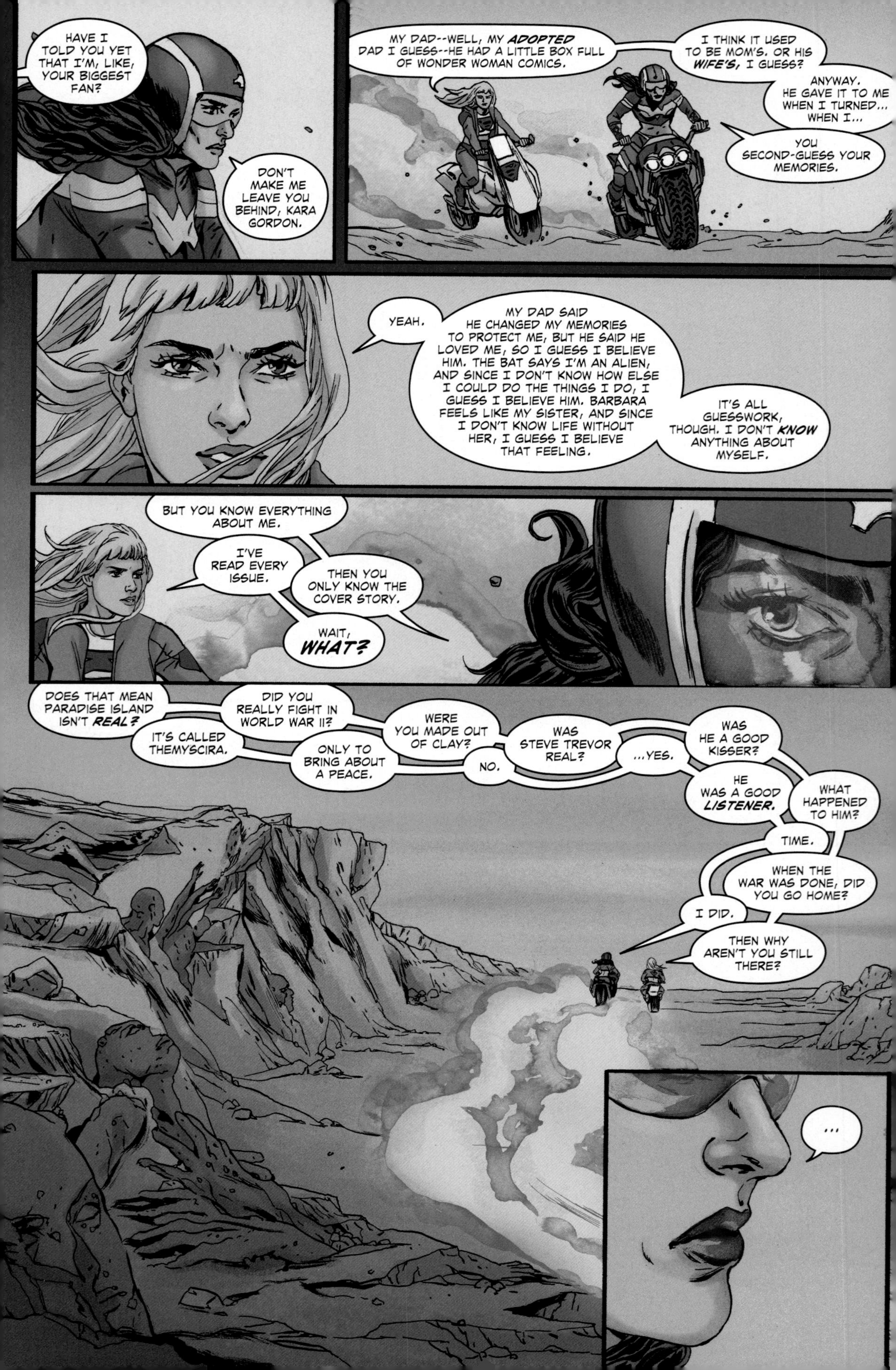
HAVE I TOLD YOU YET THAT I'M, LIKE, YOUR BIGGEST FAN?
DON'T MAKE ME LEAVE YOU BEHIND, KARA GORDON.
MY DAD--WELL, MY ADOPTED DAD I GUESS--HE HAD A LITTLE BOX FULL OF WONDER WOMAN COMICS.
I THINK IT USED TO BE MOM'S. OR HIS WIFE'S, I GUESS?
ANYWAY. HE GAVE IT TO ME WHEN I TURNED... WHEN I...
YOU SECOND-GUESS YOUR MEMORIES.
YEAH.
MY DAD SAID HE CHANGED MY MEMORIES TO PROTECT ME, BUT HE SAID HE LOVED ME, SO I GUESS I BELIEVE HIM. THE BAT SAYS I'M AN ALIEN, AND SINCE I DON'T KNOW HOW ELSE I COULD DO THE THINGS I DO, I GUESS I BELIEVE HIM. BARBARA FEELS LIKE MY SISTER, AND SINCE I DON'T KNOW LIFE WITHOUT HER, I GUESS I BELIEVE THAT FEELING.
IT'S ALL GUESSWORK, THOUGH. I DON'T KNOW ANYTHING ABOUT MYSELF.
BUT YOU KNOW EVERYTHING ABOUT ME.
I'VE READ EVERY ISSUE.
THEN YOU ONLY KNOW THE COVER STORY.
WAIT, WHAT?
DOES THAT MEAN PARADISE ISLAND ISN'T REAL?
IT'S CALLED THEMYSCIRA.
DID YOU REALLY FIGHT IN WORLD WAR II?
ONLY TO BRING ABOUT A PEACE.
WERE YOU MADE OUT OF CLAY?
NO.
WAS STEVE TREVOR REAL?
...YES.
WAS HE A GOOD KISSER?
HE WAS A GOOD LISTENER.
WHAT HAPPENED TO HIM?
TIME.
WHEN THE WAR WAS DONE, DID YOU GO HOME?
I DID.
THEN WHY AREN'T YOU STILL THERE?
...

HEY, I DIDN'T MEAN TO SAY... WHATEVER I SAID. I'M SORRY.

DID THEY... ARE THEY GONE?

WHAT HAPPENED?

THE WORLD THOUGHT IT COULD BURN ITSELF. THAT HATE WOULD FUEL THEIR SELF-DESTRUCTION SO THEY WOULDN'T EVEN REALIZE WHAT THEY'D DONE UNTIL TOO LATE.

BUT I CAME TO MAN'S WORLD. BROUGHT INSPIRATION. REMINDED THEM OF THINGS STRONGER THAN HATE.

AND THEY STAYED THEIR HAND. I WAS VICTORIOUS.

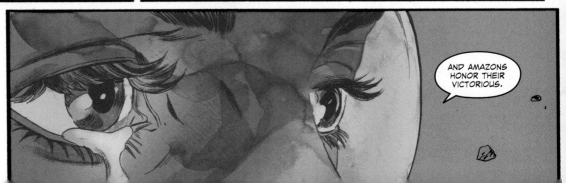

AND AMAZONS HONOR THEIR VICTORIOUS.

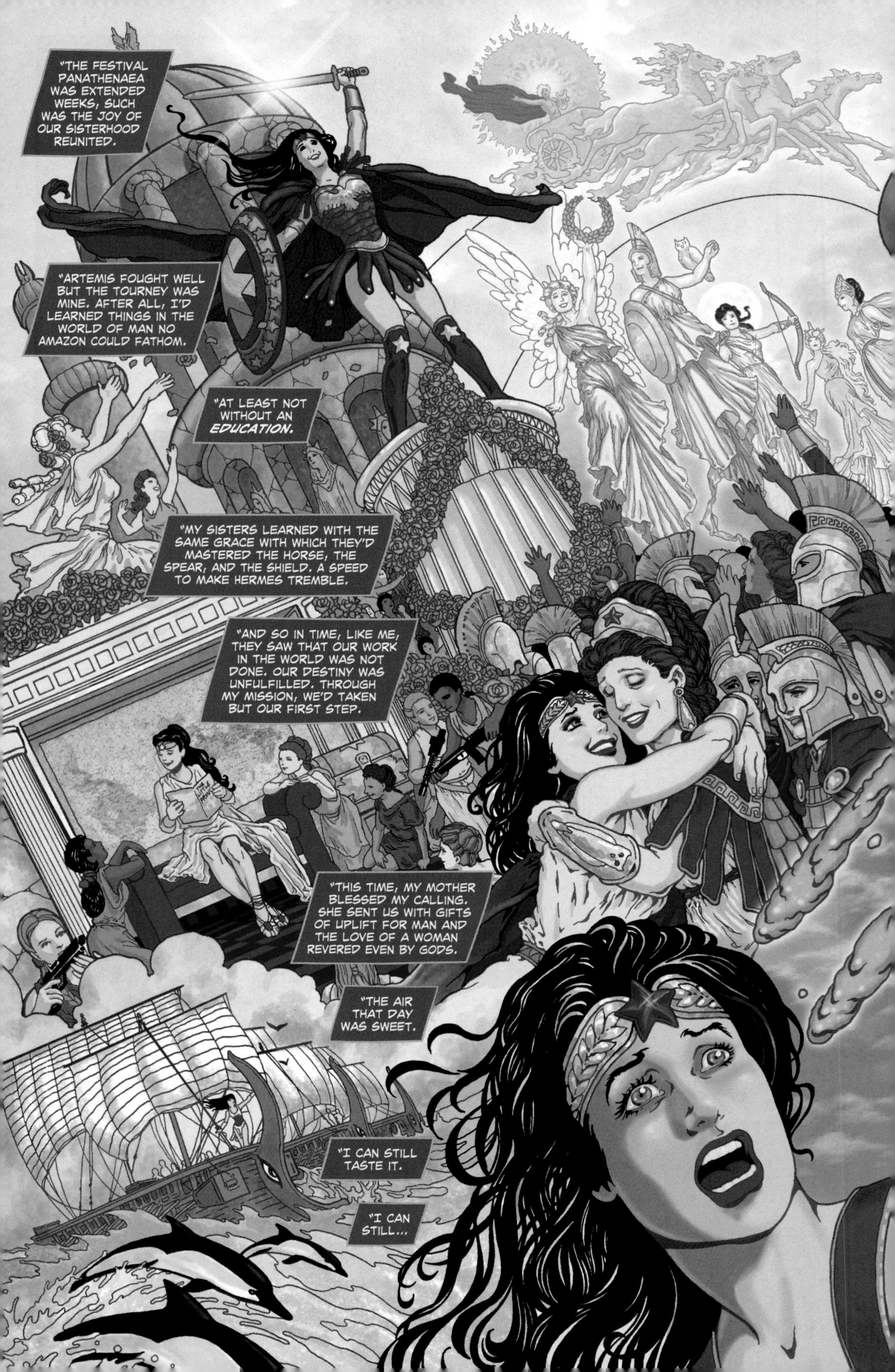
"THE FESTIVAL PANATHENAEA WAS EXTENDED WEEKS, SUCH WAS THE JOY OF OUR SISTERHOOD REUNITED.
"ARTEMIS FOUGHT WELL BUT THE TOURNEY WAS MINE. AFTER ALL, I'D LEARNED THINGS IN THE WORLD OF MAN NO AMAZON COULD FATHOM.
"AT LEAST NOT WITHOUT AN *EDUCATION.*
"MY SISTERS LEARNED WITH THE SAME GRACE WITH WHICH THEY'D MASTERED THE HORSE, THE SPEAR, AND THE SHIELD. A SPEED TO MAKE HERMES TREMBLE.
"AND SO IN TIME, LIKE ME, THEY SAW THAT OUR WORK IN THE WORLD WAS NOT DONE. OUR DESTINY WAS UNFULFILLED. THROUGH MY MISSION, WE'D TAKEN BUT OUR FIRST STEP.
"THIS TIME, MY MOTHER BLESSED MY CALLING. SHE SENT US WITH GIFTS OF UPLIFT FOR MAN AND THE LOVE OF A WOMAN REVERED EVEN BY GODS.
"THE AIR THAT DAY WAS SWEET.
"I CAN STILL TASTE IT.
"I CAN STILL...

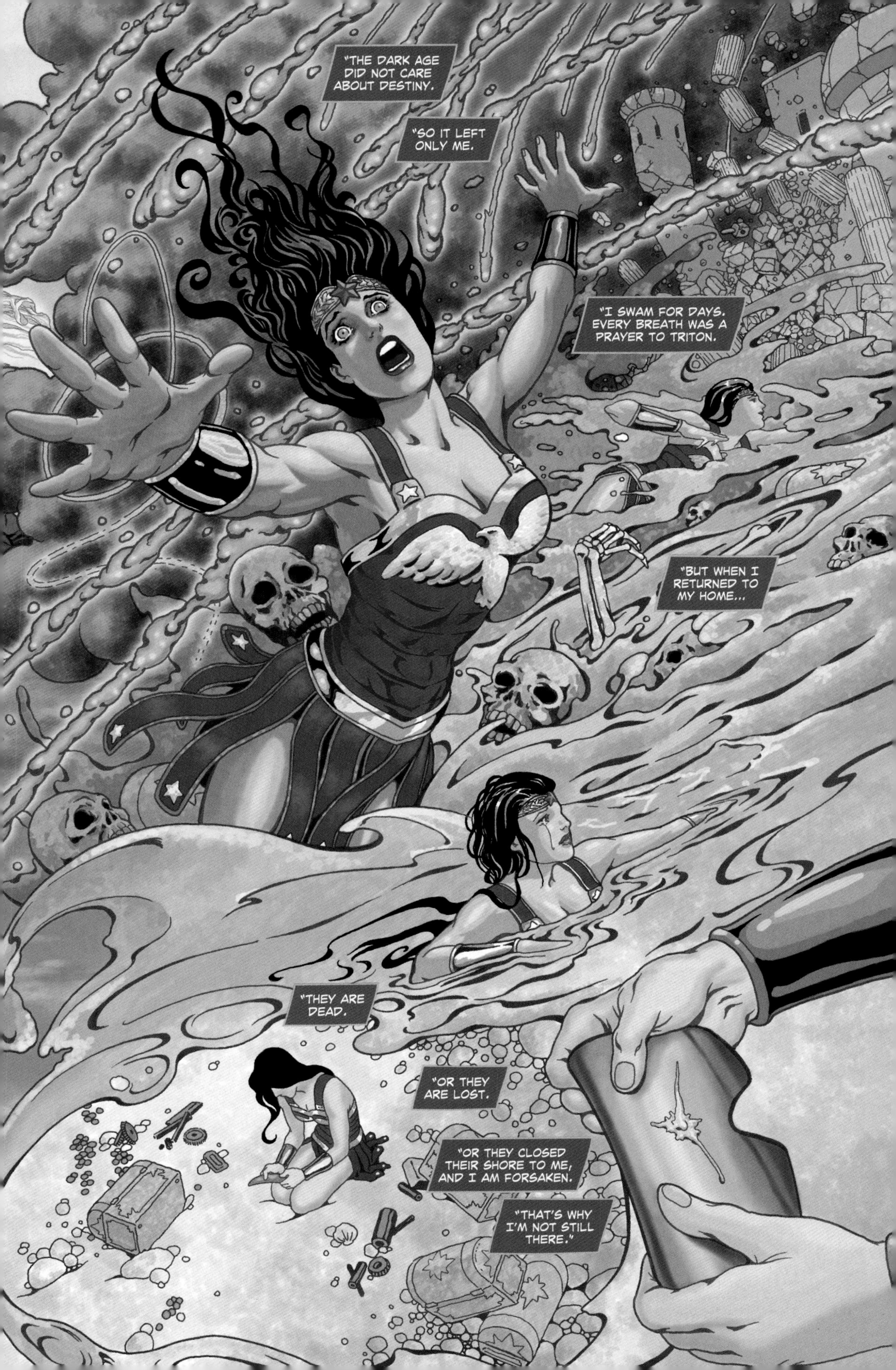
"THE DARK AGE DID NOT CARE ABOUT DESTINY.
"SO IT LEFT ONLY ME.
"I SWAM FOR DAYS. EVERY BREATH WAS A PRAYER TO TRITON.
"BUT WHEN I RETURNED TO MY HOME...
"THEY ARE DEAD.
"OR THEY ARE LOST.
"OR THEY CLOSED THEIR SHORE TO ME, AND I AM FORSAKEN.
"THAT'S WHY I'M NOT STILL THERE."

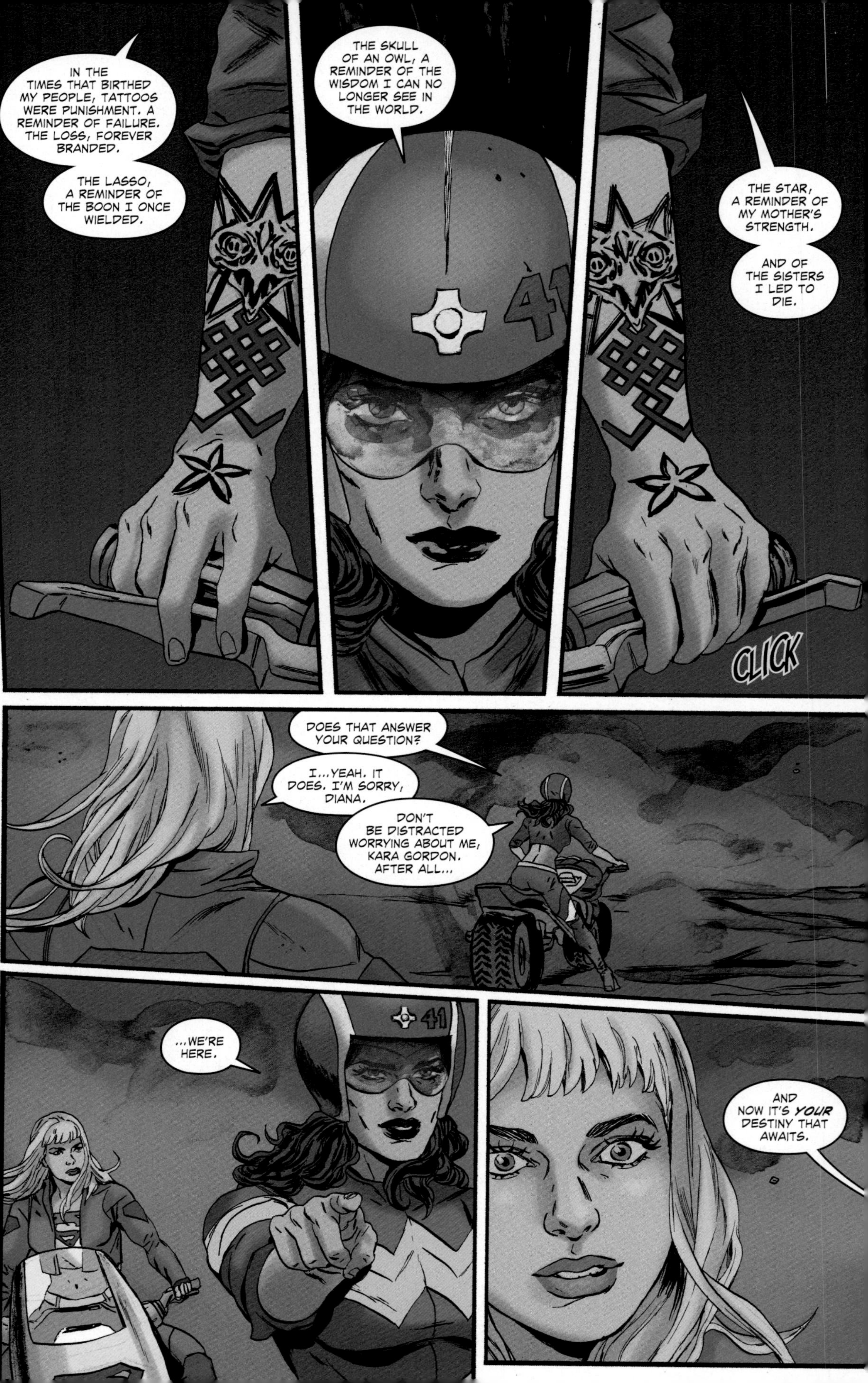
IN THE TIMES THAT BIRTHED MY PEOPLE, TATTOOS WERE PUNISHMENT. A REMINDER OF FAILURE. THE LOSS, FOREVER BRANDED.
THE LASSO, A REMINDER OF THE BOON I ONCE WIELDED.
THE SKULL OF AN OWL, A REMINDER OF THE WISDOM I CAN NO LONGER SEE IN THE WORLD.
41
THE STAR, A REMINDER OF MY MOTHER'S STRENGTH.
AND OF THE SISTERS I LED TO DIE.
CLICK
DOES THAT ANSWER YOUR QUESTION?
I...YEAH. IT DOES. I'M SORRY, DIANA.
DON'T BE DISTRACTED WORRYING ABOUT ME, KARA GORDON. AFTER ALL...
...WE'RE HERE.
41
AND NOW IT'S *YOUR* DESTINY THAT AWAITS.

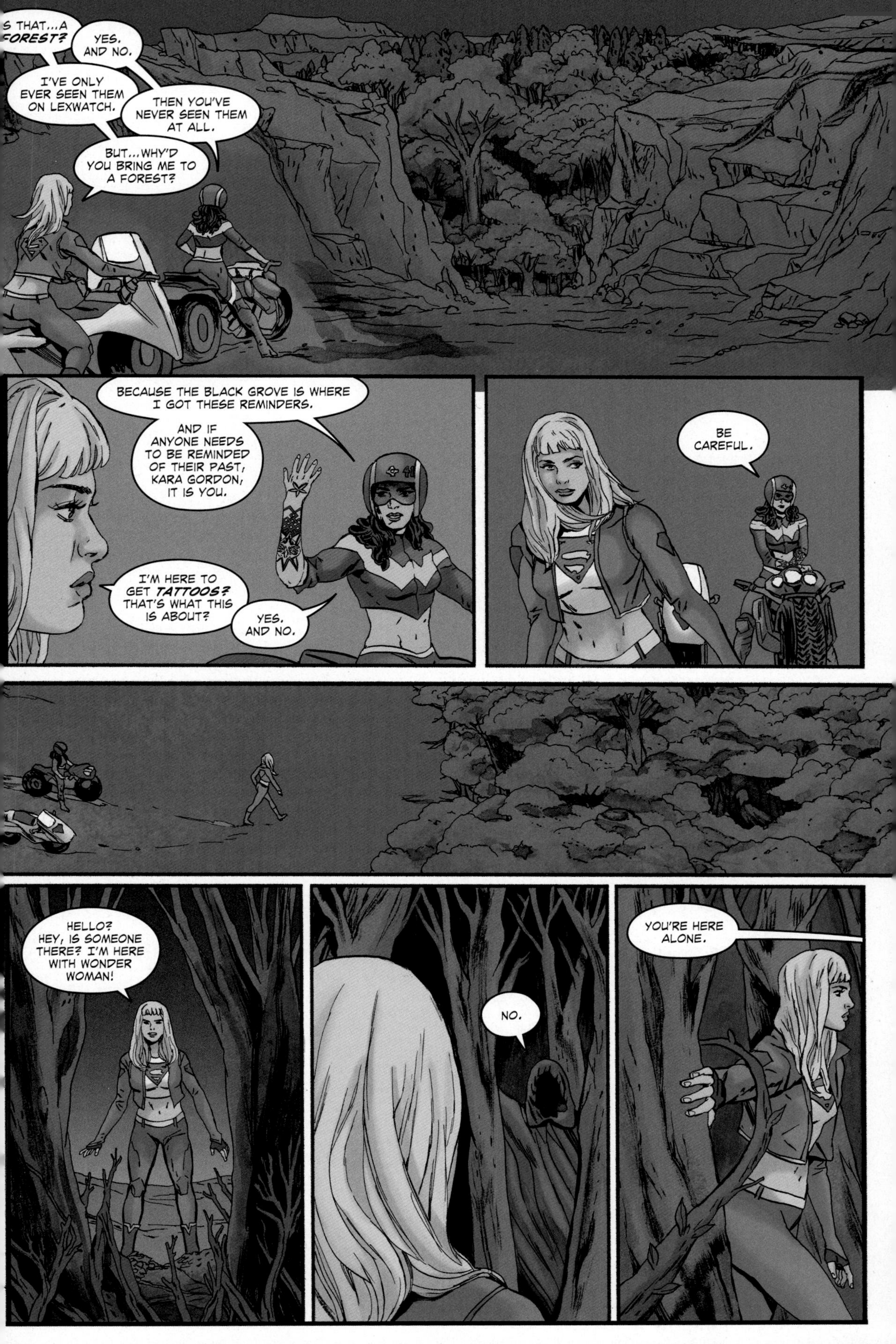
S THAT...A FOREST?
YES. AND NO.
I'VE ONLY EVER SEEN THEM ON LEXWATCH.
THEN YOU'VE NEVER SEEN THEM AT ALL.
BUT...WHY'D YOU BRING ME TO A FOREST?
BECAUSE THE BLACK GROVE IS WHERE I GOT THESE REMINDERS.
AND IF ANYONE NEEDS TO BE REMINDED OF THEIR PAST, KARA GORDON, IT IS YOU.
I'M HERE TO GET TATTOOS? THAT'S WHAT THIS IS ABOUT?
YES. AND NO.
BE CAREFUL.
HELLO? HEY, IS SOMEONE THERE? I'M HERE WITH WONDER WOMAN!
NO.
YOU'RE HERE ALONE.

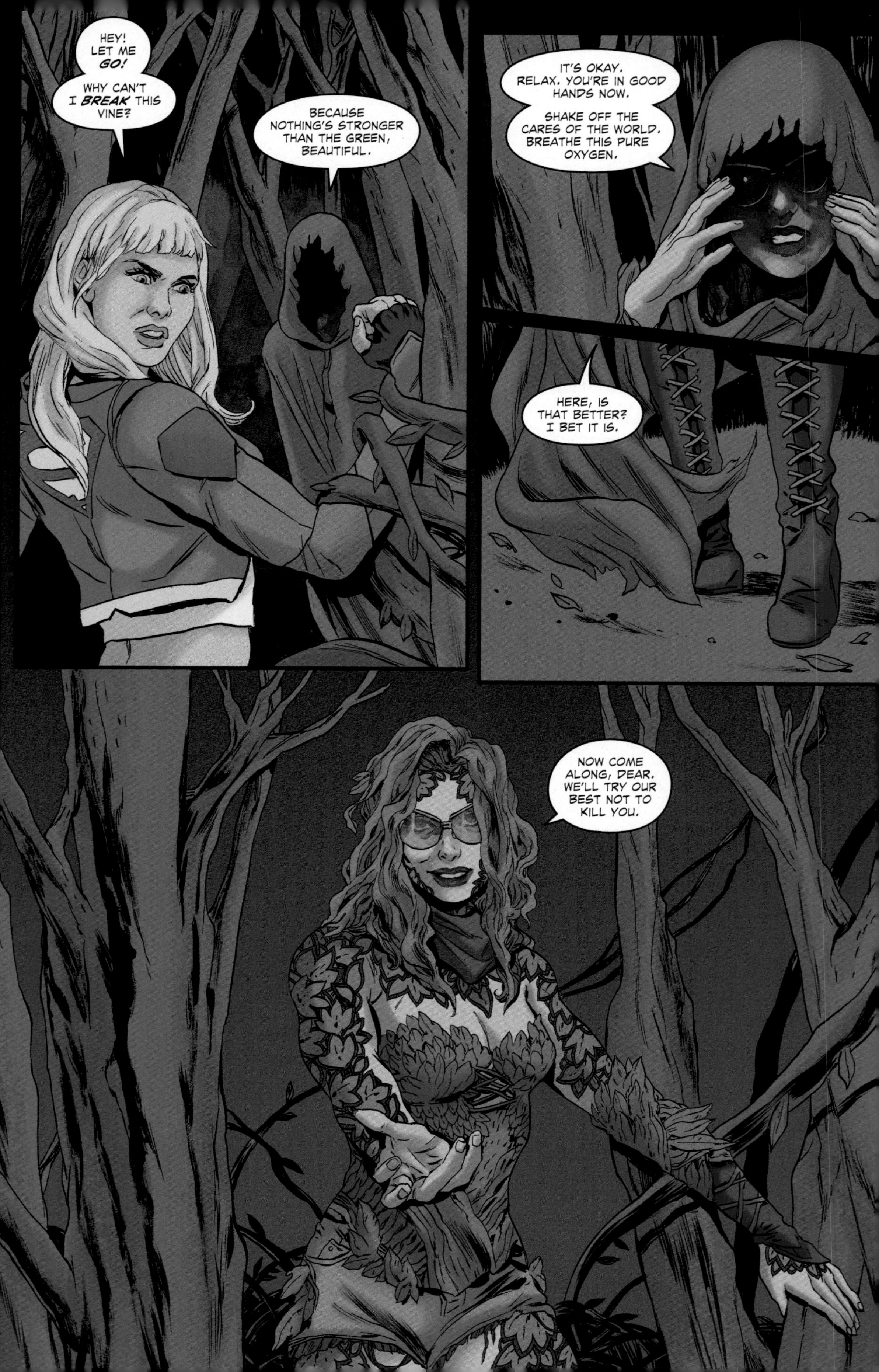

HEY! LET ME **GO!**
WHY CAN'T I **BREAK** THIS VINE?
BECAUSE NOTHING'S STRONGER THAN THE GREEN, BEAUTIFUL.
IT'S OKAY. RELAX. YOU'RE IN GOOD HANDS NOW.
SHAKE OFF THE CARES OF THE WORLD. BREATHE THIS PURE OXYGEN.
HERE, IS THAT BETTER? I BET IT IS.
NOW COME ALONG, DEAR. WE'LL TRY OUR BEST NOT TO KILL YOU.

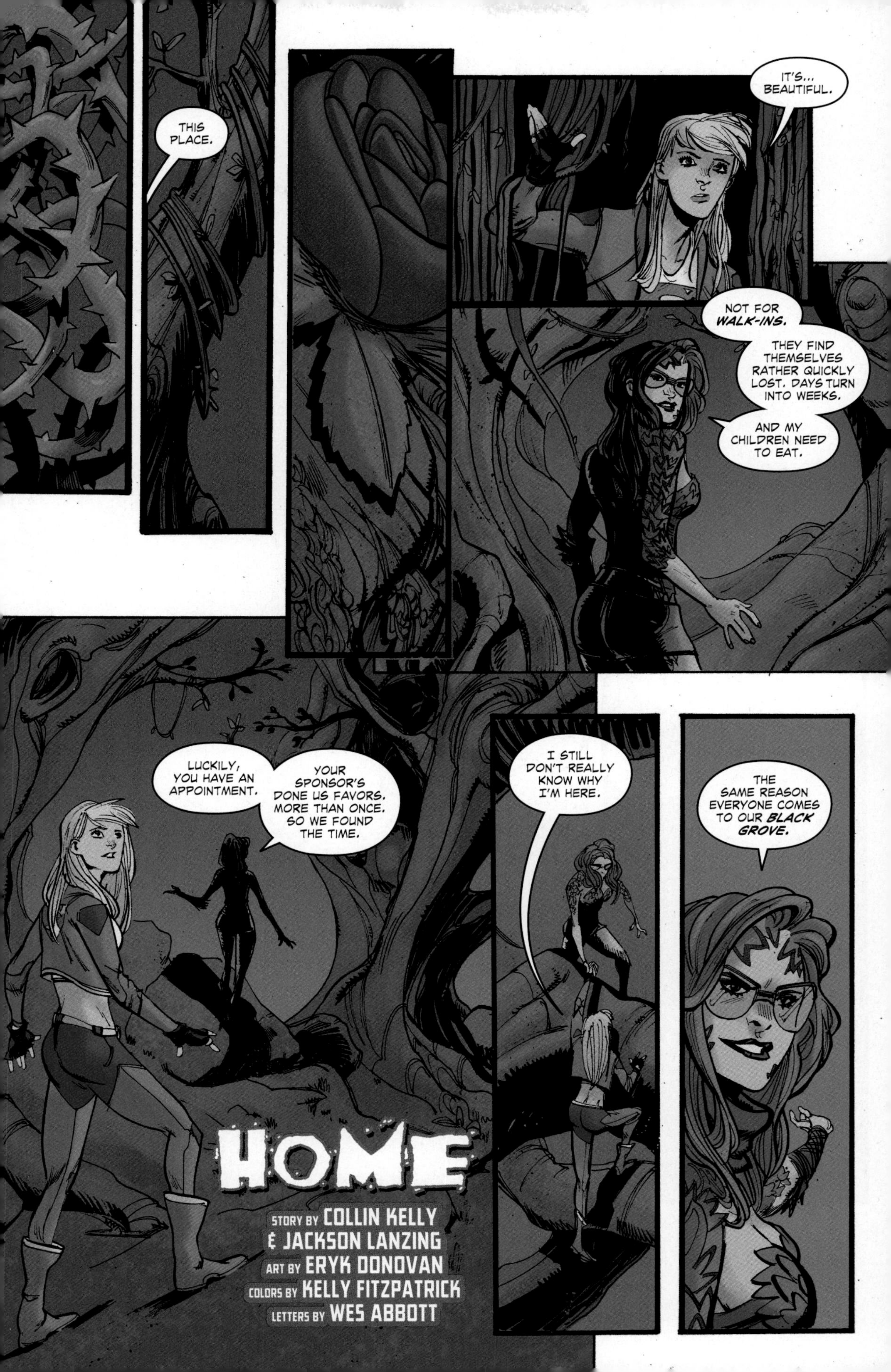

THIS PLACE.
IT'S... BEAUTIFUL.
NOT FOR *WALK-INS.*
THEY FIND THEMSELVES RATHER QUICKLY LOST. DAYS TURN INTO WEEKS.
AND MY CHILDREN NEED TO EAT.
LUCKILY, YOU HAVE AN APPOINTMENT.
YOUR SPONSOR'S DONE US FAVORS. MORE THAN ONCE. SO WE FOUND THE TIME.
I STILL DON'T REALLY KNOW WHY I'M HERE.
THE SAME REASON EVERYONE COMES TO OUR *BLACK GROVE.*
HOME
STORY BY COLLIN KELLY & JACKSON LANZING
ART BY ERYK DONOVAN
COLORS BY KELLY FITZPATRICK
LETTERS BY WES ABBOTT

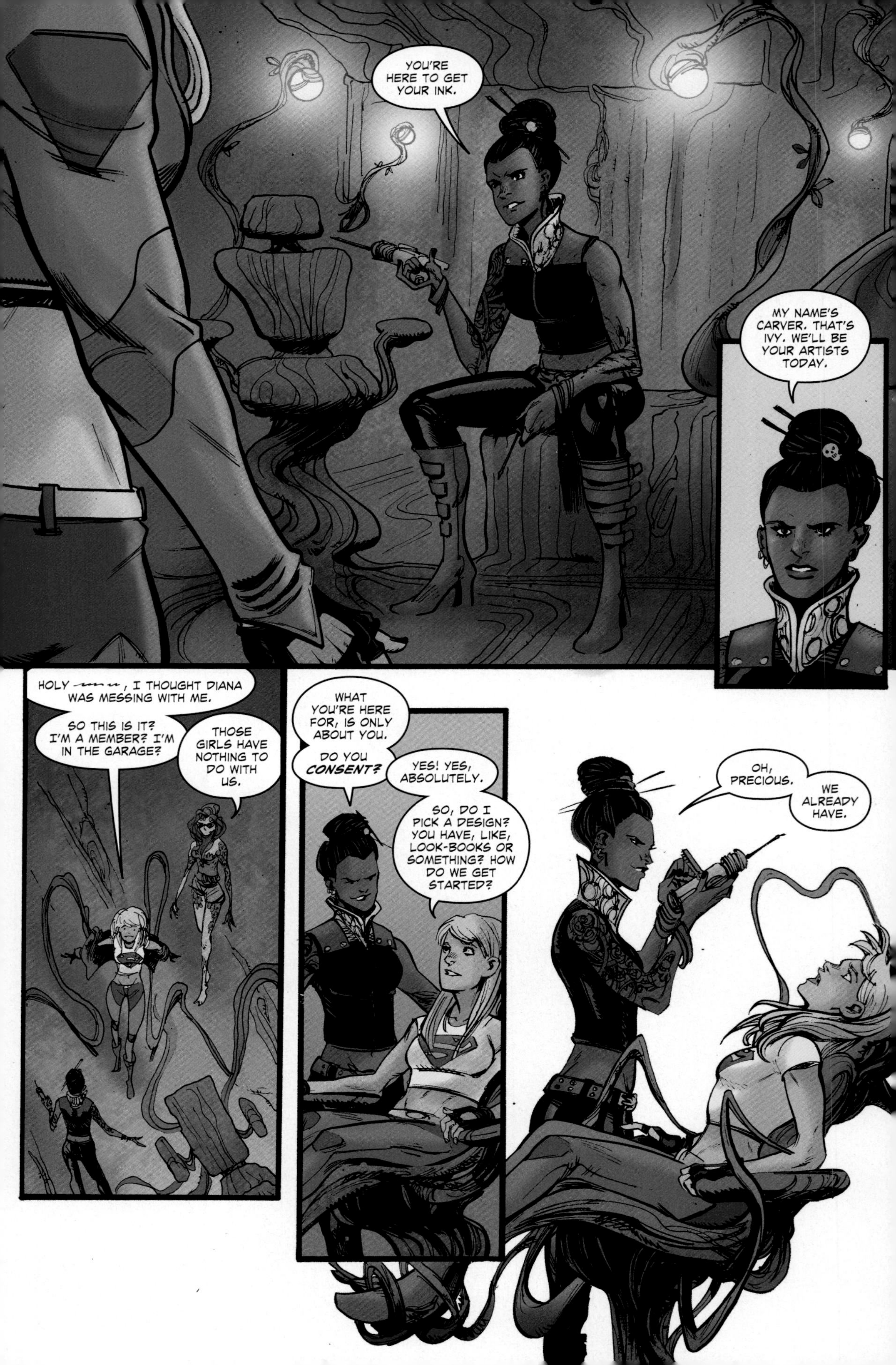
YOU'RE HERE TO GET YOUR INK.
MY NAME'S CARVER. THAT'S IVY. WE'LL BE YOUR ARTISTS TODAY.
HOLY —, I THOUGHT DIANA WAS MESSING WITH ME.
SO THIS IS IT? I'M A MEMBER? I'M IN THE GARAGE?
THOSE GIRLS HAVE NOTHING TO DO WITH US.
WHAT YOU'RE HERE FOR, IS ONLY ABOUT YOU.
DO YOU *CONSENT?*
YES! YES, ABSOLUTELY.
SO, DO I PICK A DESIGN? YOU HAVE, LIKE, LOOK-BOOKS OR SOMETHING? HOW DO WE GET STARTED?
OH, PRECIOUS.
WE ALREADY HAVE.

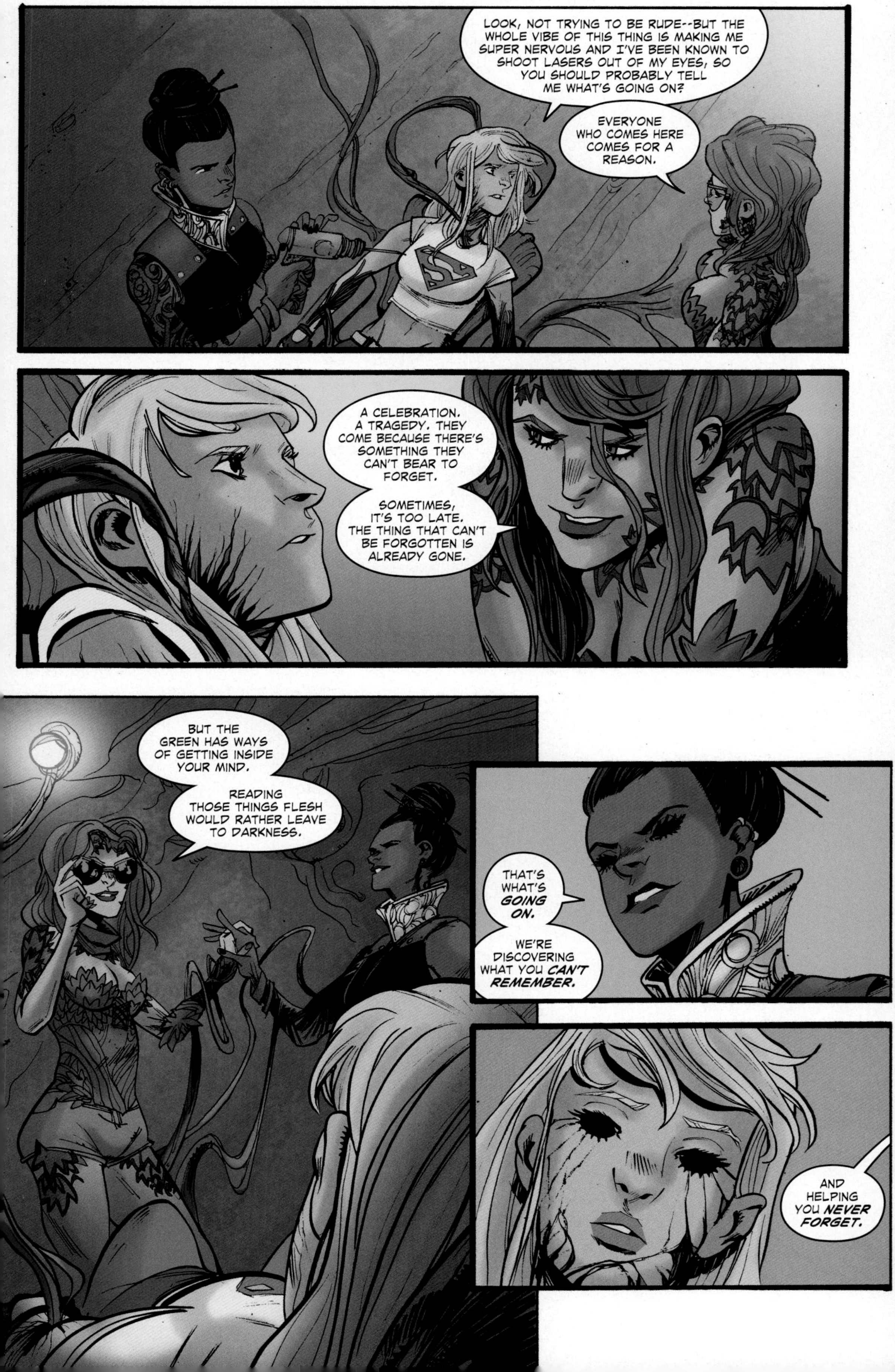
LOOK, NOT TRYING TO BE RUDE--BUT THE WHOLE VIBE OF THIS THING IS MAKING ME SUPER NERVOUS AND I'VE BEEN KNOWN TO SHOOT LASERS OUT OF MY EYES, SO YOU SHOULD PROBABLY TELL ME WHAT'S GOING ON?
EVERYONE WHO COMES HERE COMES FOR A REASON.
A CELEBRATION. A TRAGEDY. THEY COME BECAUSE THERE'S SOMETHING THEY CAN'T BEAR TO FORGET.
SOMETIMES, IT'S TOO LATE. THE THING THAT CAN'T BE FORGOTTEN IS ALREADY GONE.
BUT THE GREEN HAS WAYS OF GETTING INSIDE YOUR MIND.
READING THOSE THINGS FLESH WOULD RATHER LEAVE TO DARKNESS.
THAT'S WHAT'S *GOING ON.*
WE'RE DISCOVERING WHAT YOU *CAN'T REMEMBER.*
AND HELPING YOU *NEVER FORGET.*

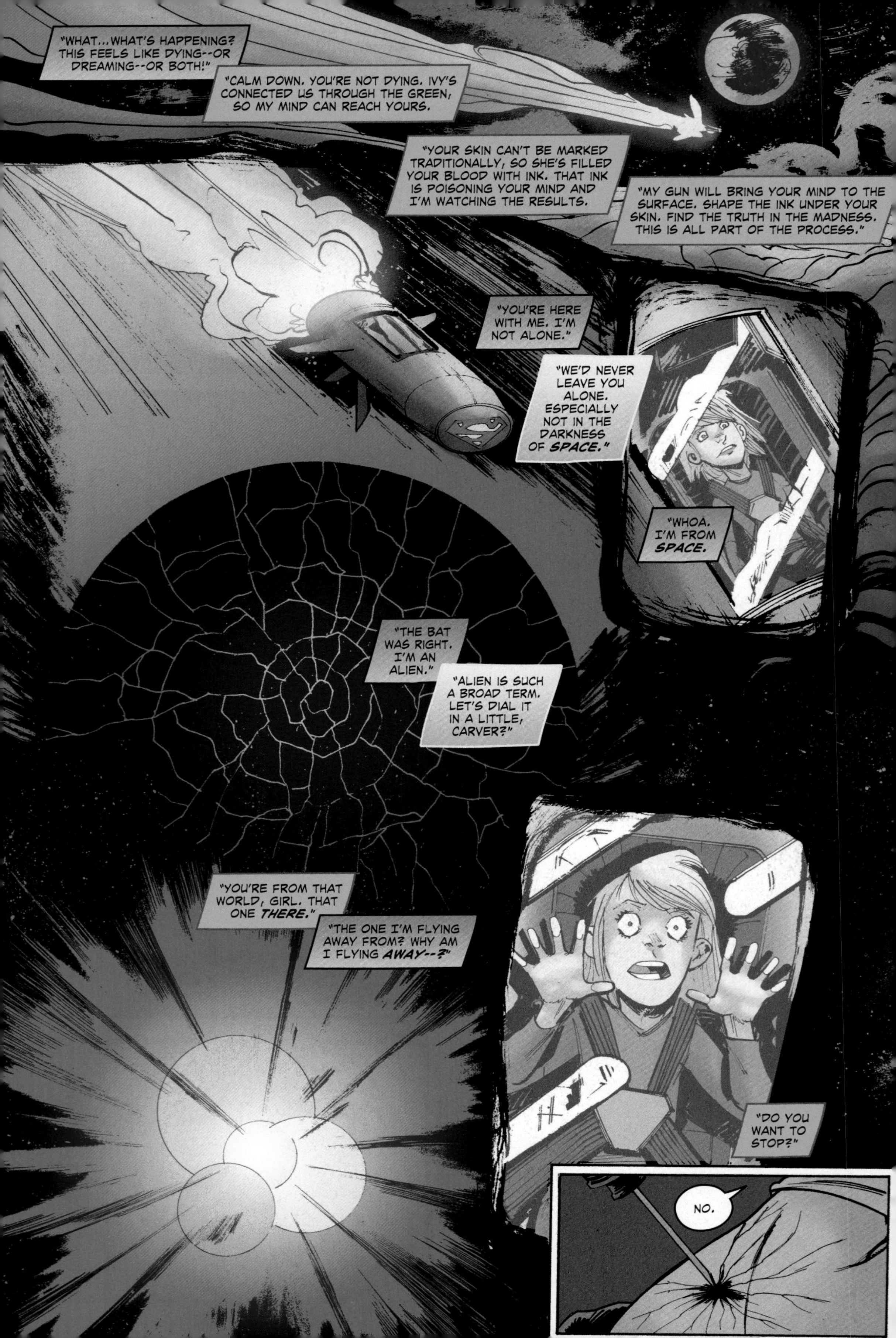
"WHAT...WHAT'S HAPPENING? THIS FEELS LIKE DYING--OR DREAMING--OR BOTH!"
"CALM DOWN. YOU'RE NOT DYING. IVY'S CONNECTED US THROUGH THE GREEN, SO MY MIND CAN REACH YOURS.
"YOUR SKIN CAN'T BE MARKED TRADITIONALLY, SO SHE'S FILLED YOUR BLOOD WITH INK. THAT INK IS POISONING YOUR MIND AND I'M WATCHING THE RESULTS.
"MY GUN WILL BRING YOUR MIND TO THE SURFACE. SHAPE THE INK UNDER YOUR SKIN. FIND THE TRUTH IN THE MADNESS. THIS IS ALL PART OF THE PROCESS."
"YOU'RE HERE WITH ME. I'M NOT ALONE."
"WE'D NEVER LEAVE YOU ALONE. ESPECIALLY NOT IN THE DARKNESS OF *SPACE.*"
"WHOA. I'M FROM *SPACE.*
"THE BAT WAS RIGHT. I'M AN ALIEN."
"ALIEN IS SUCH A BROAD TERM. LET'S DIAL IT IN A LITTLE, CARVER?"
"YOU'RE FROM THAT WORLD, GIRL. THAT ONE *THERE.*"
"THE ONE I'M FLYING AWAY FROM? WHY AM I FLYING *AWAY*--?"
"DO YOU WANT TO STOP?"
NO.

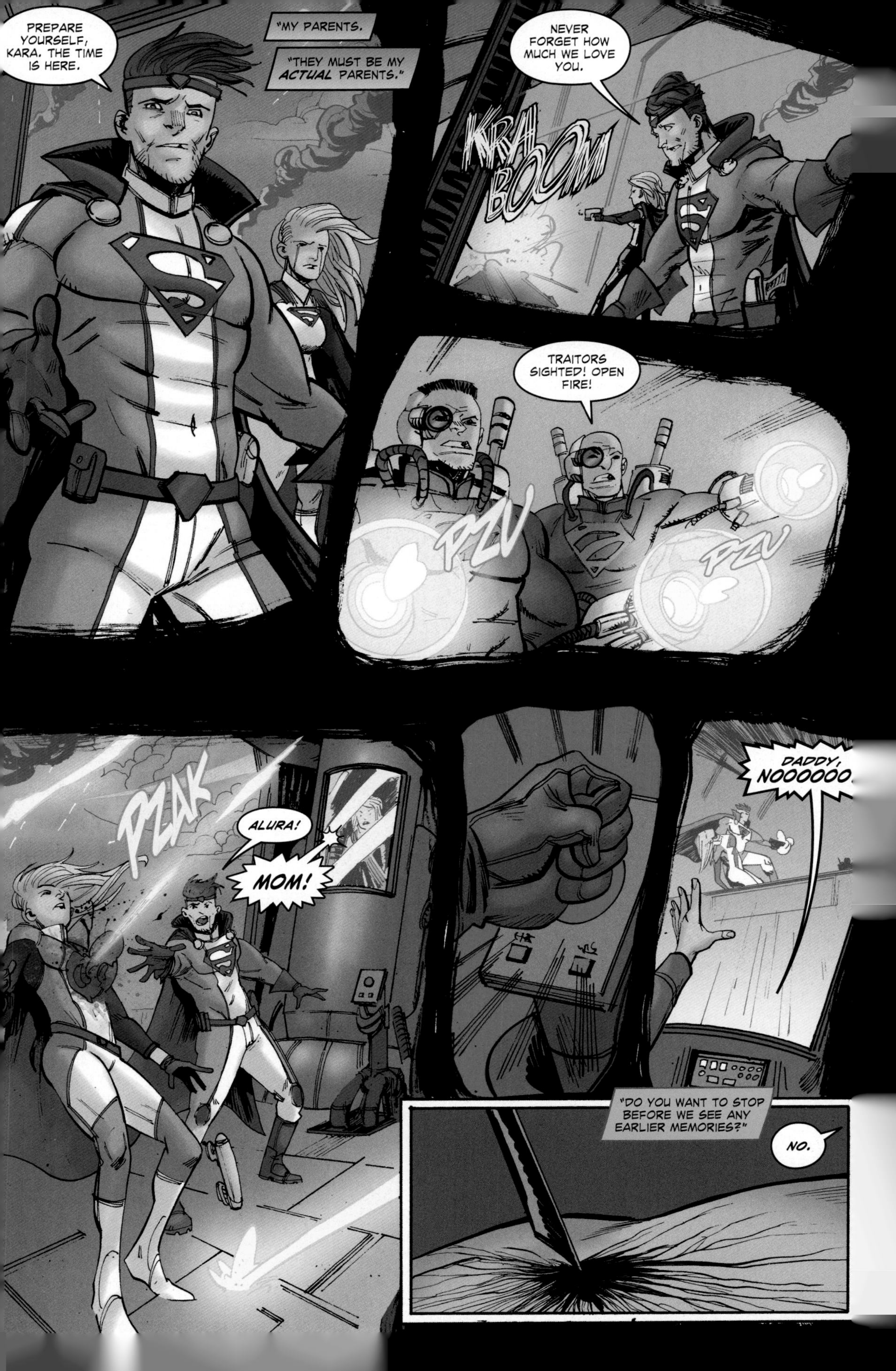
PREPARE YOURSELF, KARA. THE TIME IS HERE.
"MY PARENTS.
"THEY MUST BE MY ACTUAL PARENTS."
NEVER FORGET HOW MUCH WE LOVE YOU.
KRA BOOM
TRAITORS SIGHTED! OPEN FIRE!
PZU
PZU
PZAK
ALURA!
MOM!
DADDY, NOOOOOO
"DO YOU WANT TO STOP BEFORE WE SEE ANY EARLIER MEMORIES?"
NO.

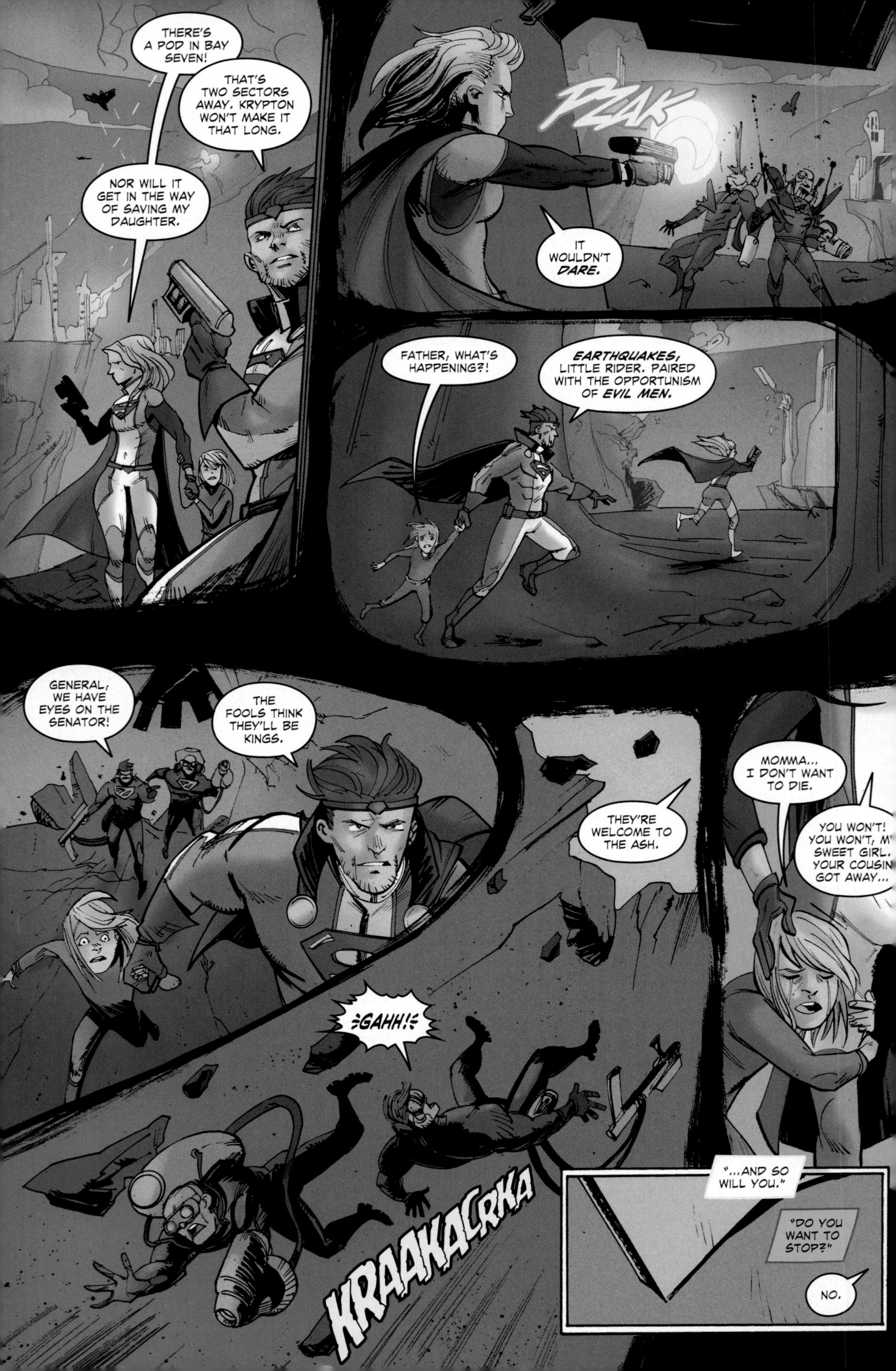
THERE'S A POD IN BAY SEVEN!
THAT'S TWO SECTORS AWAY. KRYPTON WON'T MAKE IT THAT LONG.
NOR WILL IT GET IN THE WAY OF SAVING MY DAUGHTER.
PZAK
IT WOULDN'T *DARE.*
FATHER, WHAT'S HAPPENING?!
EARTHQUAKES, LITTLE RIDER. PAIRED WITH THE OPPORTUNISM OF *EVIL MEN.*
GENERAL, WE HAVE EYES ON THE SENATOR!
THE FOOLS THINK THEY'LL BE KINGS.
THEY'RE WELCOME TO THE ASH.
GAHH!
KRAAKACRKA
MOMMA... I DON'T WANT TO DIE.
YOU WON'T! YOU WON'T, M' SWEET GIRL. YOUR COUSIN GOT AWAY...
"...AND SO WILL YOU."
"DO YOU WANT TO STOP?"
NO.

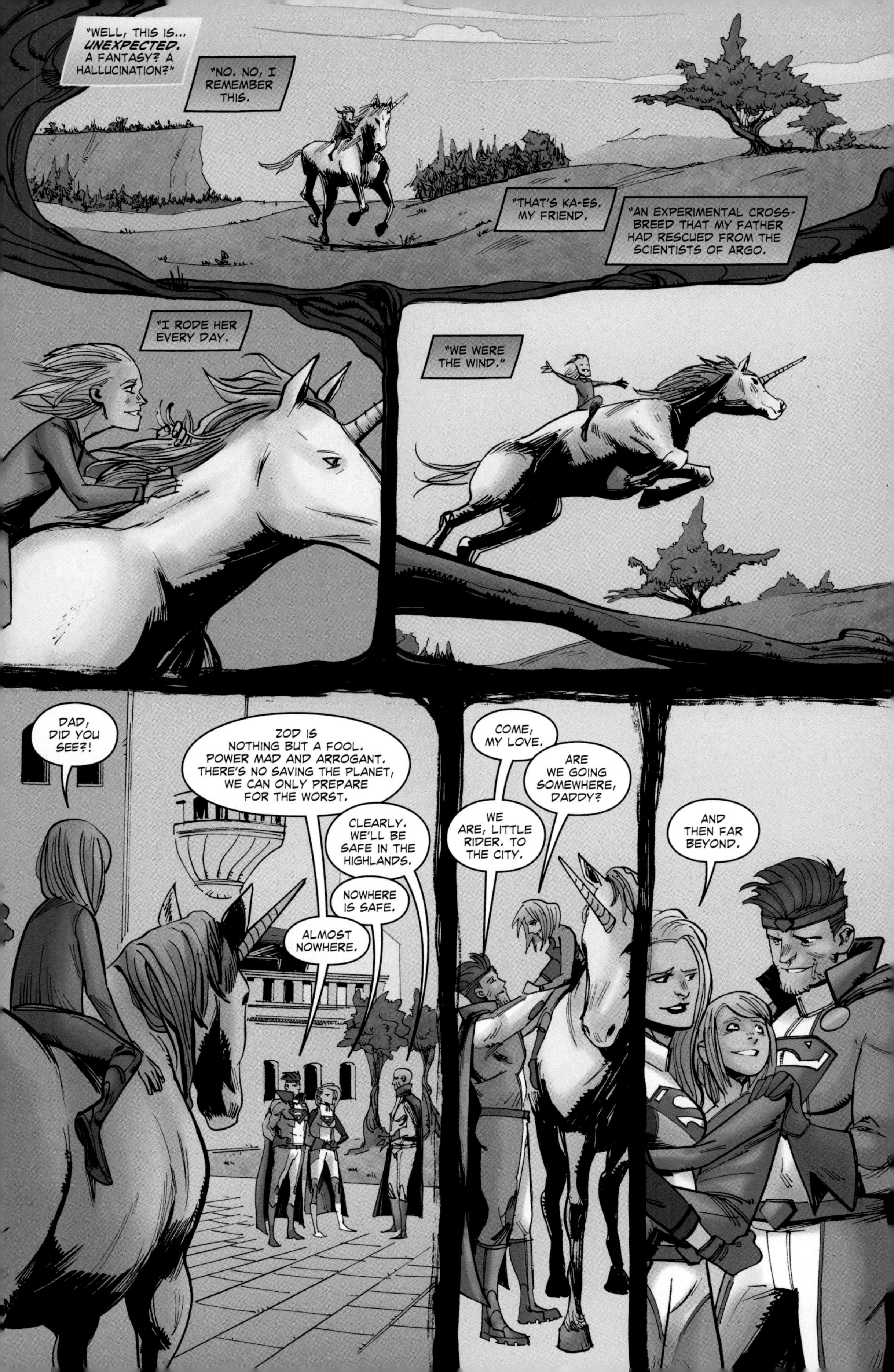
"WELL, THIS IS... *UNEXPECTED.* A FANTASY? A HALLUCINATION?"
"NO. NO, I REMEMBER THIS.
"THAT'S KA-ES. MY FRIEND.
"AN EXPERIMENTAL CROSS-BREED THAT MY FATHER HAD RESCUED FROM THE SCIENTISTS OF ARGO.
"I RODE HER EVERY DAY.
"WE WERE THE WIND."
DAD, DID YOU SEE?!
ZOD IS NOTHING BUT A FOOL. POWER MAD AND ARROGANT. THERE'S NO SAVING THE PLANET, WE CAN ONLY PREPARE FOR THE WORST.
CLEARLY. WE'LL BE SAFE IN THE HIGHLANDS.
NOWHERE IS SAFE.
ALMOST NOWHERE.
COME, MY LOVE.
ARE WE GOING SOMEWHERE, DADDY?
WE ARE, LITTLE RIDER. TO THE CITY.
AND THEN FAR BEYOND.

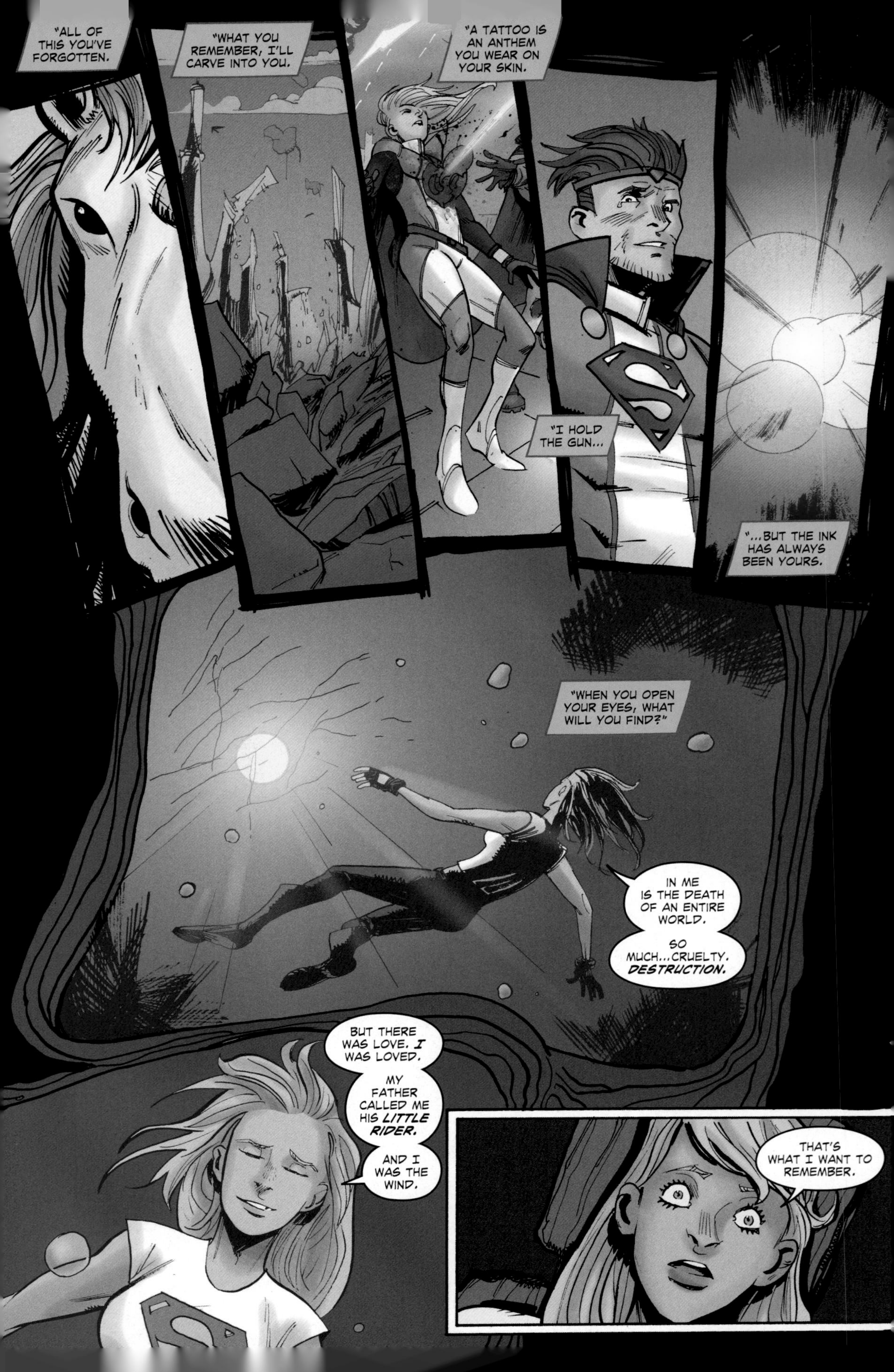
"ALL OF THIS YOU'VE FORGOTTEN.
"WHAT YOU REMEMBER, I'LL CARVE INTO YOU.
"A TATTOO IS AN ANTHEM YOU WEAR ON YOUR SKIN.
"I HOLD THE GUN...
"...BUT THE INK HAS ALWAYS BEEN YOURS.
"WHEN YOU OPEN YOUR EYES, WHAT WILL YOU FIND?"
IN ME IS THE DEATH OF AN ENTIRE WORLD.
SO MUCH...CRUELTY. DESTRUCTION.
BUT THERE WAS LOVE. I WAS LOVED.
MY FATHER CALLED ME HIS LITTLE RIDER.
AND I WAS THE WIND.
THAT'S WHAT I WANT TO REMEMBER.

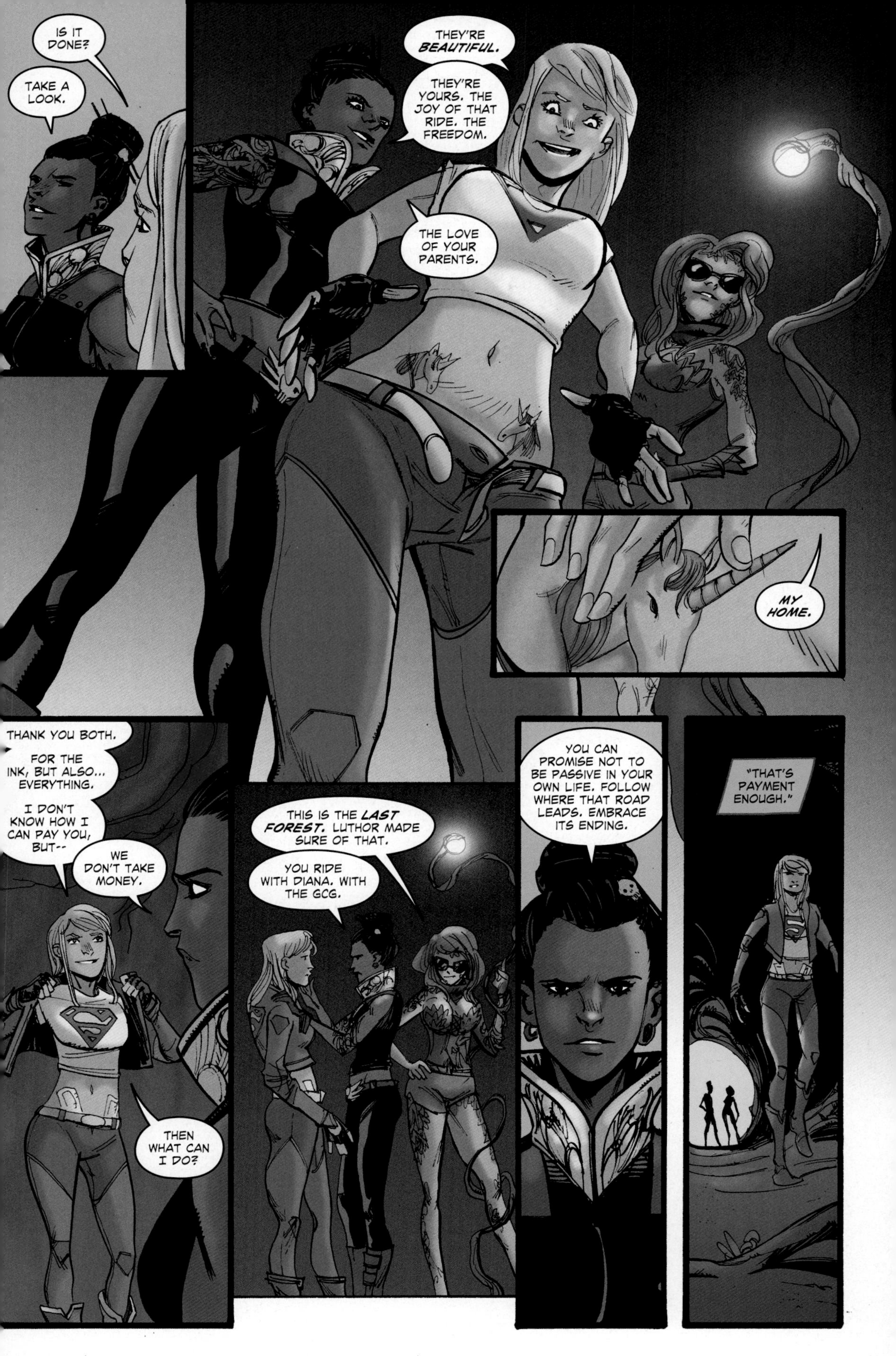

IS IT DONE?
TAKE A LOOK.
THEY'RE *BEAUTIFUL.*
THEY'RE YOURS. THE JOY OF THAT RIDE. THE FREEDOM.
THE LOVE OF YOUR PARENTS.
MY HOME.
THANK YOU BOTH.
FOR THE INK, BUT ALSO... EVERYTHING.
I DON'T KNOW HOW I CAN PAY YOU, BUT--
WE DON'T TAKE MONEY.
THEN WHAT CAN I DO?
THIS IS THE *LAST FOREST.* LUTHOR MADE SURE OF THAT.
YOU RIDE WITH DIANA. WITH THE GCG.
YOU CAN PROMISE NOT TO BE PASSIVE IN YOUR OWN LIFE. FOLLOW WHERE THAT ROAD LEADS. EMBRACE ITS ENDING.
"THAT'S PAYMENT ENOUGH."

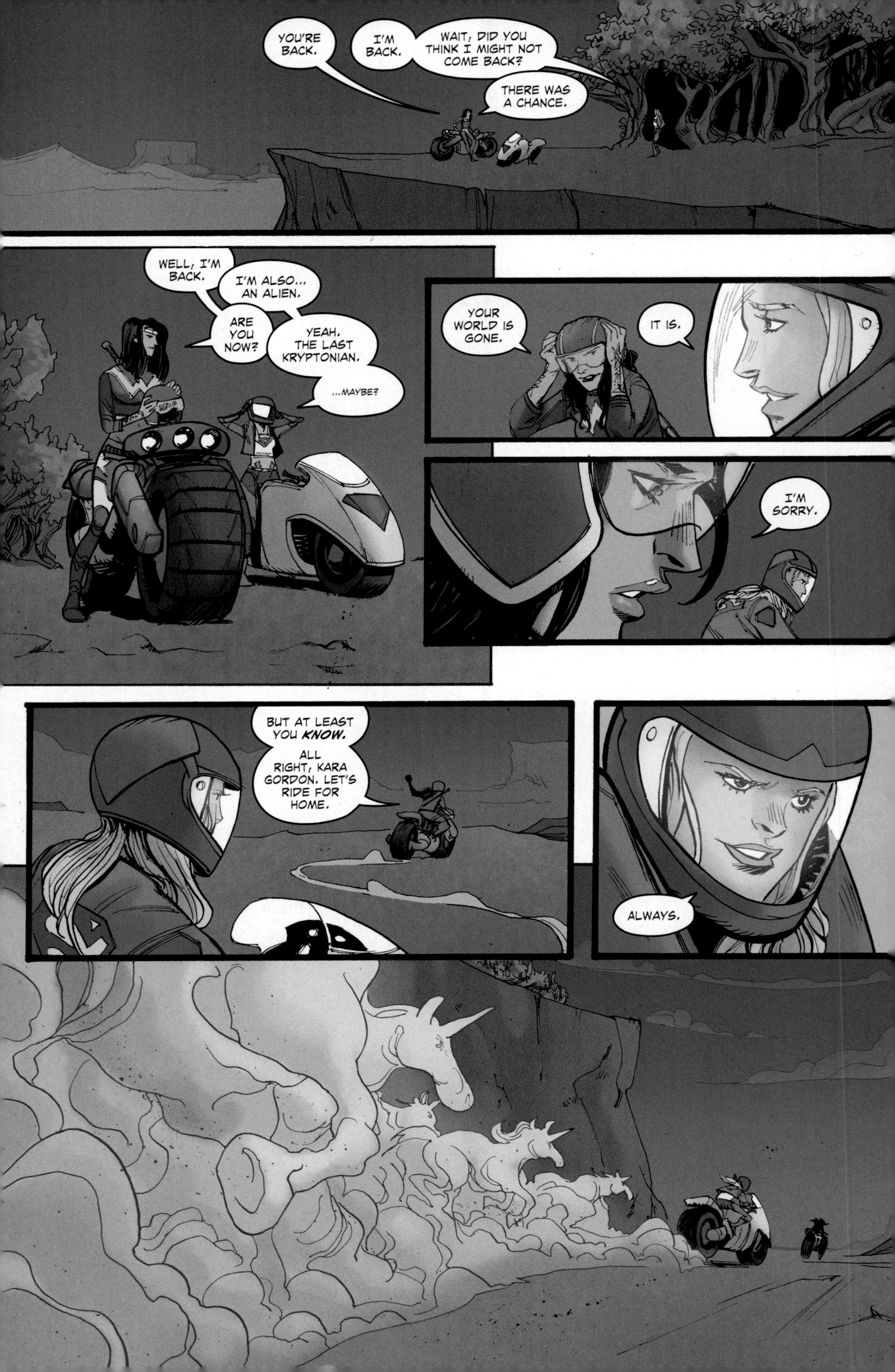

YOU'RE BACK.
I'M BACK.
WAIT, DID YOU THINK I MIGHT NOT COME BACK?
THERE WAS A CHANCE.
WELL, I'M BACK.
I'M ALSO... AN ALIEN.
ARE YOU NOW?
YEAH. THE LAST KRYPTONIAN.
...MAYBE?
YOUR WORLD IS GONE.
IT IS.
I'M SORRY.
BUT AT LEAST YOU KNOW.
ALL RIGHT, KARA GORDON. LET'S RIDE FOR HOME.
ALWAYS.

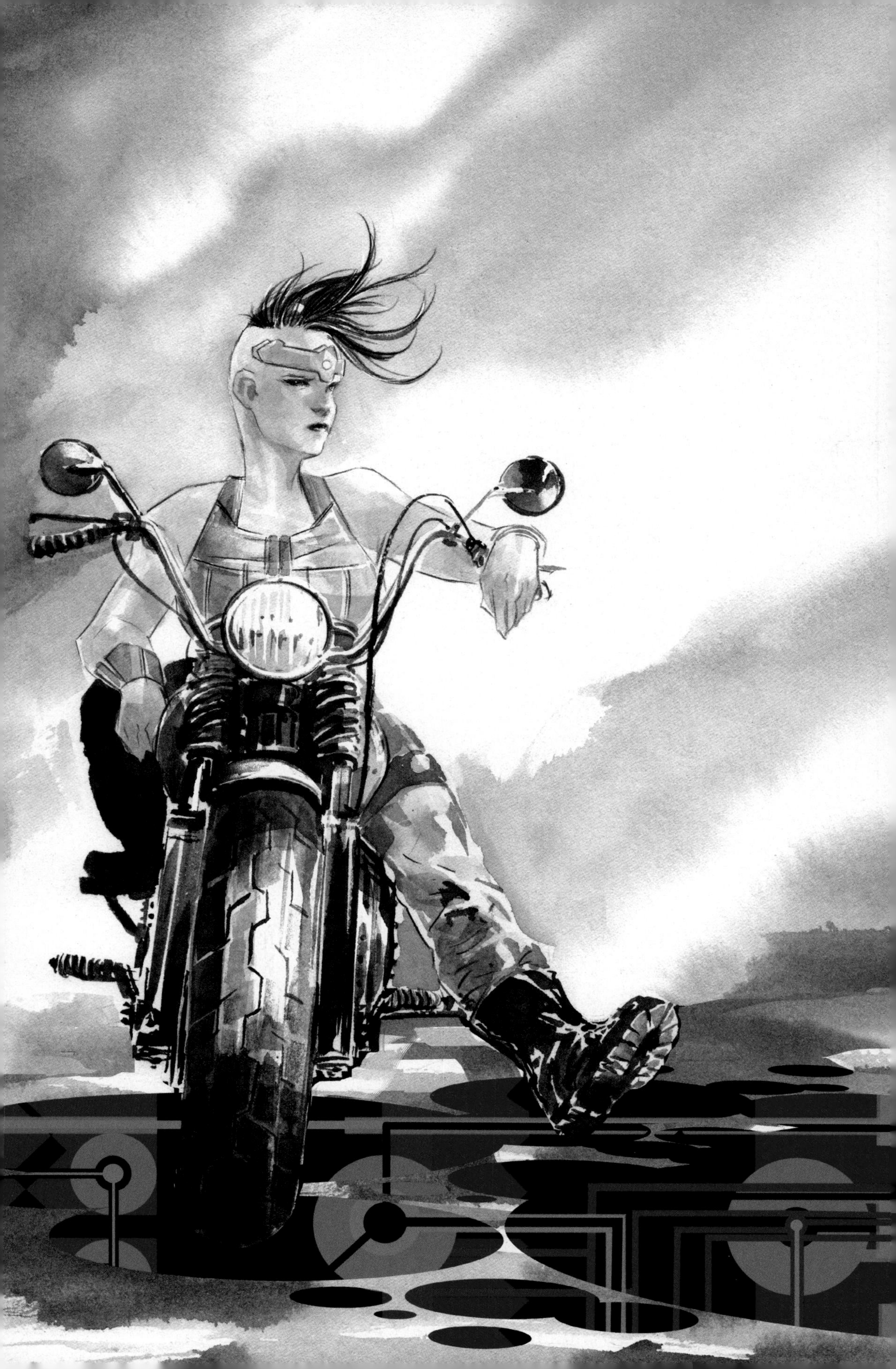

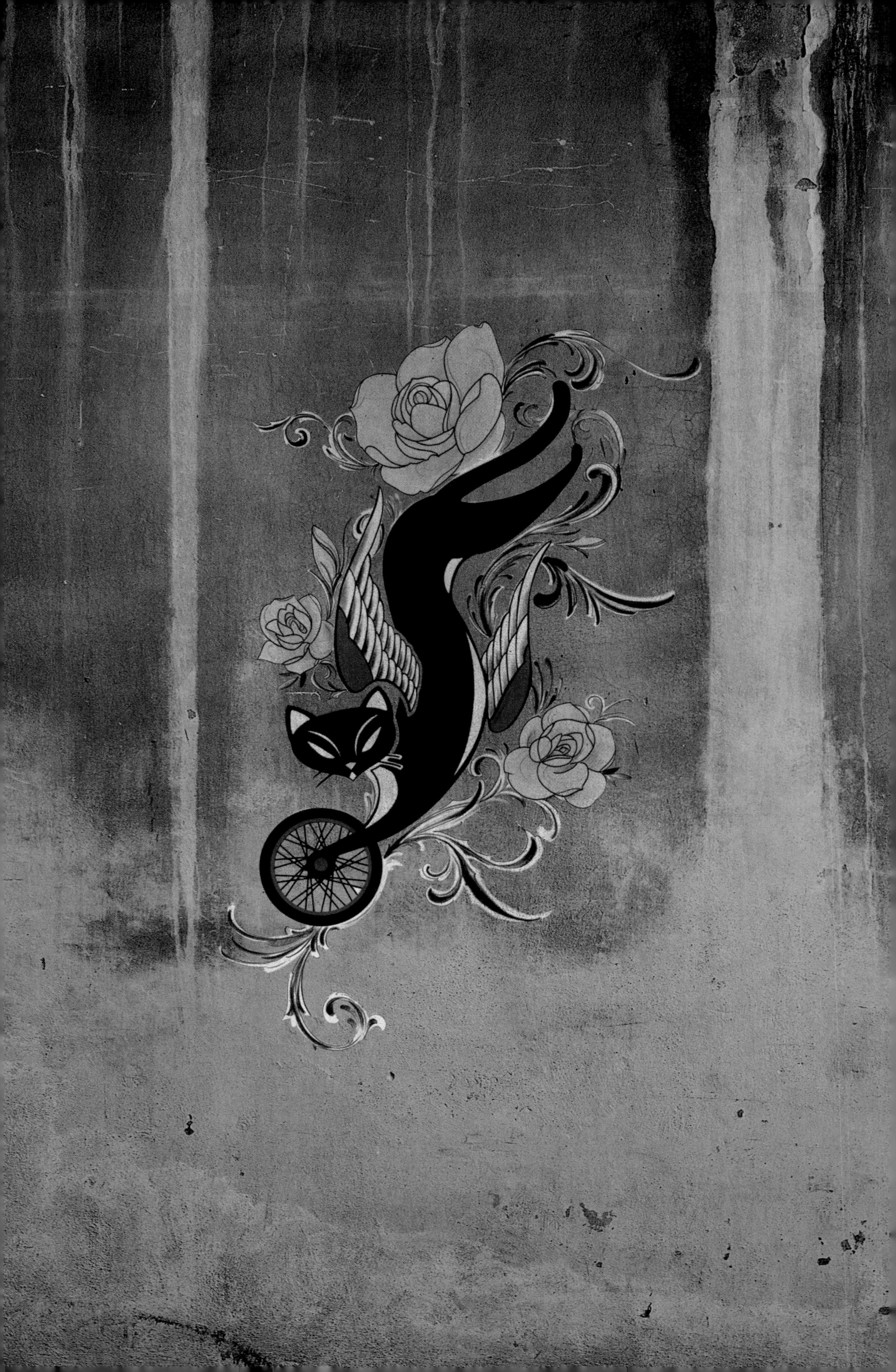

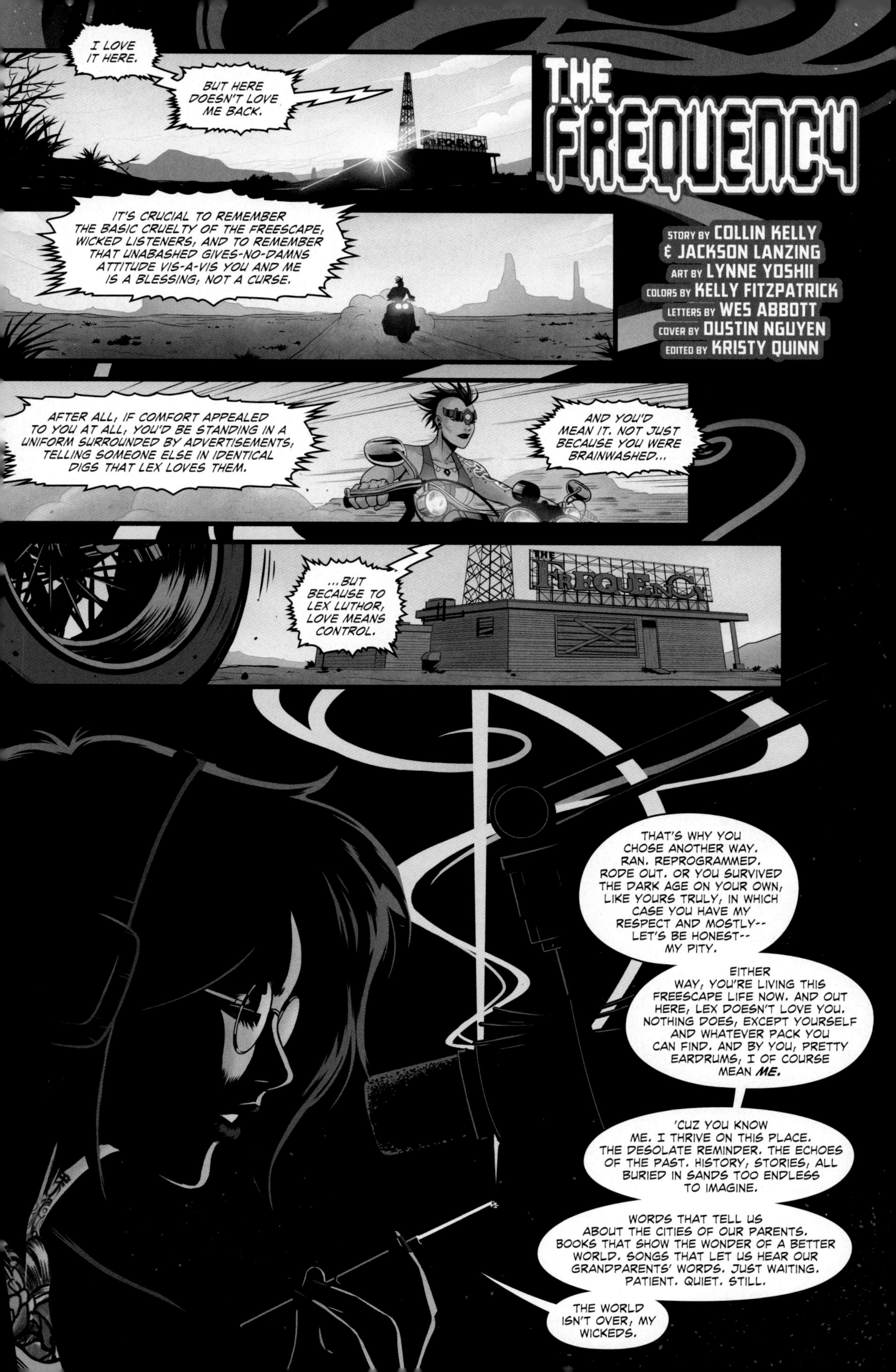
THE FREQUENCY
STORY BY COLLIN KELLY & JACKSON LANZING
ART BY LYNNE YOSHII
COLORS BY KELLY FITZPATRICK
LETTERS BY WES ABBOTT
COVER BY DUSTIN NGUYEN
EDITED BY KRISTY QUINN
I LOVE IT HERE.
BUT HERE DOESN'T LOVE ME BACK.
IT'S CRUCIAL TO REMEMBER THE BASIC CRUELTY OF THE FREESCAPE, WICKED LISTENERS, AND TO REMEMBER THAT UNABASHED GIVES-NO-DAMNS ATTITUDE VIS-A-VIS YOU AND ME IS A BLESSING, NOT A CURSE.
AFTER ALL, IF COMFORT APPEALED TO YOU AT ALL, YOU'D BE STANDING IN A UNIFORM SURROUNDED BY ADVERTISEMENTS, TELLING SOMEONE ELSE IN IDENTICAL DIGS THAT LEX LOVES THEM.
AND YOU'D MEAN IT. NOT JUST BECAUSE YOU WERE BRAINWASHED...
...BUT BECAUSE TO LEX LUTHOR, LOVE MEANS CONTROL.
THE FREQUENCY
THAT'S WHY YOU CHOSE ANOTHER WAY. RAN. REPROGRAMMED. RODE OUT. OR YOU SURVIVED THE DARK AGE ON YOUR OWN, LIKE YOURS TRULY, IN WHICH CASE YOU HAVE MY RESPECT AND MOSTLY-- LET'S BE HONEST-- MY PITY.
EITHER WAY, YOU'RE LIVING THIS FREESCAPE LIFE NOW. AND OUT HERE, LEX DOESN'T LOVE YOU. NOTHING DOES, EXCEPT YOURSELF AND WHATEVER PACK YOU CAN FIND. AND BY YOU, PRETTY EARDRUMS, I OF COURSE MEAN *ME.*
'CUZ YOU KNOW ME. I THRIVE ON THIS PLACE. THE DESOLATE REMINDER. THE ECHOES OF THE PAST. HISTORY, STORIES, ALL BURIED IN SANDS TOO ENDLESS TO IMAGINE.
WORDS THAT TELL US ABOUT THE CITIES OF OUR PARENTS. BOOKS THAT SHOW THE WONDER OF A BETTER WORLD. SONGS THAT LET US HEAR OUR GRANDPARENTS' WORDS. JUST WAITING. PATIENT. QUIET. STILL.
THE WORLD ISN'T OVER, MY WICKEDS.

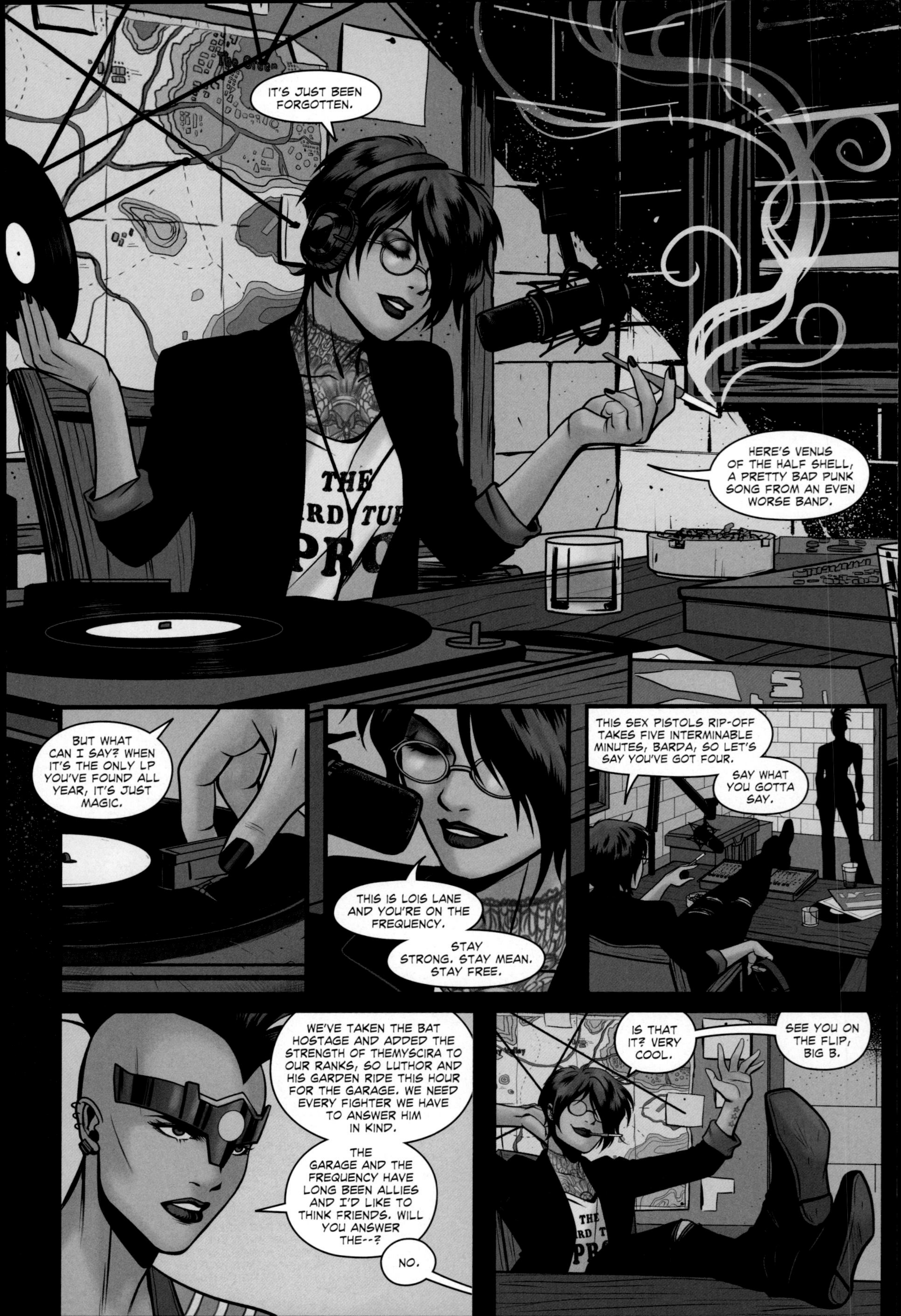
IT'S JUST BEEN FORGOTTEN.
HERE'S VENUS OF THE HALF SHELL, A PRETTY BAD PUNK SONG FROM AN EVEN WORSE BAND.
BUT WHAT CAN I SAY? WHEN IT'S THE ONLY LP YOU'VE FOUND ALL YEAR, IT'S JUST MAGIC.
THIS IS LOIS LANE AND YOU'RE ON THE FREQUENCY.
STAY STRONG. STAY MEAN. STAY FREE.
THIS SEX PISTOLS RIP-OFF TAKES FIVE INTERMINABLE MINUTES, BARDA, SO LET'S SAY YOU'VE GOT FOUR.
SAY WHAT YOU GOTTA SAY.
WE'VE TAKEN THE BAT HOSTAGE AND ADDED THE STRENGTH OF THEMYSCIRA TO OUR RANKS, SO LUTHOR AND HIS GARDEN RIDE THIS HOUR FOR THE GARAGE. WE NEED EVERY FIGHTER WE HAVE TO ANSWER HIM IN KIND.
THE GARAGE AND THE FREQUENCY HAVE LONG BEEN ALLIES AND I'D LIKE TO THINK FRIENDS. WILL YOU ANSWER THE--?
NO.
IS THAT IT? VERY COOL.
SEE YOU ON THE FLIP, BIG B.

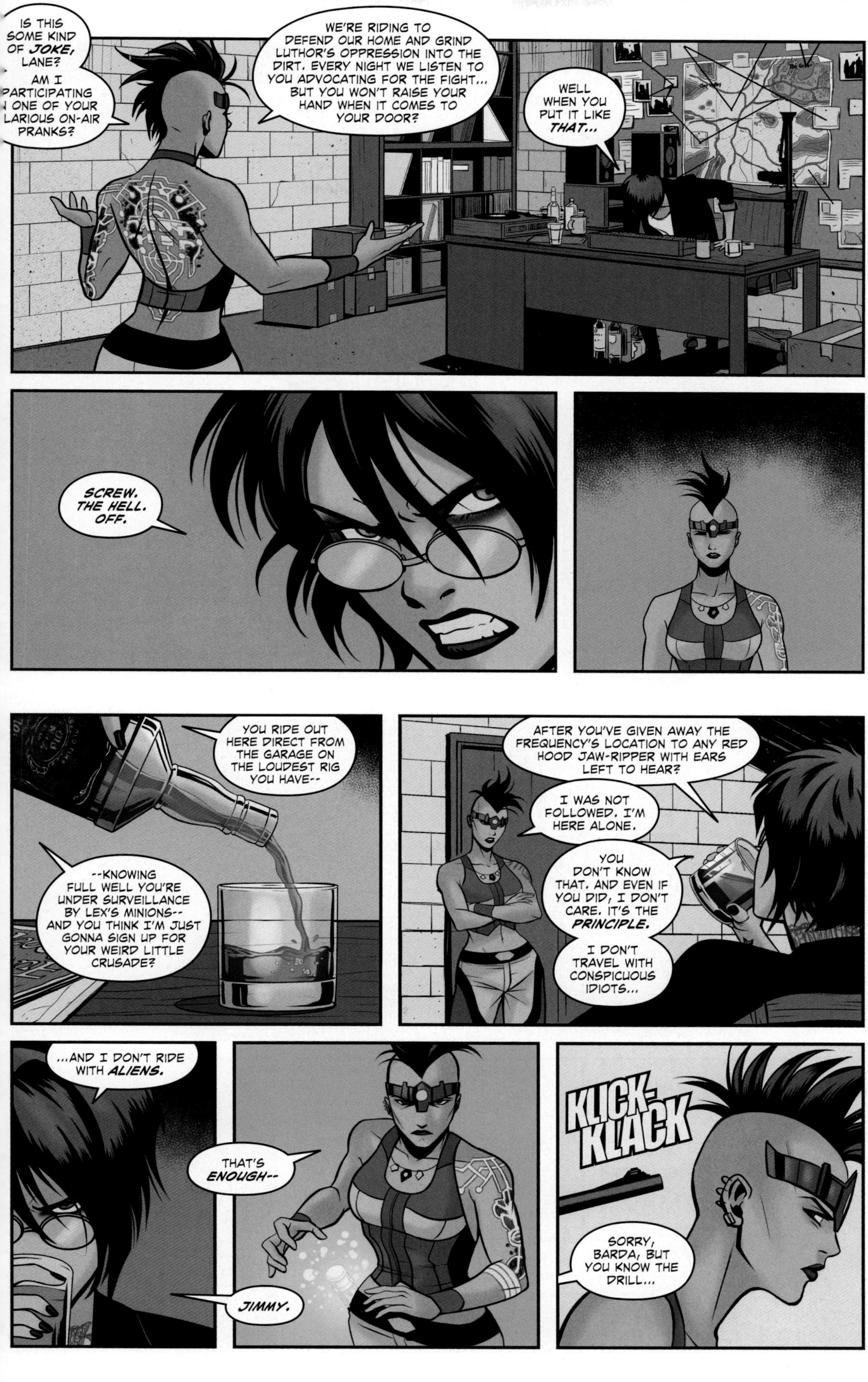
IS THIS SOME KIND OF JOKE, LANE?
AM I PARTICIPATING IN ONE OF YOUR HILARIOUS ON-AIR PRANKS?
WE'RE RIDING TO DEFEND OUR HOME AND GRIND LUTHOR'S OPPRESSION INTO THE DIRT. EVERY NIGHT WE LISTEN TO YOU ADVOCATING FOR THE FIGHT... BUT YOU WON'T RAISE YOUR HAND WHEN IT COMES TO YOUR DOOR?
WELL WHEN YOU PUT IT LIKE THAT...
SCREW. THE HELL. OFF.
YOU RIDE OUT HERE DIRECT FROM THE GARAGE ON THE LOUDEST RIG YOU HAVE--
--KNOWING FULL WELL YOU'RE UNDER SURVEILLANCE BY LEX'S MINIONS-- AND YOU THINK I'M JUST GONNA SIGN UP FOR YOUR WEIRD LITTLE CRUSADE?
AFTER YOU'VE GIVEN AWAY THE FREQUENCY'S LOCATION TO ANY RED HOOD JAW-RIPPER WITH EARS LEFT TO HEAR?
I WAS NOT FOLLOWED. I'M HERE ALONE.
YOU DON'T KNOW THAT. AND EVEN IF YOU DID, I DON'T CARE. IT'S THE PRINCIPLE.
I DON'T TRAVEL WITH CONSPICUOUS IDIOTS...
...AND I DON'T RIDE WITH ALIENS.
THAT'S ENOUGH--
JIMMY.
KLICK-KLACK
SORRY, BARDA, BUT YOU KNOW THE DRILL...

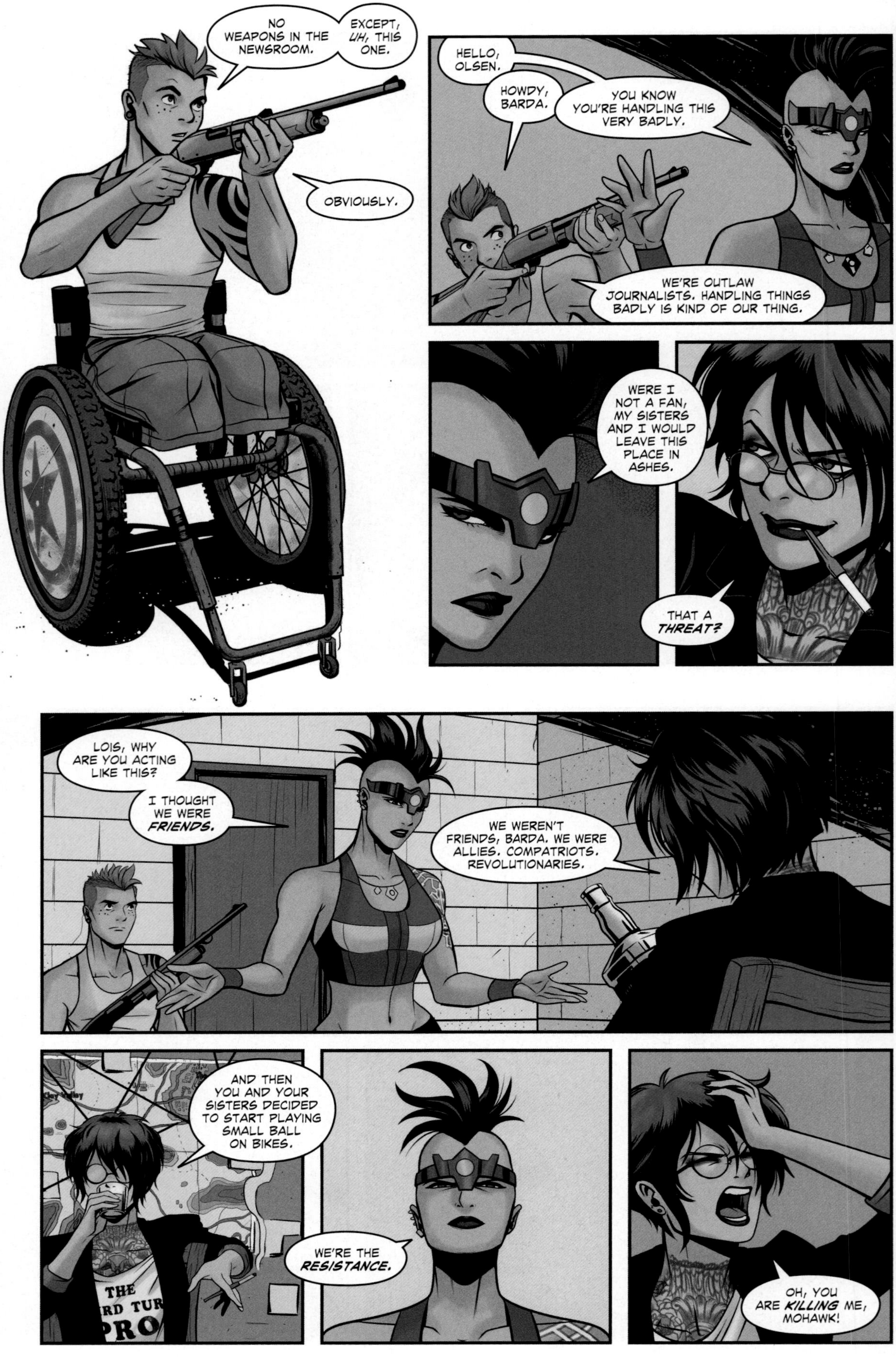
NO WEAPONS IN THE NEWSROOM.
EXCEPT, *UH*, THIS ONE.
OBVIOUSLY.
HELLO, OLSEN.
HOWDY, BARDA.
YOU KNOW YOU'RE HANDLING THIS VERY BADLY.
WE'RE OUTLAW JOURNALISTS. HANDLING THINGS BADLY IS KIND OF OUR THING.
WERE I NOT A FAN, MY SISTERS AND I WOULD LEAVE THIS PLACE IN ASHES.
THAT A ***THREAT?***
LOIS, WHY ARE YOU ACTING LIKE THIS?
I THOUGHT WE WERE ***FRIENDS.***
WE WEREN'T FRIENDS, BARDA. WE WERE ALLIES. COMPATRIOTS. REVOLUTIONARIES.
AND THEN YOU AND YOUR SISTERS DECIDED TO START PLAYING SMALL BALL ON BIKES.
WE'RE THE ***RESISTANCE.***
OH, YOU ARE ***KILLING*** ME, MOHAWK!

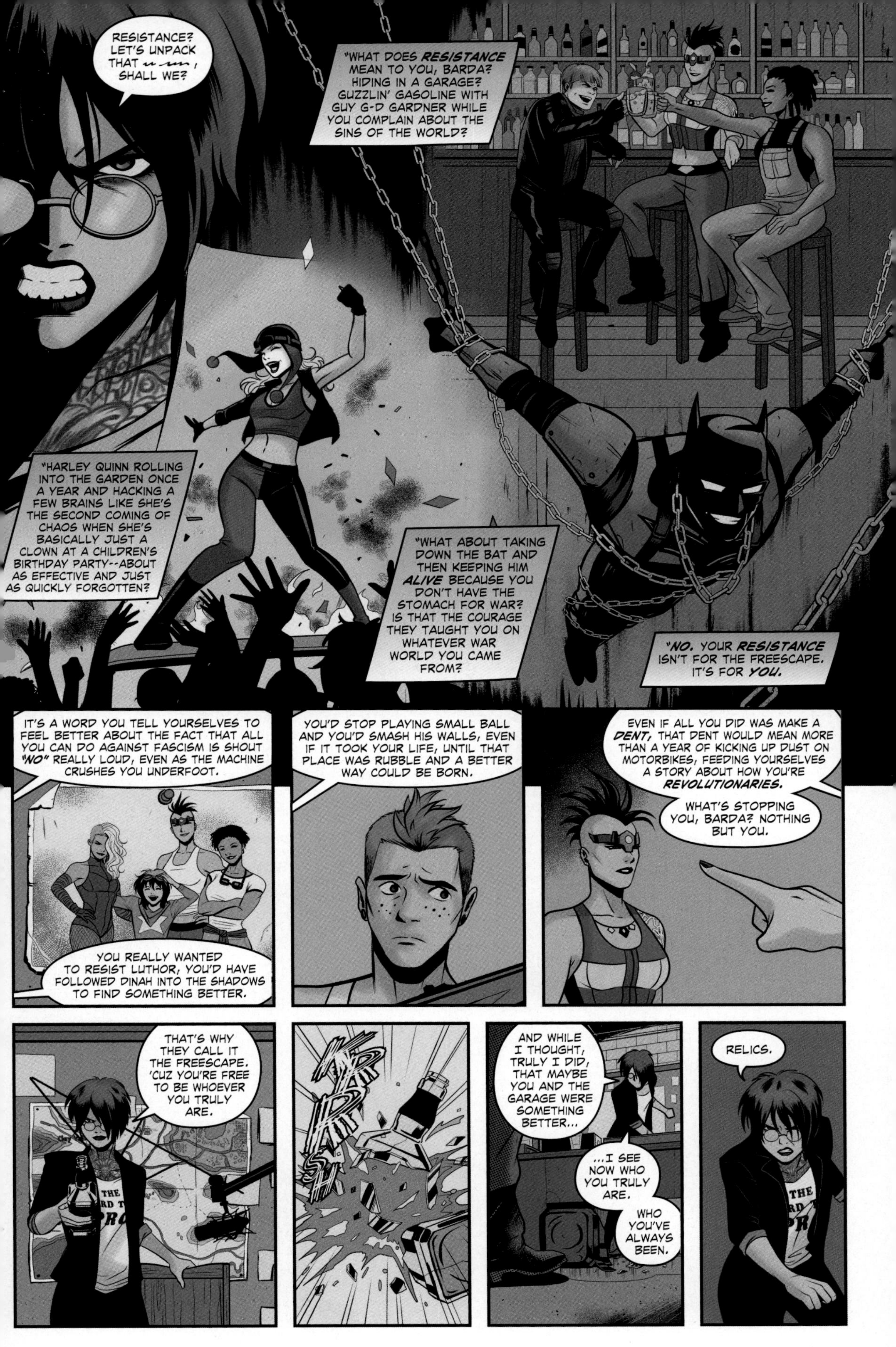
RESISTANCE? LET'S UNPACK THAT, SHALL WE?
"WHAT DOES RESISTANCE MEAN TO YOU, BARDA? HIDING IN A GARAGE? GUZZLIN' GASOLINE WITH GUY G-D GARDNER WHILE YOU COMPLAIN ABOUT THE SINS OF THE WORLD?
"HARLEY QUINN ROLLING INTO THE GARDEN ONCE A YEAR AND HACKING A FEW BRAINS LIKE SHE'S THE SECOND COMING OF CHAOS WHEN SHE'S BASICALLY JUST A CLOWN AT A CHILDREN'S BIRTHDAY PARTY--ABOUT AS EFFECTIVE AND JUST AS QUICKLY FORGOTTEN?
"WHAT ABOUT TAKING DOWN THE BAT AND THEN KEEPING HIM ALIVE BECAUSE YOU DON'T HAVE THE STOMACH FOR WAR? IS THAT THE COURAGE THEY TAUGHT YOU ON WHATEVER WAR WORLD YOU CAME FROM?
"NO. YOUR RESISTANCE ISN'T FOR THE FREESCAPE. IT'S FOR YOU.
IT'S A WORD YOU TELL YOURSELVES TO FEEL BETTER ABOUT THE FACT THAT ALL YOU CAN DO AGAINST FASCISM IS SHOUT "NO" REALLY LOUD, EVEN AS THE MACHINE CRUSHES YOU UNDERFOOT.
YOU REALLY WANTED TO RESIST LUTHOR, YOU'D HAVE FOLLOWED DINAH INTO THE SHADOWS TO FIND SOMETHING BETTER.
YOU'D STOP PLAYING SMALL BALL AND YOU'D SMASH HIS WALLS, EVEN IF IT TOOK YOUR LIFE, UNTIL THAT PLACE WAS RUBBLE AND A BETTER WAY COULD BE BORN.
EVEN IF ALL YOU DID WAS MAKE A DENT, THAT DENT WOULD MEAN MORE THAN A YEAR OF KICKING UP DUST ON MOTORBIKES, FEEDING YOURSELVES A STORY ABOUT HOW YOU'RE REVOLUTIONARIES.
WHAT'S STOPPING YOU, BARDA? NOTHING BUT YOU.
THAT'S WHY THEY CALL IT THE FREESCAPE. 'CUZ YOU'RE FREE TO BE WHOEVER YOU TRULY ARE.
AND WHILE I THOUGHT, TRULY I DID, THAT MAYBE YOU AND THE GARAGE WERE SOMETHING BETTER...
...I SEE NOW WHO YOU TRULY ARE.
WHO YOU'VE ALWAYS BEEN.
RELICS.

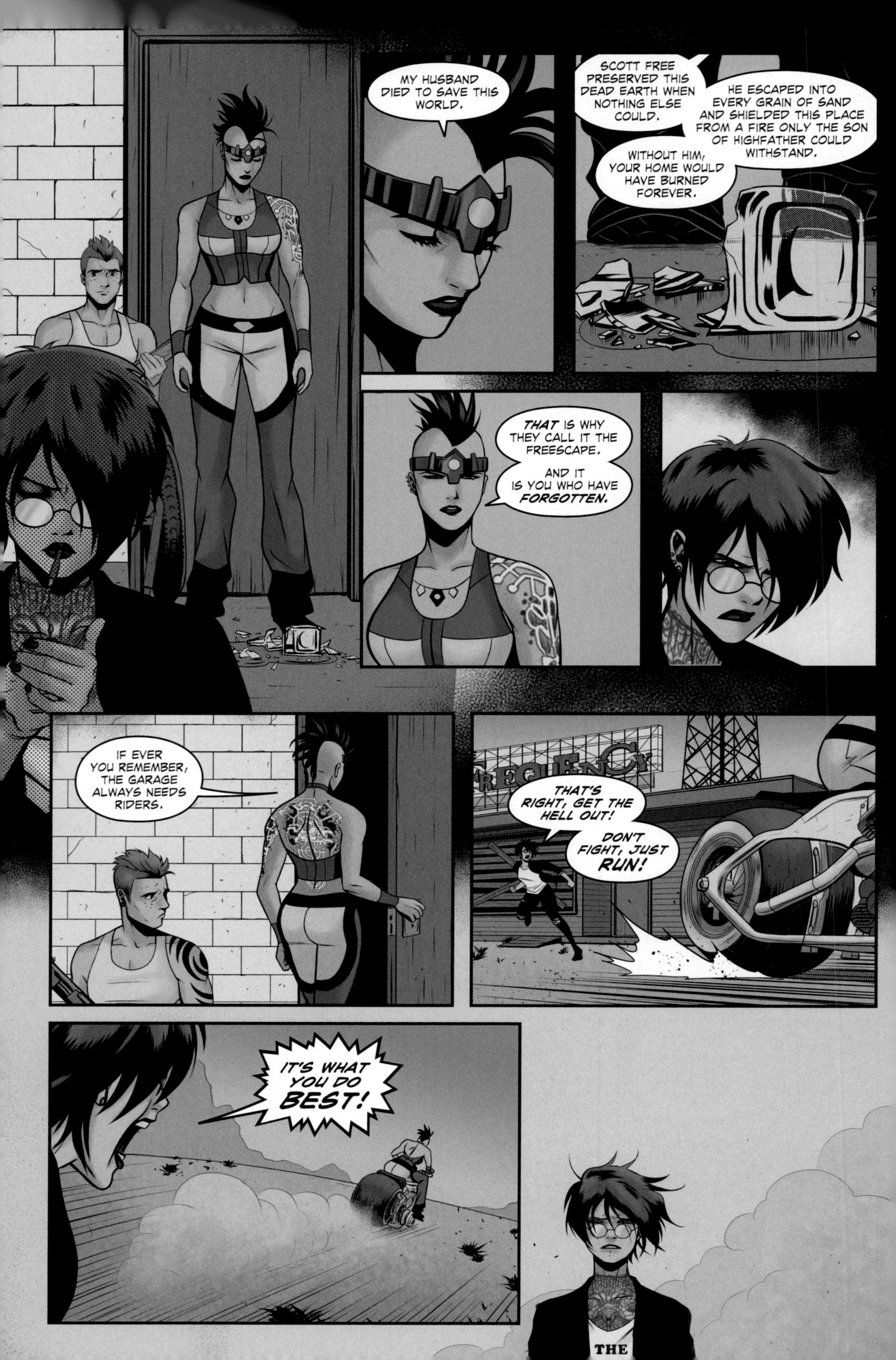
MY HUSBAND DIED TO SAVE THIS WORLD.
SCOTT FREE PRESERVED THIS DEAD EARTH WHEN NOTHING ELSE COULD.
HE ESCAPED INTO EVERY GRAIN OF SAND AND SHIELDED THIS PLACE FROM A FIRE ONLY THE SON OF HIGHFATHER COULD WITHSTAND.
WITHOUT HIM, YOUR HOME WOULD HAVE BURNED FOREVER.
THAT IS WHY THEY CALL IT THE FREESCAPE.
AND IT IS YOU WHO HAVE FORGOTTEN.
IF EVER YOU REMEMBER, THE GARAGE ALWAYS NEEDS RIDERS.
THAT'S RIGHT, GET THE HELL OUT!
DON'T FIGHT, JUST RUN!
IT'S WHAT YOU DO BEST!
THE

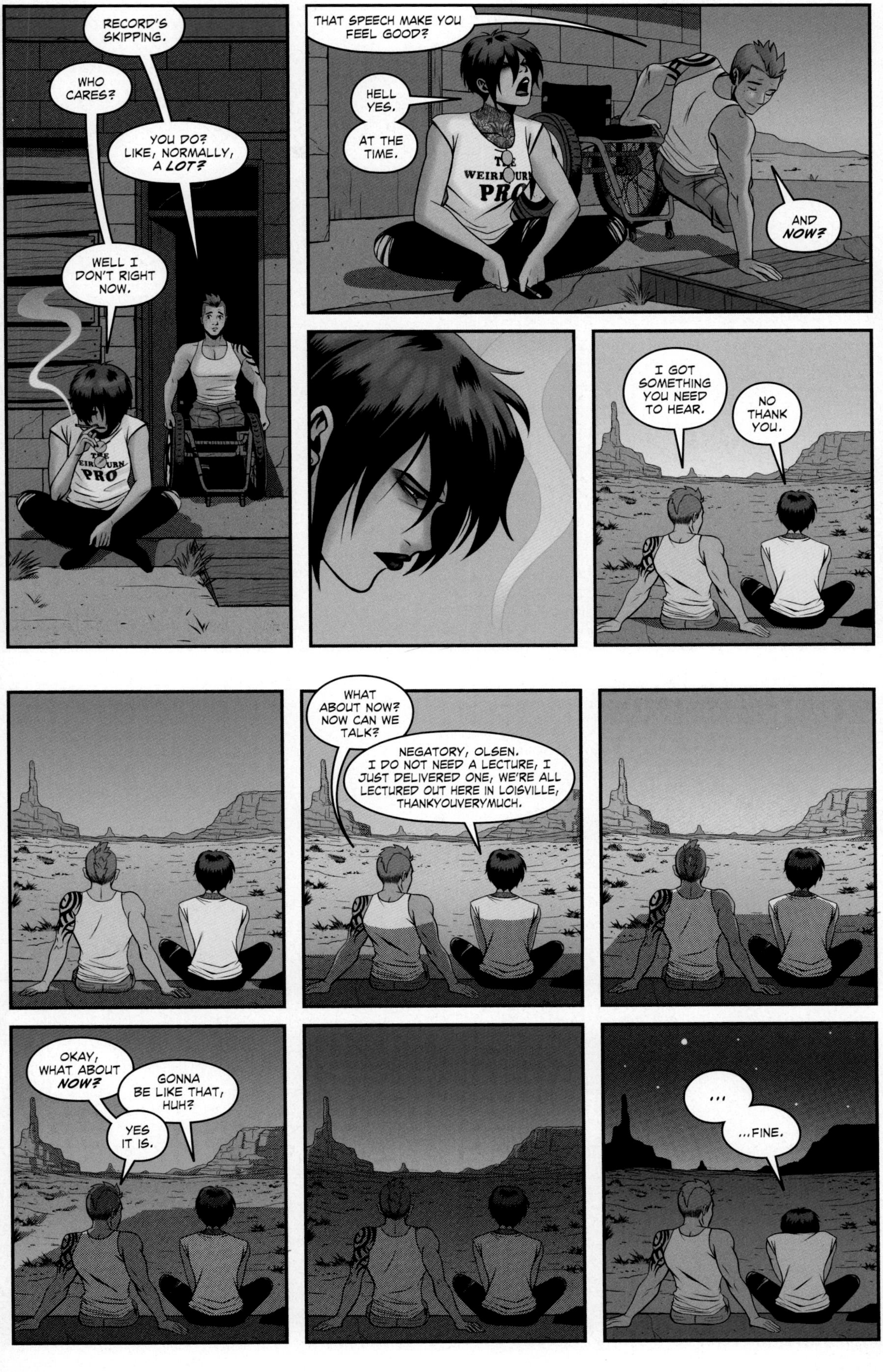
RECORD'S SKIPPING.
WHO CARES?
YOU DO? LIKE, NORMALLY, A *LOT?*
WELL I DON'T RIGHT NOW.
THE WEIRDBURN PRO
THAT SPEECH MAKE YOU FEEL GOOD?
HELL YES.
AT THE TIME.
AND *NOW?*
I GOT SOMETHING YOU NEED TO HEAR.
NO THANK YOU.
WHAT ABOUT NOW? NOW CAN WE TALK?
NEGATORY, OLSEN. I DO NOT NEED A LECTURE, I JUST DELIVERED ONE, WE'RE ALL LECTURED OUT HERE IN LOISVILLE, THANKYOUVERYMUCH.
OKAY, WHAT ABOUT *NOW?*
GONNA BE LIKE THAT, HUH?
YES IT IS.
...
...FINE.

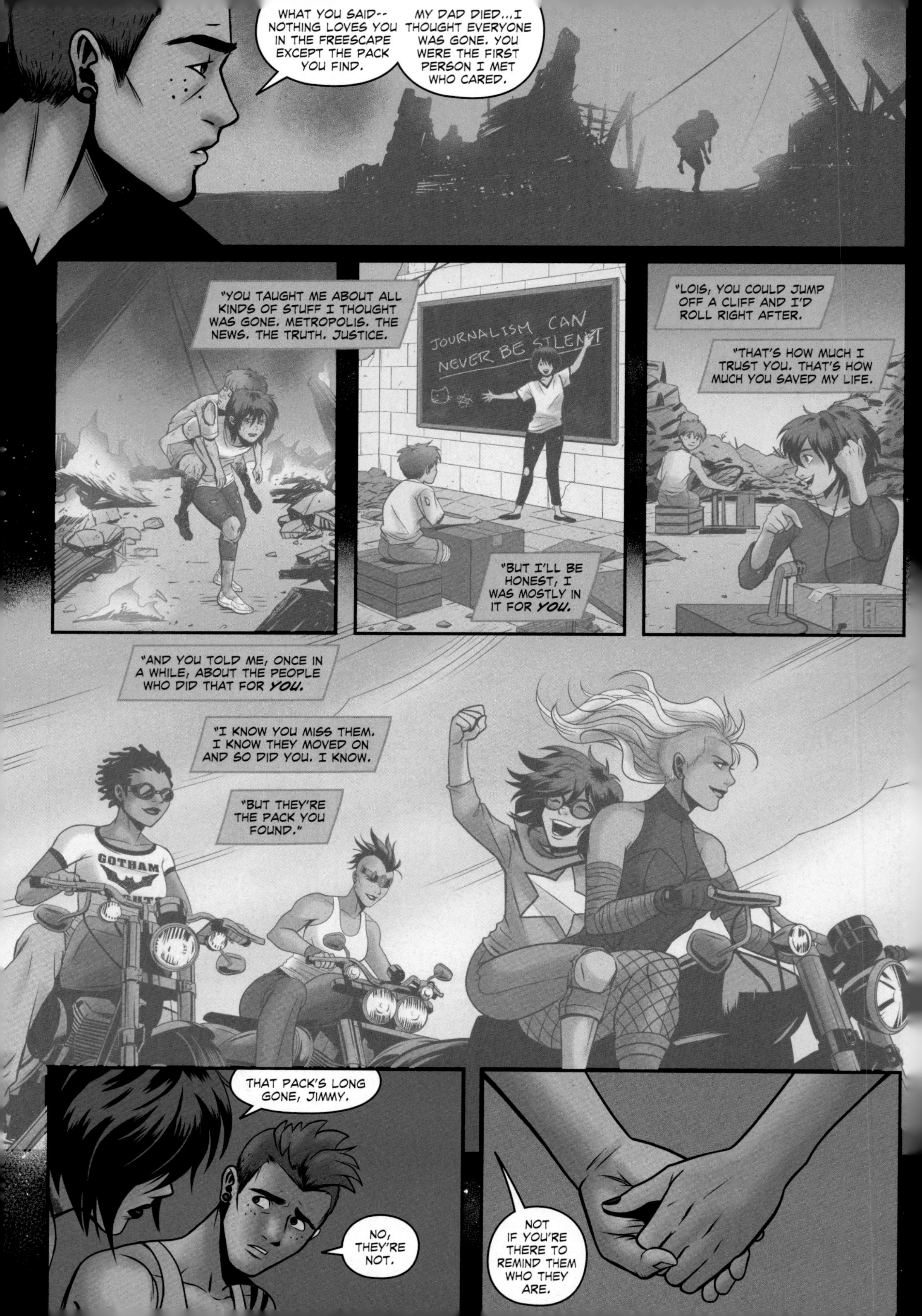
WHAT YOU SAID-- NOTHING LOVES YOU IN THE FREESCAPE EXCEPT THE PACK YOU FIND.
MY DAD DIED...I THOUGHT EVERYONE WAS GONE. YOU WERE THE FIRST PERSON I MET WHO CARED.
"YOU TAUGHT ME ABOUT ALL KINDS OF STUFF I THOUGHT WAS GONE. METROPOLIS. THE NEWS. THE TRUTH. JUSTICE.
JOURNALISM CAN NEVER BE SILENT
"BUT I'LL BE HONEST, I WAS MOSTLY IN IT FOR *YOU.*
"LOIS, YOU COULD JUMP OFF A CLIFF AND I'D ROLL RIGHT AFTER.
"THAT'S HOW MUCH I TRUST YOU. THAT'S HOW MUCH YOU SAVED MY LIFE.
"AND YOU TOLD ME, ONCE IN A WHILE, ABOUT THE PEOPLE WHO DID THAT FOR *YOU.*
"I KNOW YOU MISS THEM. I KNOW THEY MOVED ON AND SO DID YOU. I KNOW.
"BUT THEY'RE THE PACK YOU FOUND."
GOTHAM
THAT PACK'S LONG GONE, JIMMY.
NO, THEY'RE NOT.
NOT IF YOU'RE THERE TO REMIND THEM WHO THEY ARE.

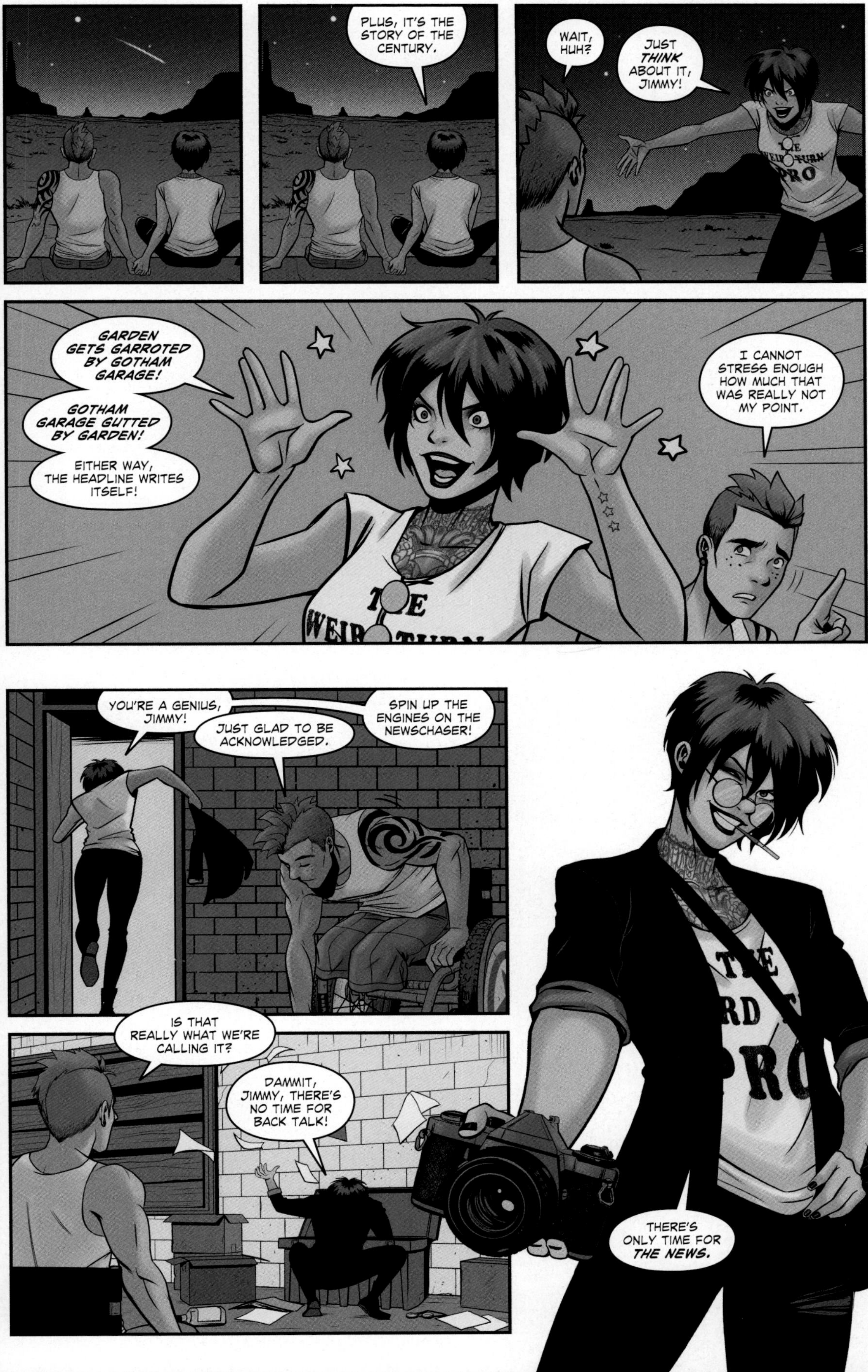

PLUS, IT'S THE STORY OF THE CENTURY.
WAIT, HUH?
JUST THINK ABOUT IT, JIMMY!
THE WEIRD TURN PRO
GARDEN GETS GARROTED BY GOTHAM GARAGE!
GOTHAM GARAGE GUTTED BY GARDEN!
EITHER WAY, THE HEADLINE WRITES ITSELF!
I CANNOT STRESS ENOUGH HOW MUCH THAT WAS REALLY NOT MY POINT.
YOU'RE A GENIUS, JIMMY!
JUST GLAD TO BE ACKNOWLEDGED.
SPIN UP THE ENGINES ON THE NEWSCHASER!
IS THAT REALLY WHAT WE'RE CALLING IT?
DAMMIT, JIMMY, THERE'S NO TIME FOR BACK TALK!
THERE'S ONLY TIME FOR THE NEWS.

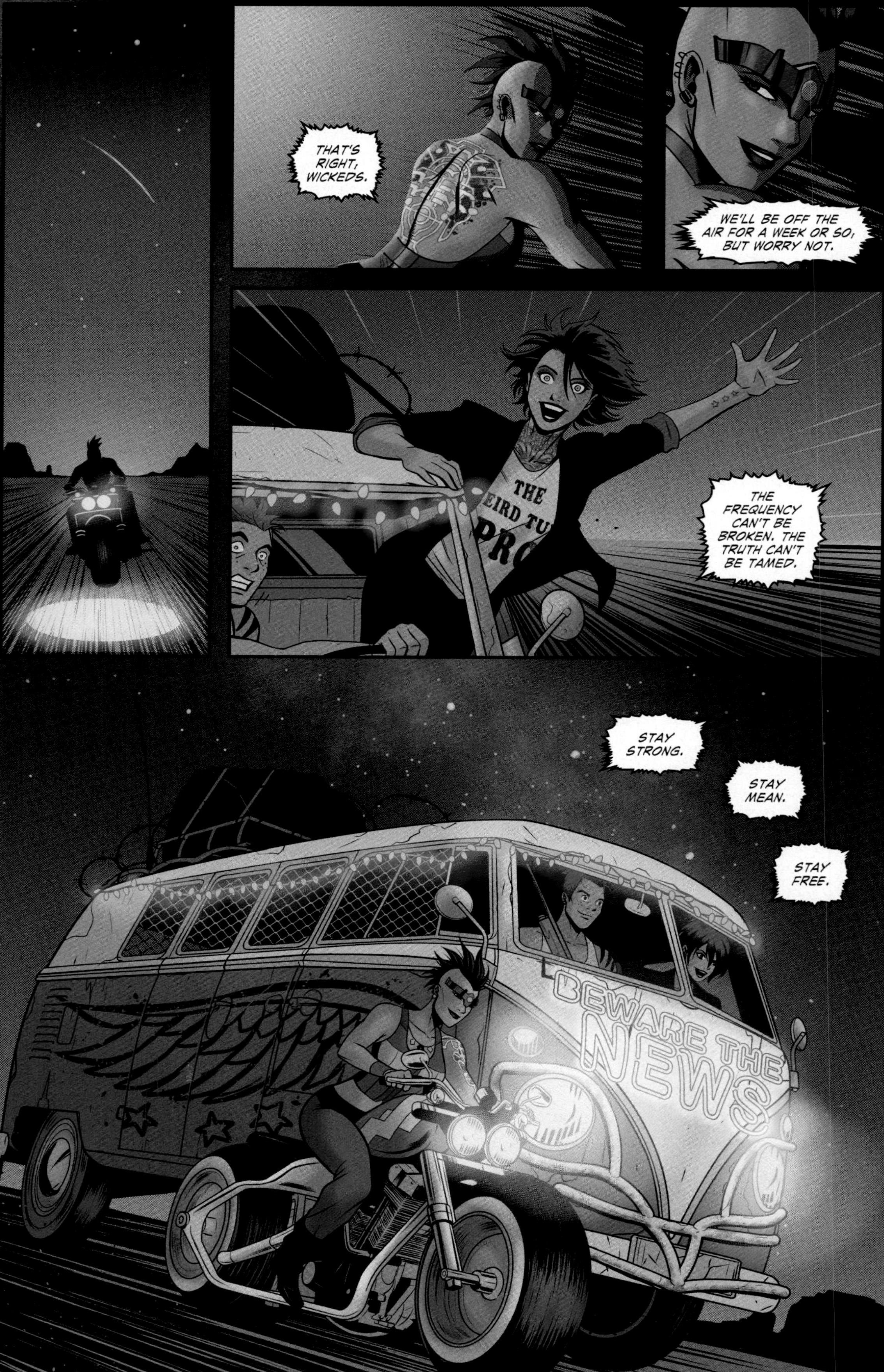
THAT'S RIGHT, WICKEDS.
WE'LL BE OFF THE AIR FOR A WEEK OR SO, BUT WORRY NOT.
THE EIRD TU PRO
THE FREQUENCY CAN'T BE BROKEN. THE TRUTH CAN'T BE TAMED.
STAY STRONG.
STAY MEAN.
STAY FREE.
BEWARE THE NEWS

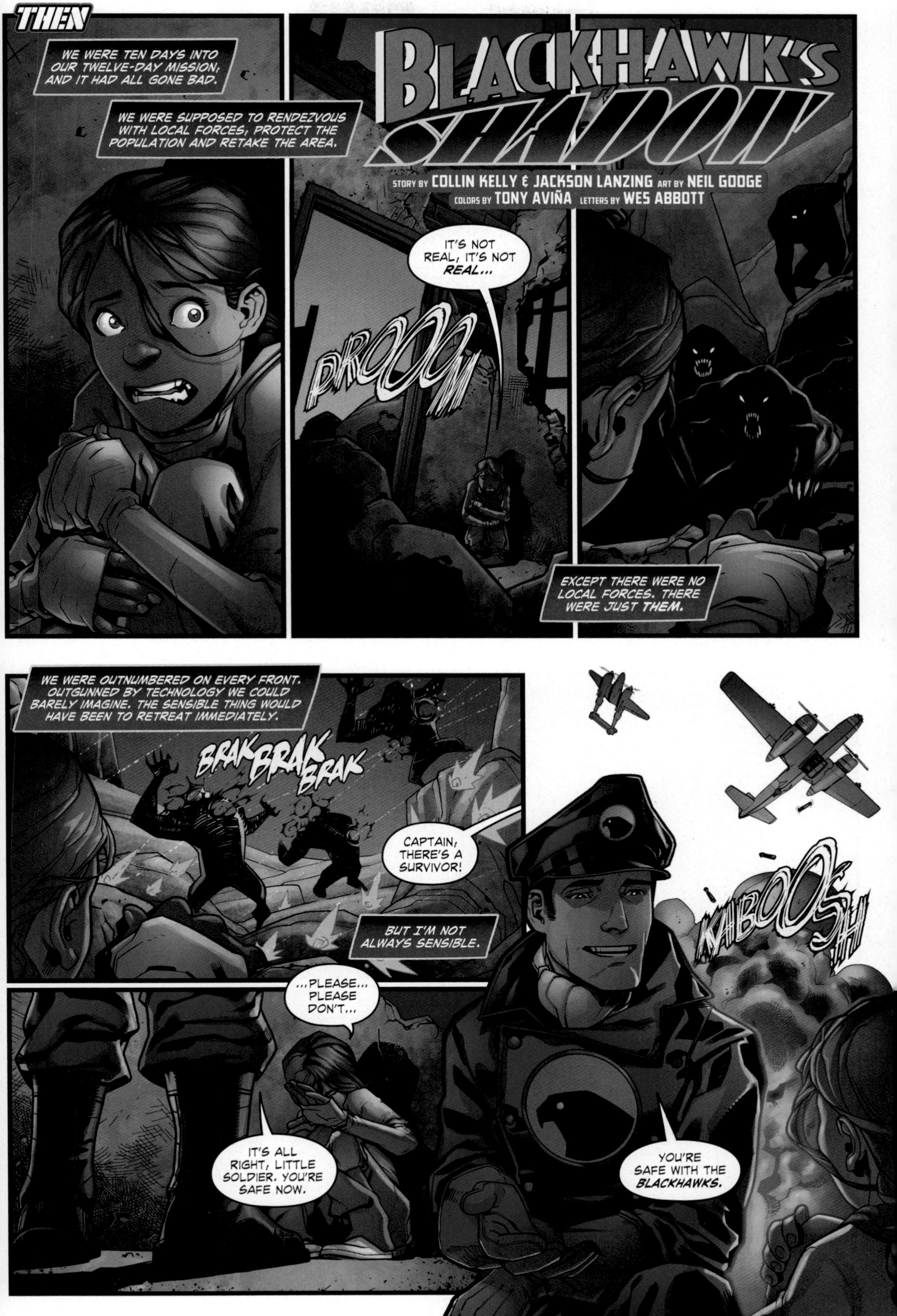
THEN
WE WERE TEN DAYS INTO OUR TWELVE-DAY MISSION, AND IT HAD ALL GONE BAD.
WE WERE SUPPOSED TO RENDEZVOUS WITH LOCAL FORCES, PROTECT THE POPULATION AND RETAKE THE AREA.
BLACKHAWK'S SHADOW
STORY BY COLLIN KELLY & JACKSON LANZING ART BY NEIL GOOGE
COLORS BY TONY AVIÑA LETTERS BY WES ABBOTT
IT'S NOT REAL, IT'S NOT REAL...
DROOOM
EXCEPT THERE WERE NO LOCAL FORCES. THERE WERE JUST THEM.
WE WERE OUTNUMBERED ON EVERY FRONT. OUTGUNNED BY TECHNOLOGY WE COULD BARELY IMAGINE. THE SENSIBLE THING WOULD HAVE BEEN TO RETREAT IMMEDIATELY.
BRAK BRAK BRAK
CAPTAIN, THERE'S A SURVIVOR!
BUT I'M NOT ALWAYS SENSIBLE.
KABOOSH
...PLEASE... PLEASE DON'T...
IT'S ALL RIGHT, LITTLE SOLDIER. YOU'RE SAFE NOW.
YOU'RE SAFE WITH THE BLACKHAWKS.

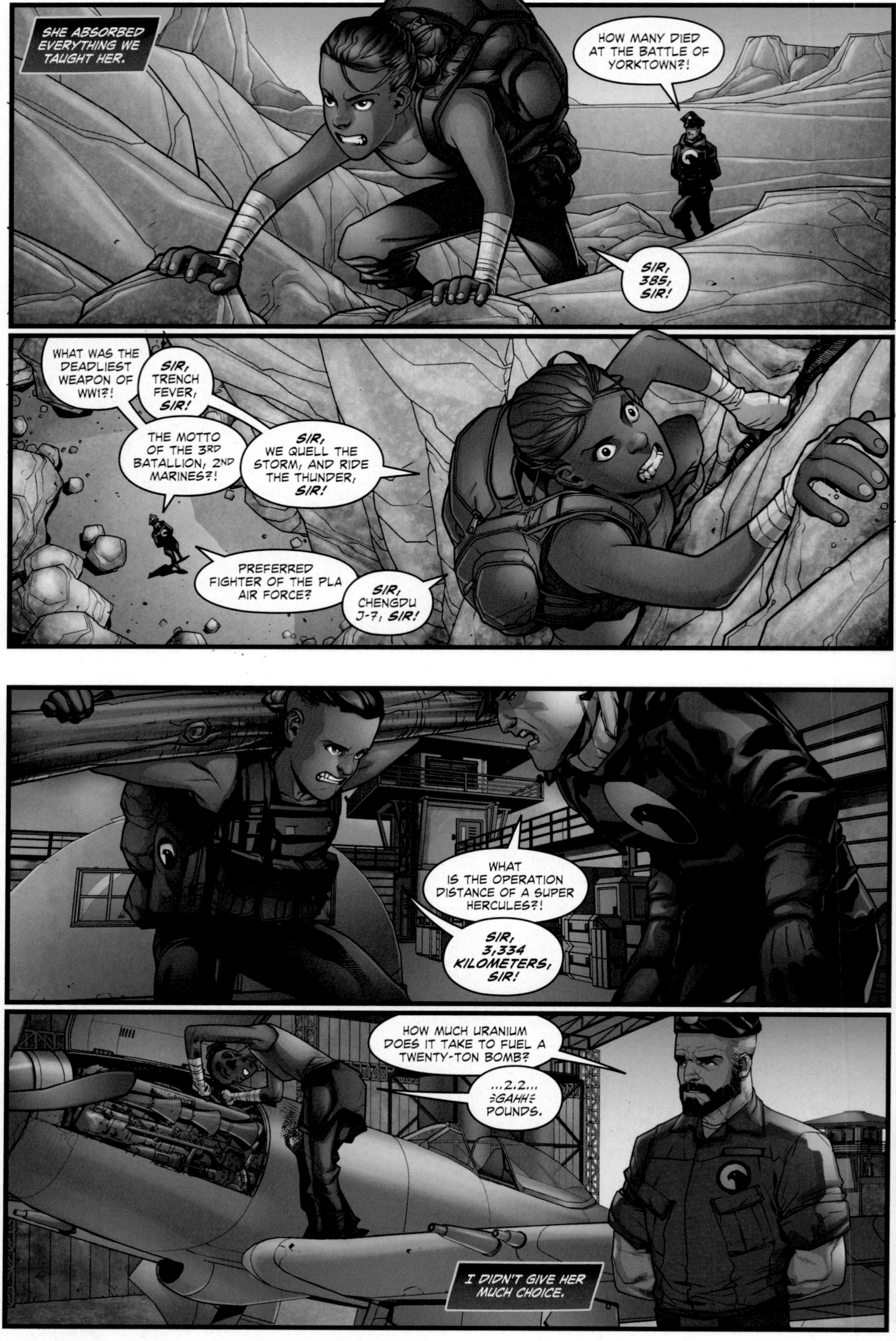
SHE ABSORBED EVERYTHING WE TAUGHT HER.
HOW MANY DIED AT THE BATTLE OF YORKTOWN?!
SIR, 385, SIR!
WHAT WAS THE DEADLIEST WEAPON OF WW1?!
SIR, TRENCH FEVER, SIR!
THE MOTTO OF THE 3RD BATALLION, 2ND MARINES?!
SIR, WE QUELL THE STORM, AND RIDE THE THUNDER, SIR!
PREFERRED FIGHTER OF THE PLA AIR FORCE?
SIR, CHENGDU J-7, SIR!
WHAT IS THE OPERATION DISTANCE OF A SUPER HERCULES?!
SIR, 3,334 KILOMETERS, SIR!
HOW MUCH URANIUM DOES IT TAKE TO FUEL A TWENTY-TON BOMB?
...2.2... GAHH POUNDS.
I DIDN'T GIVE HER MUCH CHOICE.

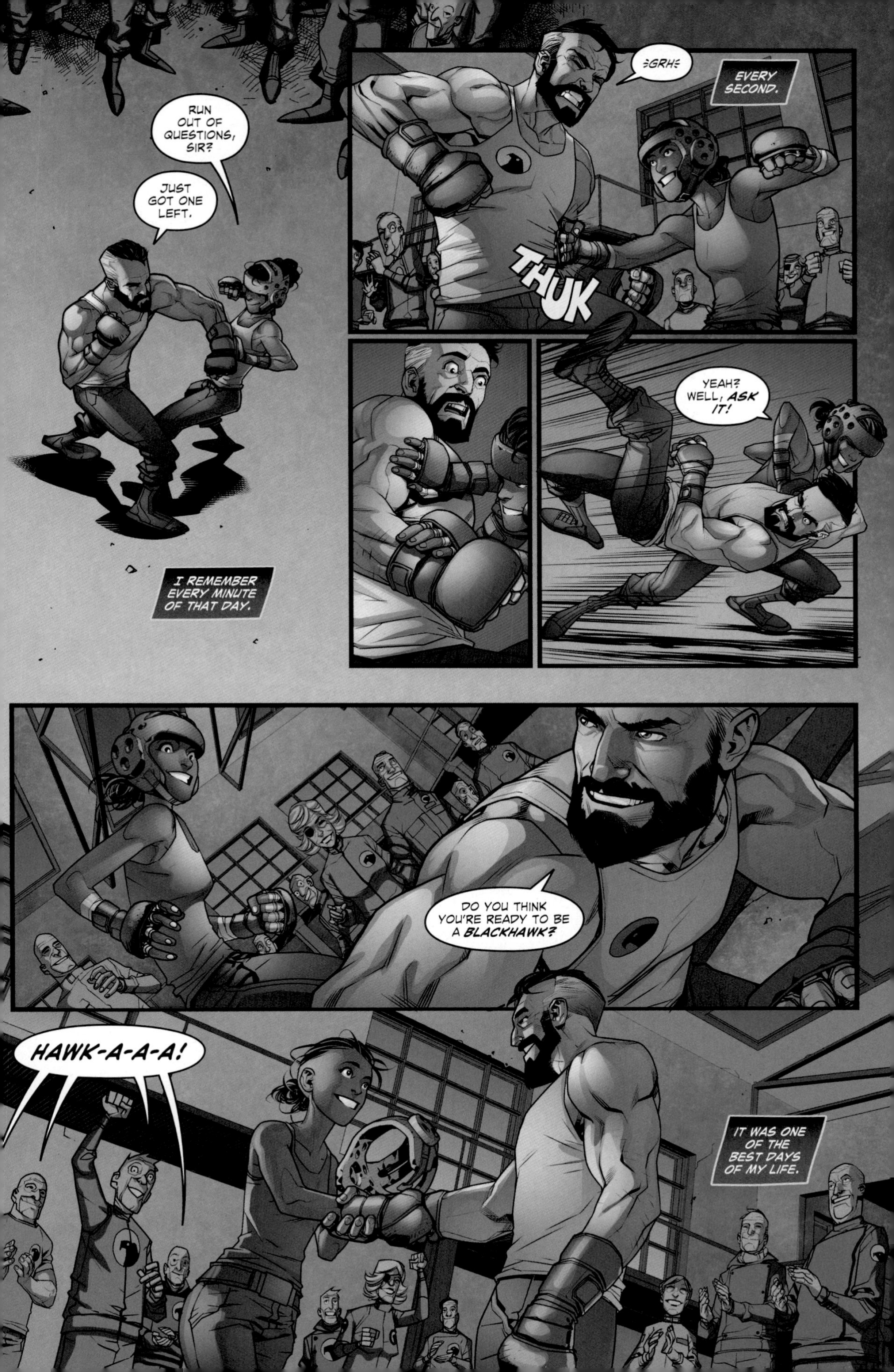
RUN OUT OF QUESTIONS, SIR?
JUST GOT ONE LEFT.
I REMEMBER EVERY MINUTE OF THAT DAY.
GRH
EVERY SECOND.
THUK
YEAH? WELL, ASK IT!
DO YOU THINK YOU'RE READY TO BE A BLACKHAWK?
HAWK-A-A-A!
IT WAS ONE OF THE BEST DAYS OF MY LIFE.

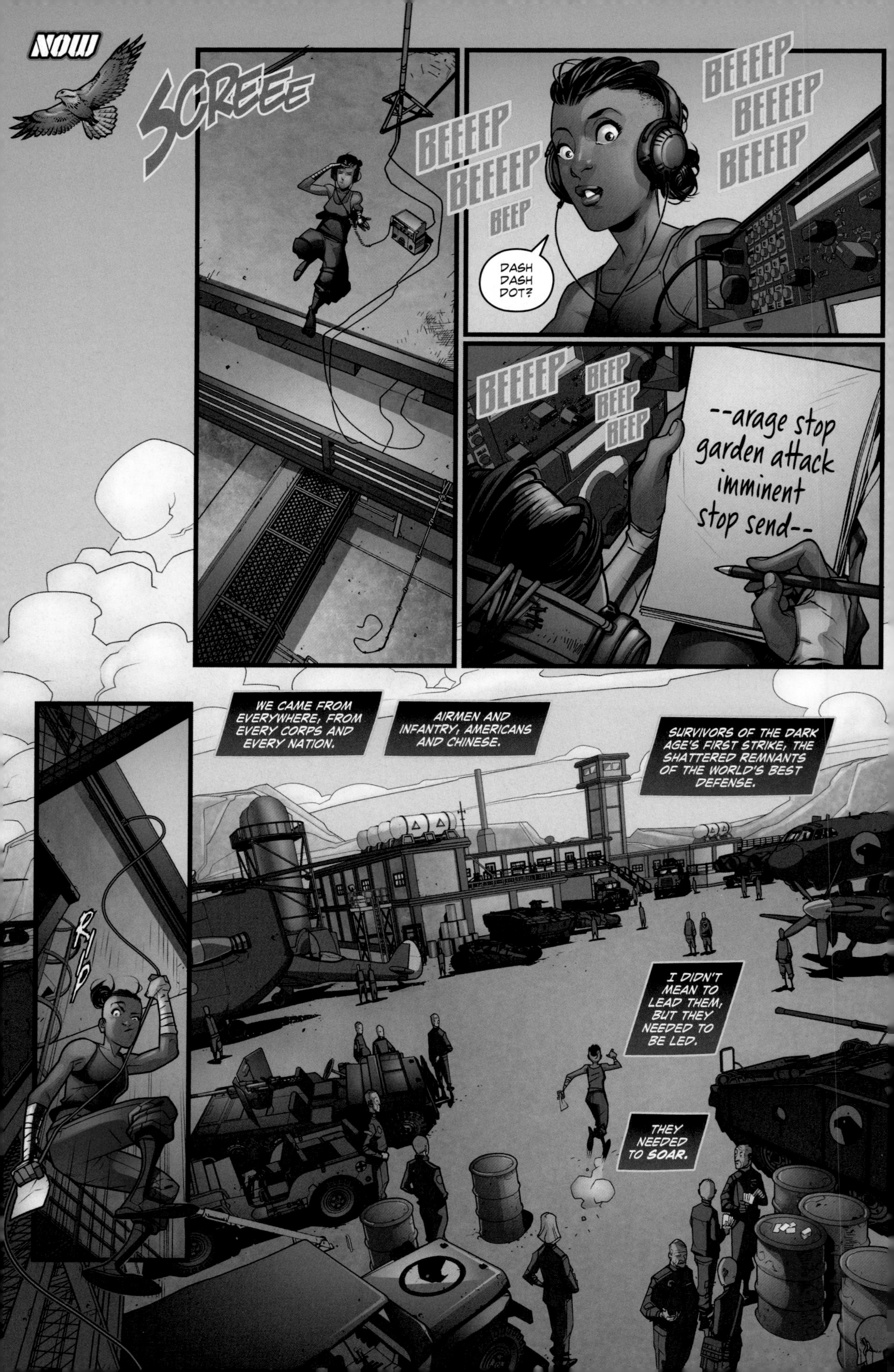
NOW
SCREEE
BEEEEP
BEEEEP
BEEP
DASH DASH DOT?
BEEEEP
BEEEEP
BEEEEP
BEEEEP
BEEP
BEEP
BEEP
--arage stop garden attack imminent stop send--
WE CAME FROM EVERYWHERE, FROM EVERY CORPS AND EVERY NATION.
AIRMEN AND INFANTRY, AMERICANS AND CHINESE.
SURVIVORS OF THE DARK AGE'S FIRST STRIKE, THE SHATTERED REMNANTS OF THE WORLD'S BEST DEFENSE.
RIP
I DIDN'T MEAN TO LEAD THEM, BUT THEY NEEDED TO BE LED.
THEY NEEDED TO SOAR.

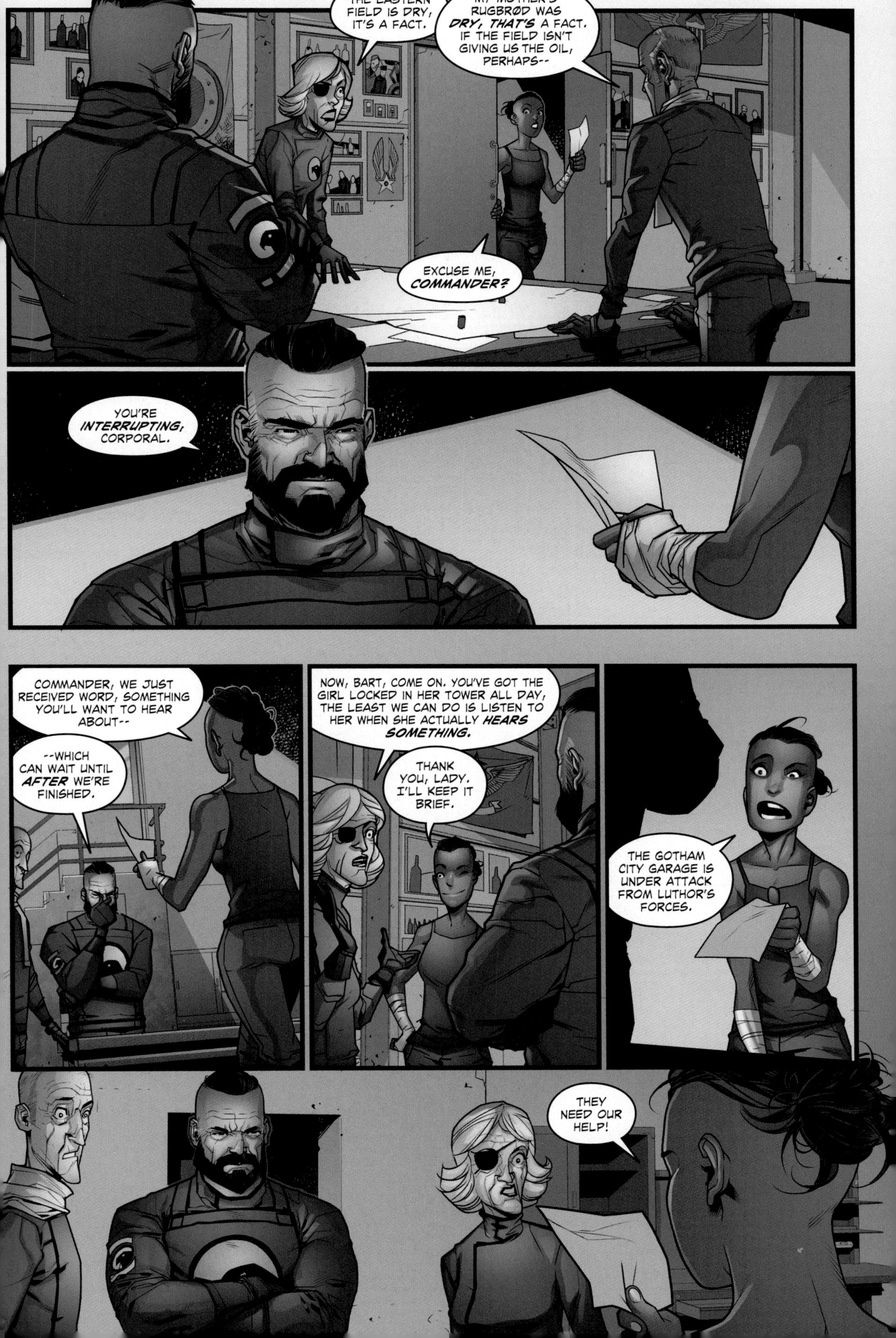
THE EASTERN FIELD IS DRY, IT'S A FACT.
MY MOTHER'S RUGBRØD WAS DRY, THAT'S A FACT. IF THE FIELD ISN'T GIVING US THE OIL, PERHAPS--
EXCUSE ME, COMMANDER?
YOU'RE INTERRUPTING, CORPORAL.
COMMANDER, WE JUST RECEIVED WORD, SOMETHING YOU'LL WANT TO HEAR ABOUT--
--WHICH CAN WAIT UNTIL AFTER WE'RE FINISHED.
NOW, BART, COME ON. YOU'VE GOT THE GIRL LOCKED IN HER TOWER ALL DAY, THE LEAST WE CAN DO IS LISTEN TO HER WHEN SHE ACTUALLY HEARS SOMETHING.
THANK YOU, LADY. I'LL KEEP IT BRIEF.
THE GOTHAM CITY GARAGE IS UNDER ATTACK FROM LUTHOR'S FORCES.
THEY NEED OUR HELP!

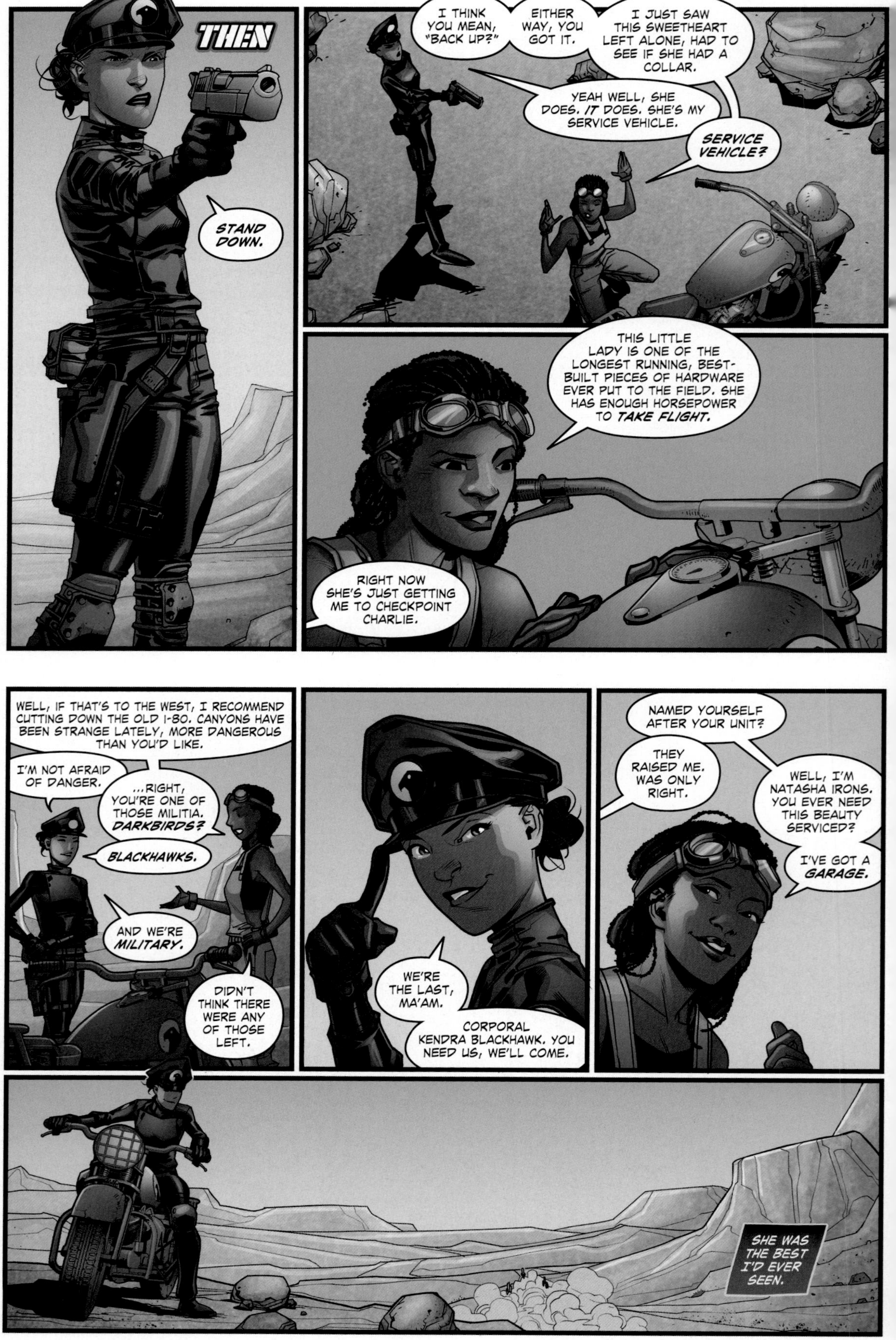
THEN
STAND DOWN.
I THINK YOU MEAN, "BACK UP?"
EITHER WAY, YOU GOT IT.
I JUST SAW THIS SWEETHEART LEFT ALONE, HAD TO SEE IF SHE HAD A COLLAR.
YEAH WELL, SHE DOES. IT DOES. SHE'S MY SERVICE VEHICLE.
SERVICE VEHICLE?
THIS LITTLE LADY IS ONE OF THE LONGEST RUNNING, BEST-BUILT PIECES OF HARDWARE EVER PUT TO THE FIELD. SHE HAS ENOUGH HORSEPOWER TO TAKE FLIGHT.
RIGHT NOW SHE'S JUST GETTING ME TO CHECKPOINT CHARLIE.
WELL, IF THAT'S TO THE WEST, I RECOMMEND CUTTING DOWN THE OLD I-80. CANYONS HAVE BEEN STRANGE LATELY, MORE DANGEROUS THAN YOU'D LIKE.
I'M NOT AFRAID OF DANGER.
...RIGHT, YOU'RE ONE OF THOSE MILITIA. DARKBIRDS?
BLACKHAWKS.
AND WE'RE MILITARY.
DIDN'T THINK THERE WERE ANY OF THOSE LEFT.
WE'RE THE LAST, MA'AM.
CORPORAL KENDRA BLACKHAWK. YOU NEED US, WE'LL COME.
NAMED YOURSELF AFTER YOUR UNIT?
THEY RAISED ME. WAS ONLY RIGHT.
WELL, I'M NATASHA IRONS. YOU EVER NEED THIS BEAUTY SERVICED?
I'VE GOT A GARAGE.
SHE WAS THE BEST I'D EVER SEEN.

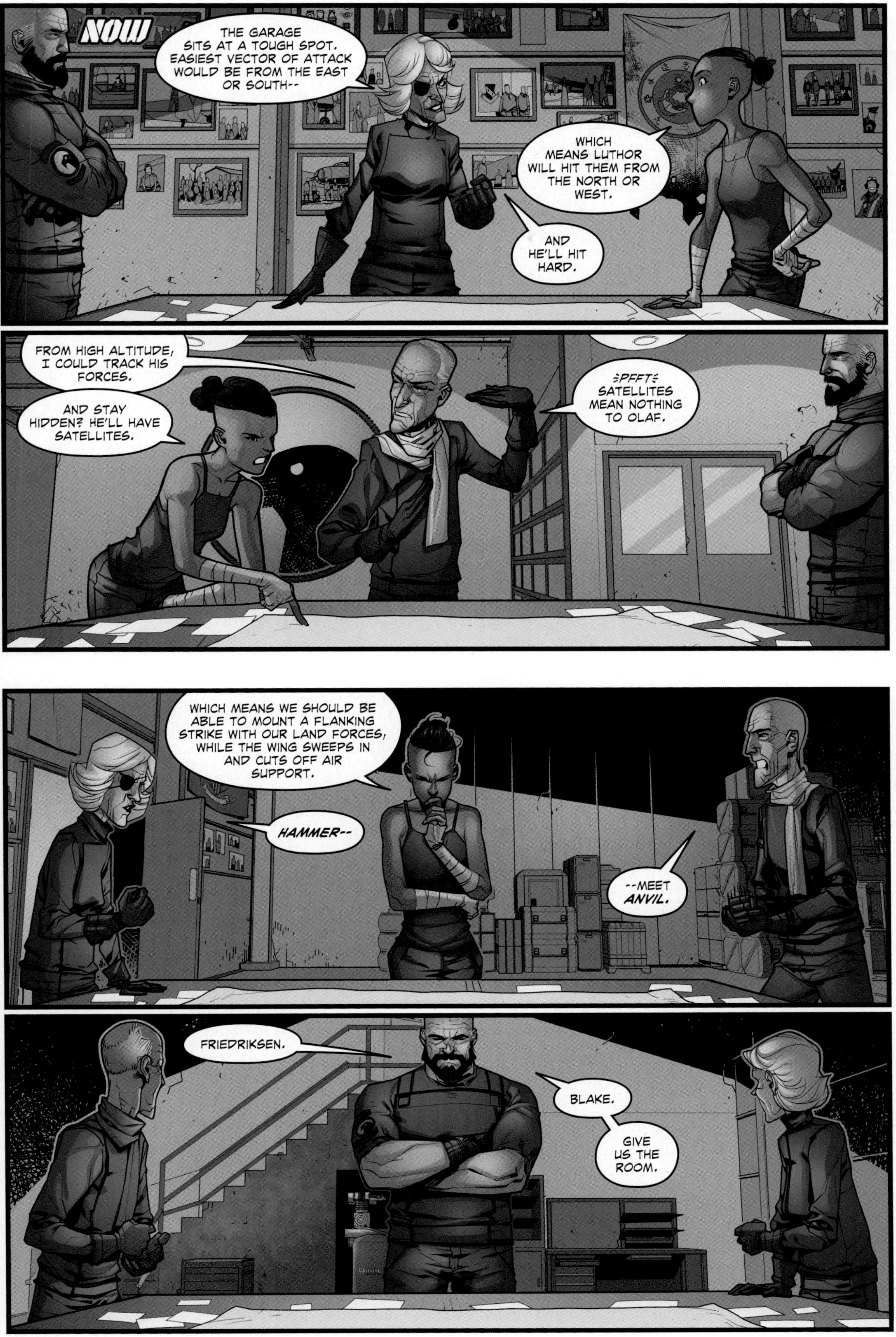
NOW
THE GARAGE SITS AT A TOUGH SPOT. EASIEST VECTOR OF ATTACK WOULD BE FROM THE EAST OR SOUTH--
WHICH MEANS LUTHOR WILL HIT THEM FROM THE NORTH OR WEST.
AND HE'LL HIT HARD.
FROM HIGH ALTITUDE, I COULD TRACK HIS FORCES.
AND STAY HIDDEN? HE'LL HAVE SATELLITES.
PFFT SATELLITES MEAN NOTHING TO OLAF.
WHICH MEANS WE SHOULD BE ABLE TO MOUNT A FLANKING STRIKE WITH OUR LAND FORCES, WHILE THE WING SWEEPS IN AND CUTS OFF AIR SUPPORT.
HAMMER--
--MEET ANVIL.
FRIEDRIKSEN.
BLAKE.
GIVE US THE ROOM.

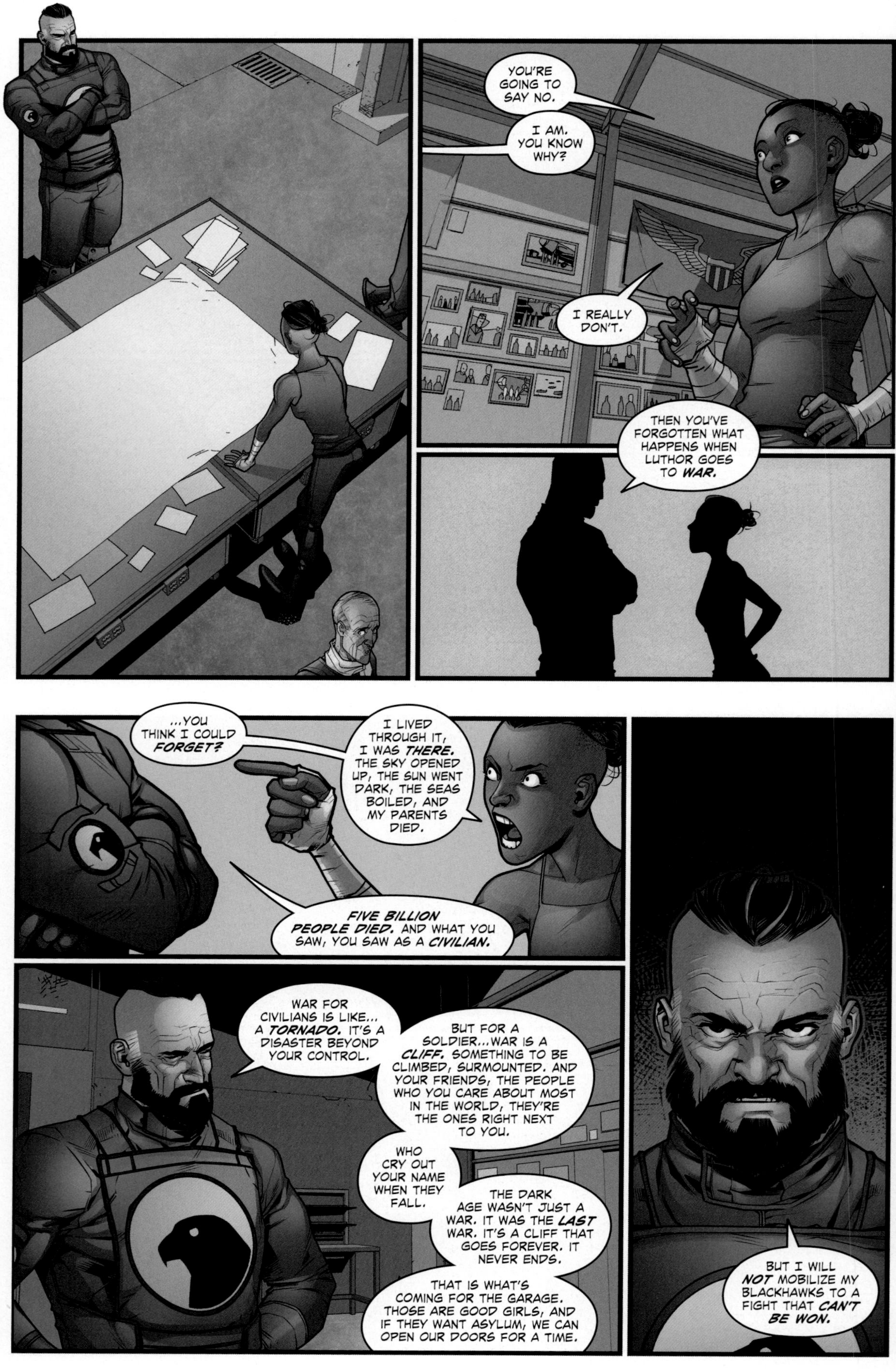
YOU'RE GOING TO SAY NO.
I AM. YOU KNOW WHY?
I REALLY DON'T.
THEN YOU'VE FORGOTTEN WHAT HAPPENS WHEN LUTHOR GOES TO WAR.
...YOU THINK I COULD FORGET?
I LIVED THROUGH IT, I WAS THERE. THE SKY OPENED UP, THE SUN WENT DARK, THE SEAS BOILED, AND MY PARENTS DIED.
FIVE BILLION PEOPLE DIED. AND WHAT YOU SAW, YOU SAW AS A CIVILIAN.
WAR FOR CIVILIANS IS LIKE... A TORNADO. IT'S A DISASTER BEYOND YOUR CONTROL.
BUT FOR A SOLDIER...WAR IS A CLIFF. SOMETHING TO BE CLIMBED, SURMOUNTED. AND YOUR FRIENDS, THE PEOPLE WHO YOU CARE ABOUT MOST IN THE WORLD, THEY'RE THE ONES RIGHT NEXT TO YOU.
WHO CRY OUT YOUR NAME WHEN THEY FALL.
THE DARK AGE WASN'T JUST A WAR. IT WAS THE LAST WAR. IT'S A CLIFF THAT GOES FOREVER. IT NEVER ENDS.
THAT IS WHAT'S COMING FOR THE GARAGE. THOSE ARE GOOD GIRLS, AND IF THEY WANT ASYLUM, WE CAN OPEN OUR DOORS FOR A TIME.
BUT I WILL NOT MOBILIZE MY BLACKHAWKS TO A FIGHT THAT CAN'T BE WON.

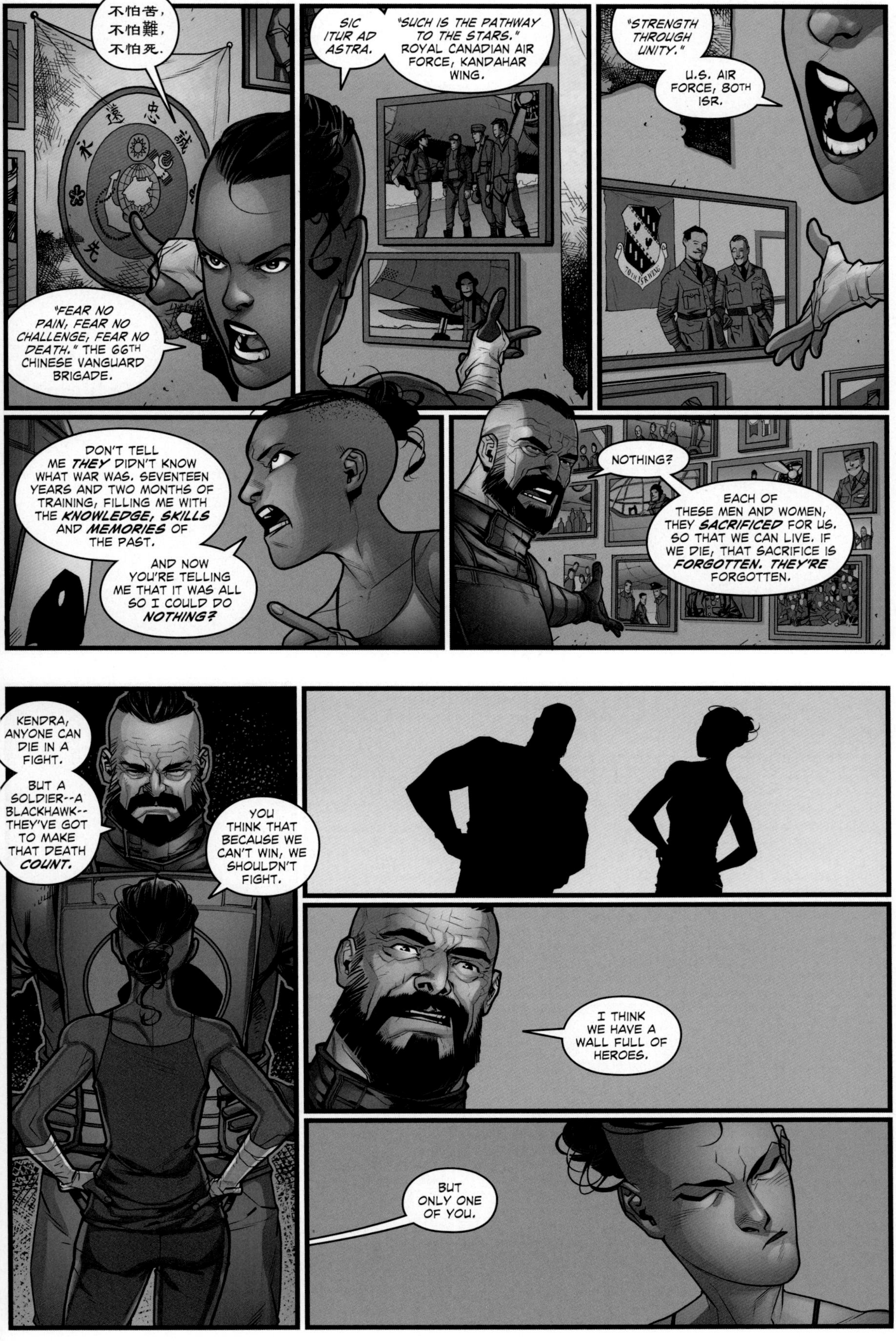
不怕苦，
不怕難，
不怕死.
"FEAR NO PAIN, FEAR NO CHALLENGE, FEAR NO DEATH." THE 66TH CHINESE VANGUARD BRIGADE.
SIC ITUR AD ASTRA.
"SUCH IS THE PATHWAY TO THE STARS." ROYAL CANADIAN AIR FORCE, KANDAHAR WING.
"STRENGTH THROUGH UNITY."
U.S. AIR FORCE, 80TH ISR.
70TH ISR WING
DON'T TELL ME THEY DIDN'T KNOW WHAT WAR WAS. SEVENTEEN YEARS AND TWO MONTHS OF TRAINING, FILLING ME WITH THE KNOWLEDGE, SKILLS AND MEMORIES OF THE PAST.
AND NOW YOU'RE TELLING ME THAT IT WAS ALL SO I COULD DO NOTHING?
NOTHING?
EACH OF THESE MEN AND WOMEN, THEY SACRIFICED FOR US. SO THAT WE CAN LIVE. IF WE DIE, THAT SACRIFICE IS FORGOTTEN. THEY'RE FORGOTTEN.
KENDRA, ANYONE CAN DIE IN A FIGHT.
BUT A SOLDIER--A BLACKHAWK--THEY'VE GOT TO MAKE THAT DEATH COUNT.
YOU THINK THAT BECAUSE WE CAN'T WIN, WE SHOULDN'T FIGHT.
I THINK WE HAVE A WALL FULL OF HEROES.
BUT ONLY ONE OF YOU.

YOU'RE RIGHT.

AND IF WAR IS A CLIFF, NOW IT'S *MY FRIENDS* WHO ARE HANGING FROM THE EDGE.

THANKS TO YOU, I KNOW WAR. EVEN IF I'VE NEVER LIVED IT.

BUT I WILL NOT DISRESPECT THEM BY ASSUMING THAT'S ALL THEY'D WANT FROM ME.

KENDRA--

I'M SORRY, *COMMANDER.*

AND WITH EVERY BREATH I'VE GOT, I'LL REMEMBER EVERYONE WHOSE SACRIFICE GOT ME HERE.

I'M RESIGNING MY COMMISSION.

SEVENTEEN YEARS.

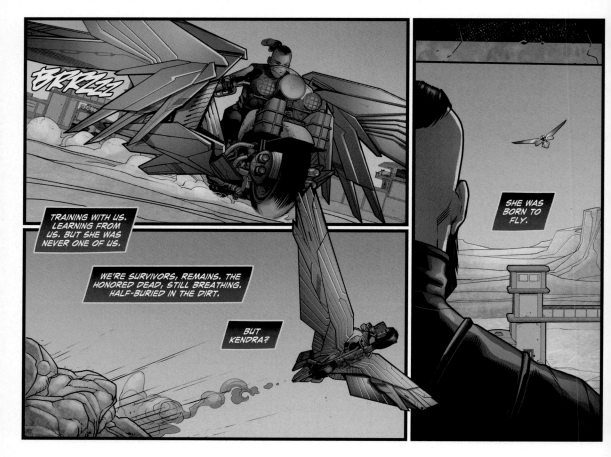

BRRZZZ

TRAINING WITH US. LEARNING FROM US. BUT SHE WAS NEVER ONE OF US.

WE'RE SURVIVORS, REMAINS. THE HONORED DEAD, STILL BREATHING. HALF-BURIED IN THE DIRT.

BUT KENDRA?

SHE WAS BORN TO FLY.

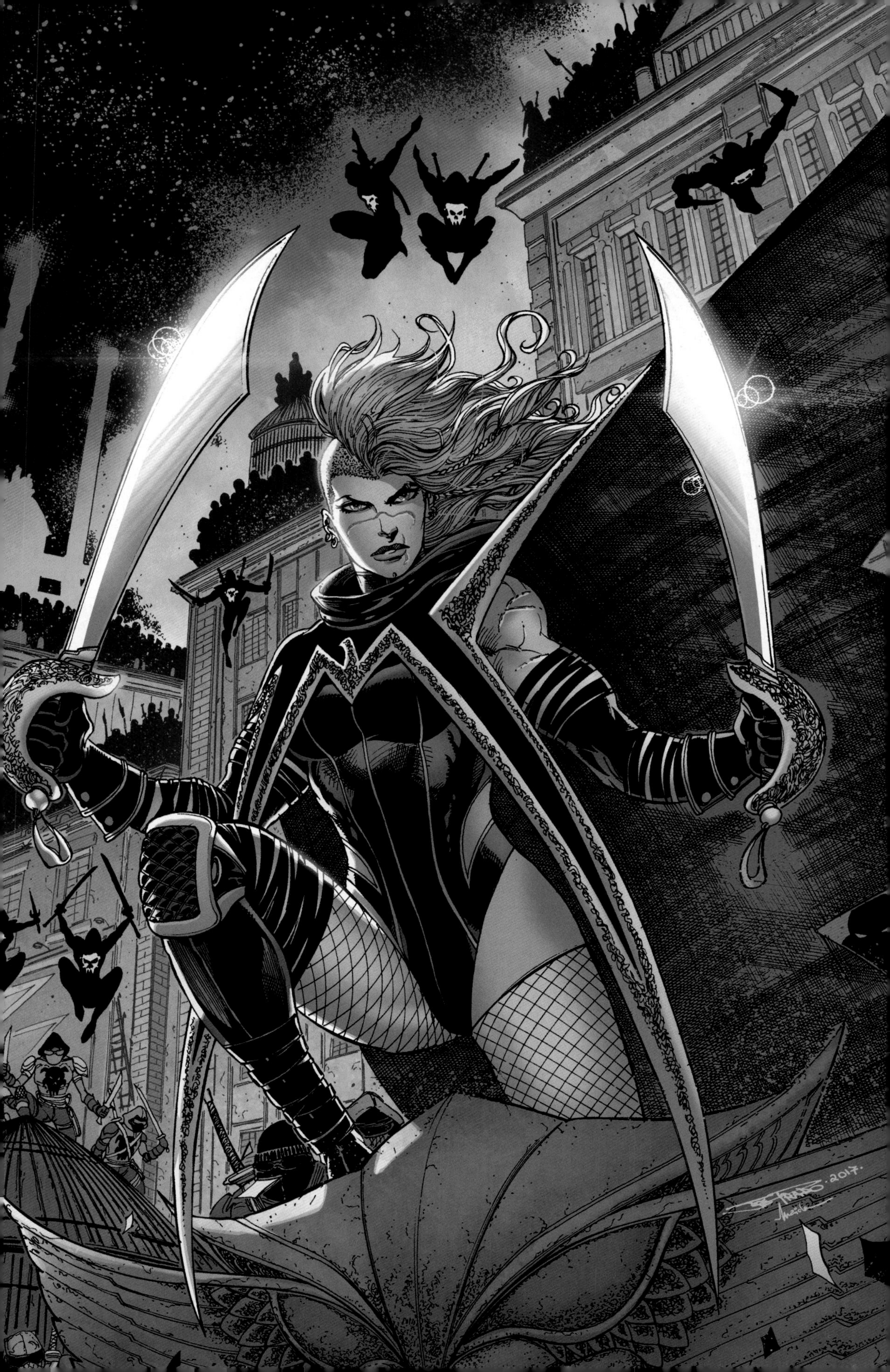

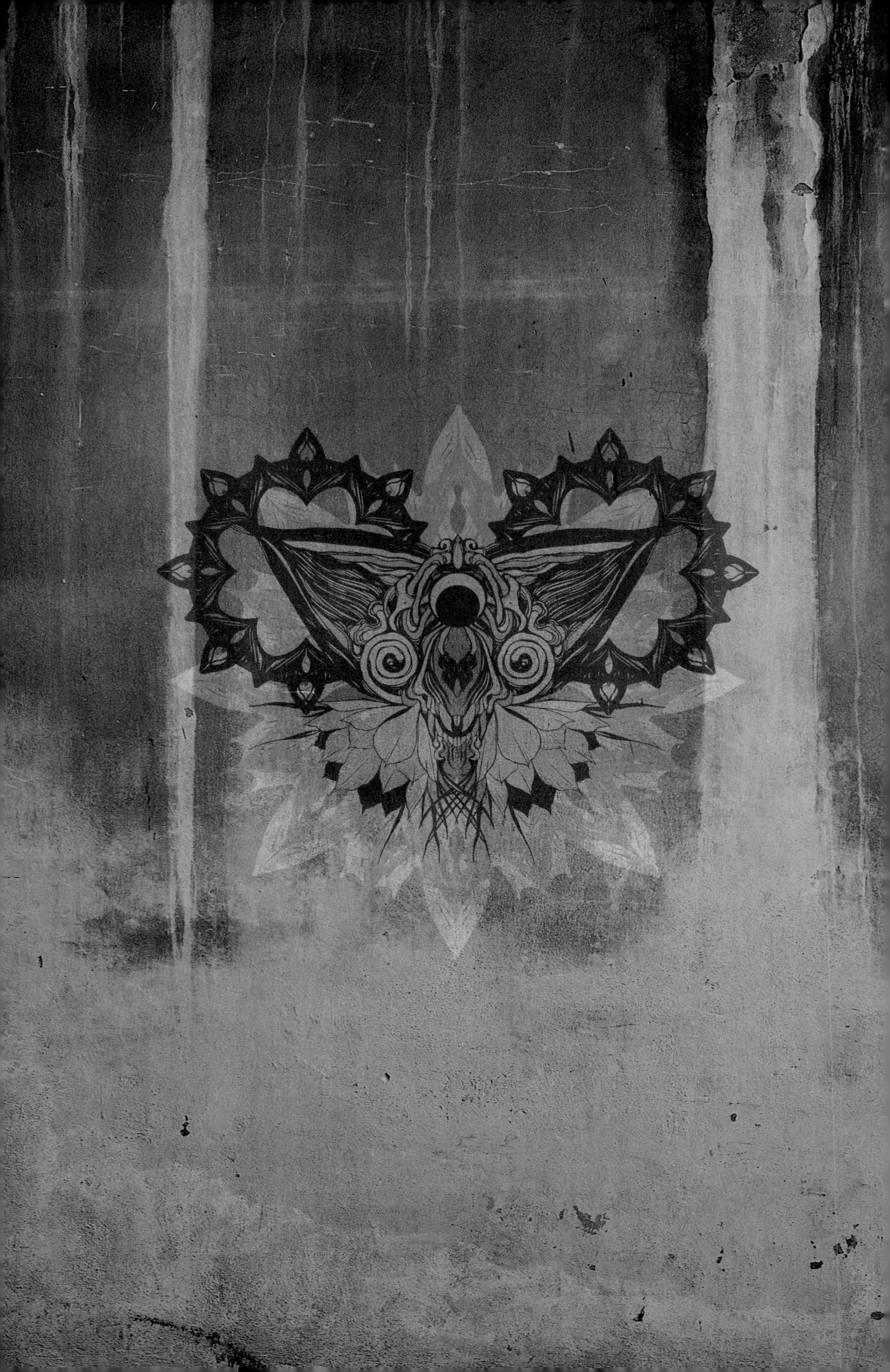

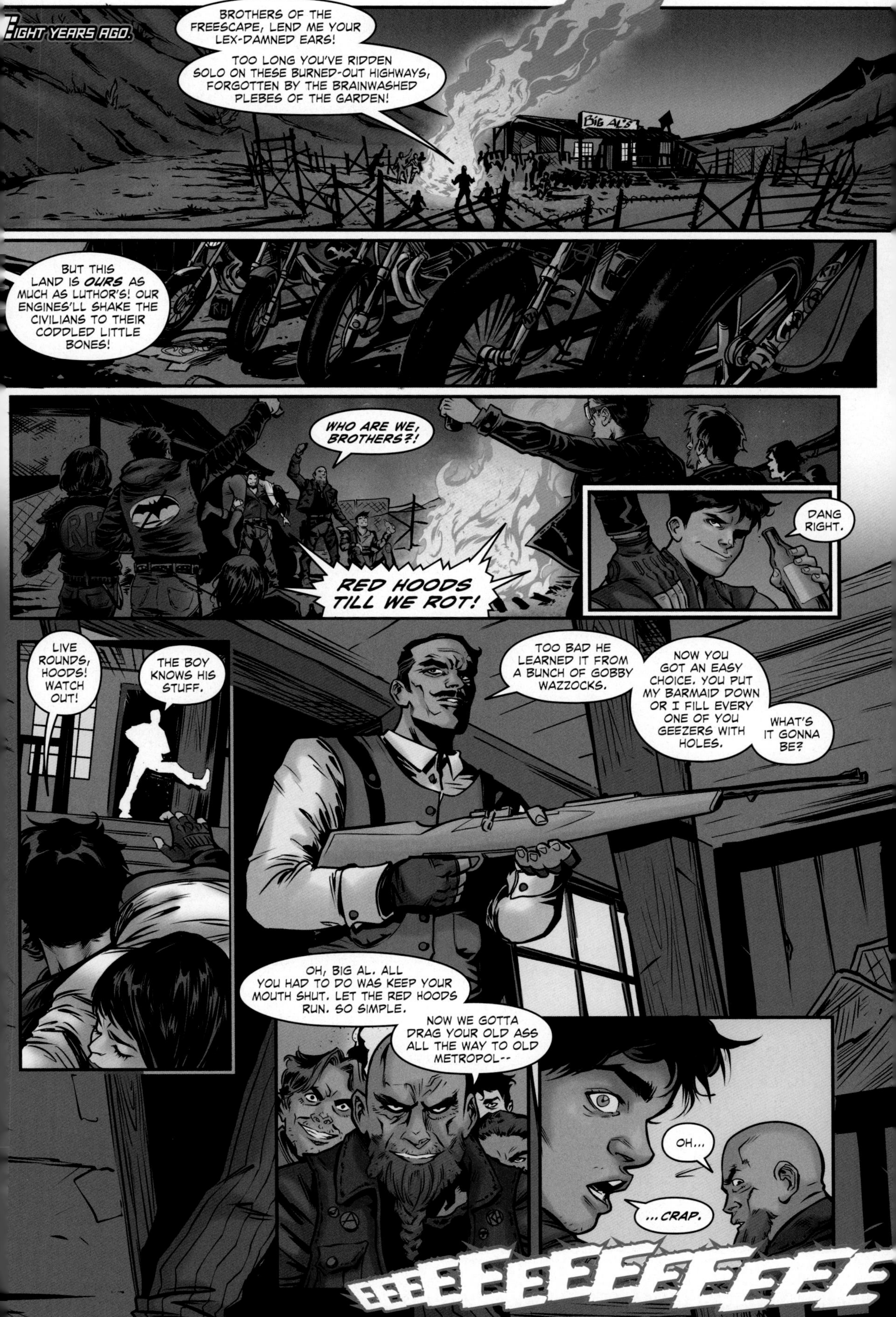
EIGHT YEARS AGO.
BROTHERS OF THE FREESCAPE, LEND ME YOUR LEX-DAMNED EARS!
TOO LONG YOU'VE RIDDEN SOLO ON THESE BURNED-OUT HIGHWAYS, FORGOTTEN BY THE BRAINWASHED PLEBES OF THE GARDEN!
BIG AL'S
BUT THIS LAND IS OURS AS MUCH AS LUTHOR'S! OUR ENGINES'LL SHAKE THE CIVILIANS TO THEIR CODDLED LITTLE BONES!
WHO ARE WE, BROTHERS?!
RED HOODS TILL WE ROT!
DANG RIGHT.
LIVE ROUNDS, HOODS! WATCH OUT!
THE BOY KNOWS HIS STUFF.
TOO BAD HE LEARNED IT FROM A BUNCH OF GOBBY WAZZOCKS.
NOW YOU GOT AN EASY CHOICE. YOU PUT MY BARMAID DOWN OR I FILL EVERY ONE OF YOU GEEZERS WITH HOLES.
WHAT'S IT GONNA BE?
OH, BIG AL. ALL YOU HAD TO DO WAS KEEP YOUR MOUTH SHUT. LET THE RED HOODS RUN. SO SIMPLE.
NOW WE GOTTA DRAG YOUR OLD ASS ALL THE WAY TO OLD METROPOL--
OH...
...CRAP.
EEEEEEEEEEEEEE

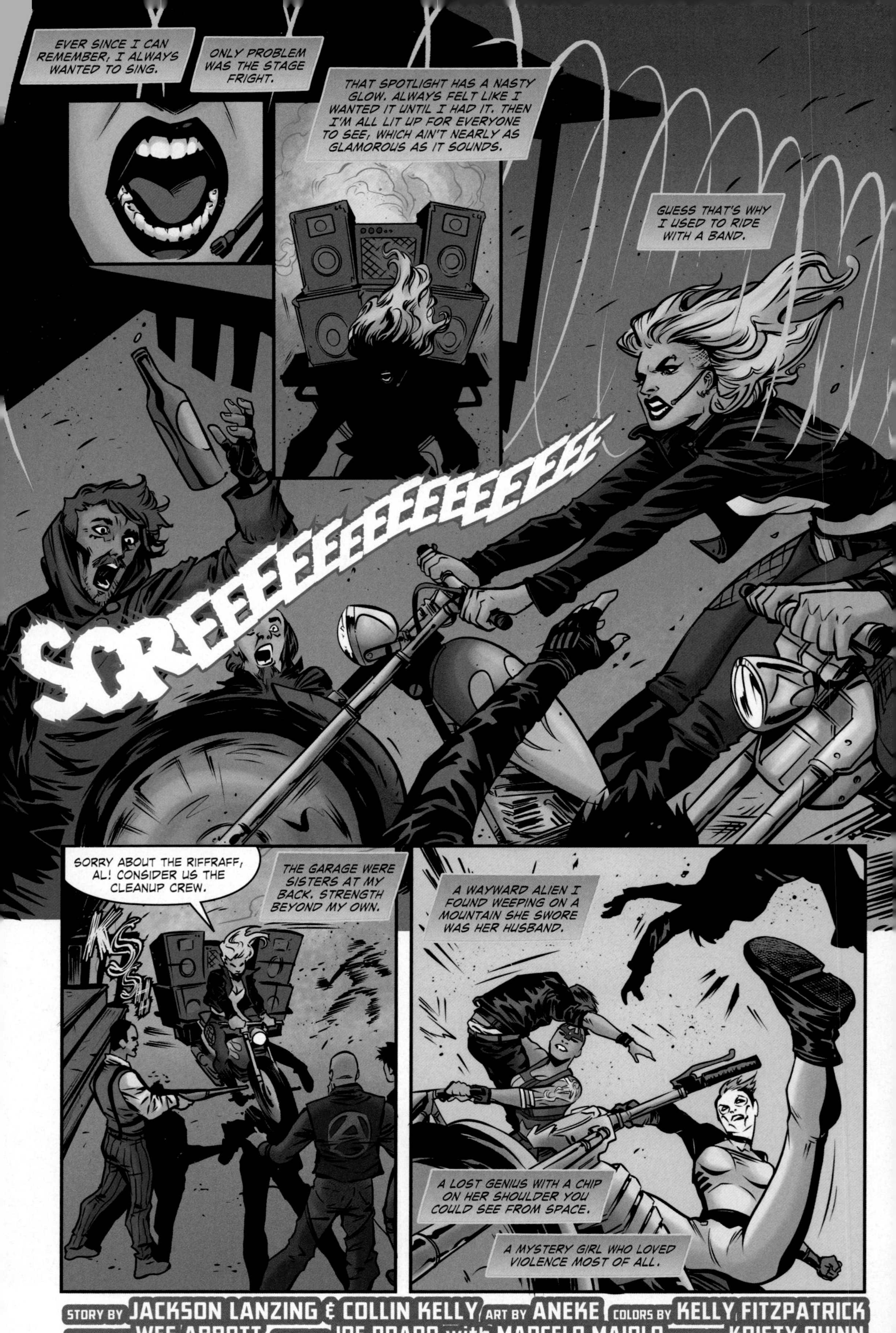
EVER SINCE I CAN REMEMBER, I ALWAYS WANTED TO SING.
ONLY PROBLEM WAS THE STAGE FRIGHT.
THAT SPOTLIGHT HAS A NASTY GLOW. ALWAYS FELT LIKE I WANTED IT UNTIL I HAD IT. THEN I'M ALL LIT UP FOR EVERYONE TO SEE, WHICH AIN'T NEARLY AS GLAMOROUS AS IT SOUNDS.
GUESS THAT'S WHY I USED TO RIDE WITH A BAND.
SCREEEEEEEEEEEEEEEE
SORRY ABOUT THE RIFFRAFF, AL! CONSIDER US THE CLEANUP CREW.
THE GARAGE WERE SISTERS AT MY BACK. STRENGTH BEYOND MY OWN.
KSSH
A WAYWARD ALIEN I FOUND WEEPING ON A MOUNTAIN SHE SWORE WAS HER HUSBAND.
A LOST GENIUS WITH A CHIP ON HER SHOULDER YOU COULD SEE FROM SPACE.
A MYSTERY GIRL WHO LOVED VIOLENCE MOST OF ALL.

STORY BY JACKSON LANZING & COLLIN KELLY ART BY ANEKE COLORS BY KELLY FITZPATRICK
LETTERS BY WES ABBOTT COVER BY JOE PRADO with MARCELO MAIOLO EDITED BY KRISTY QUINN

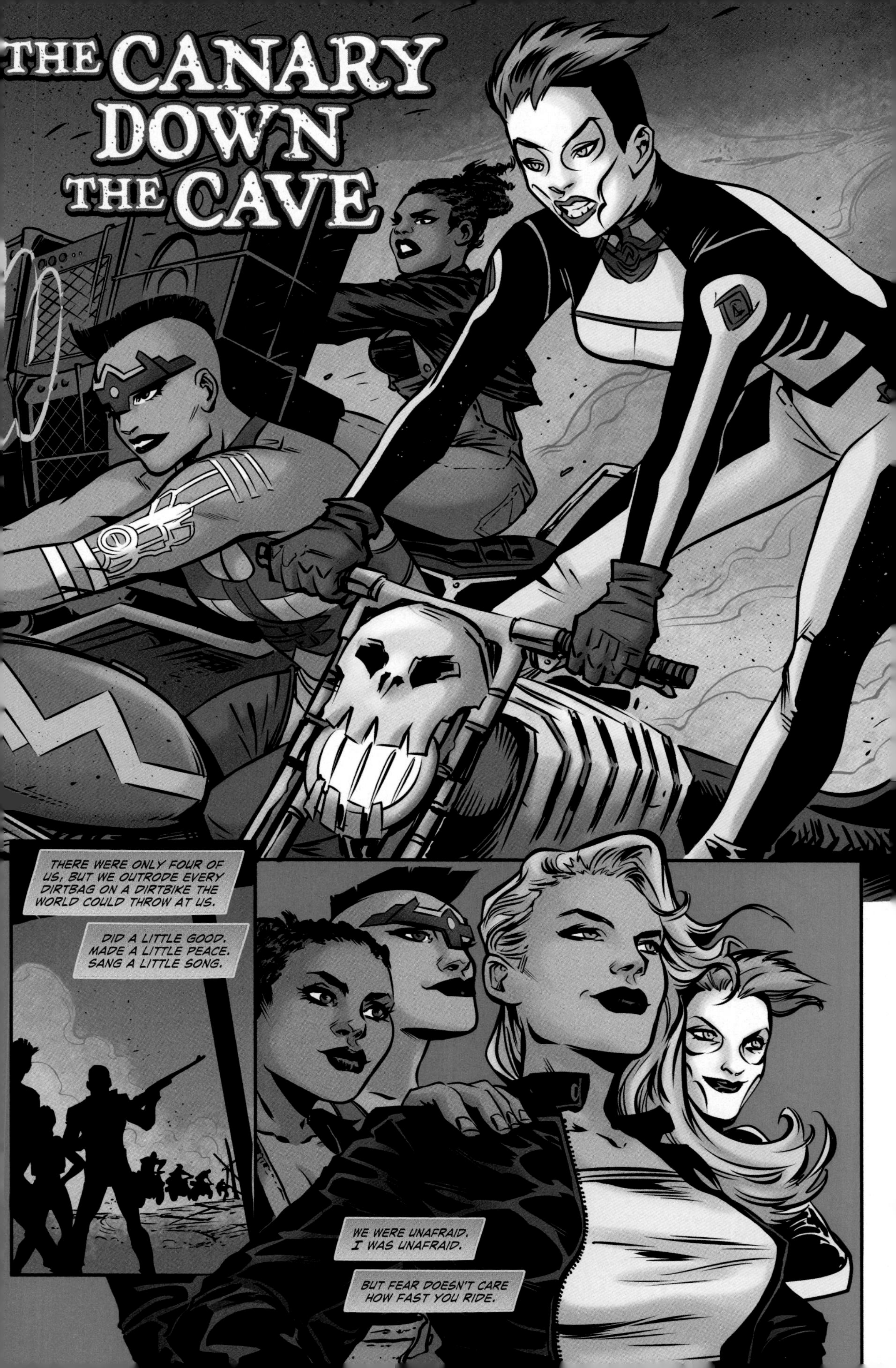
THE CANARY DOWN THE CAVE
THERE WERE ONLY FOUR OF US, BUT WE OUTRODE EVERY DIRTBAG ON A DIRTBIKE THE WORLD COULD THROW AT US.
DID A LITTLE GOOD. MADE A LITTLE PEACE. SANG A LITTLE SONG.
WE WERE UNAFRAID. I WAS UNAFRAID.
BUT FEAR DOESN'T CARE HOW FAST YOU RIDE.

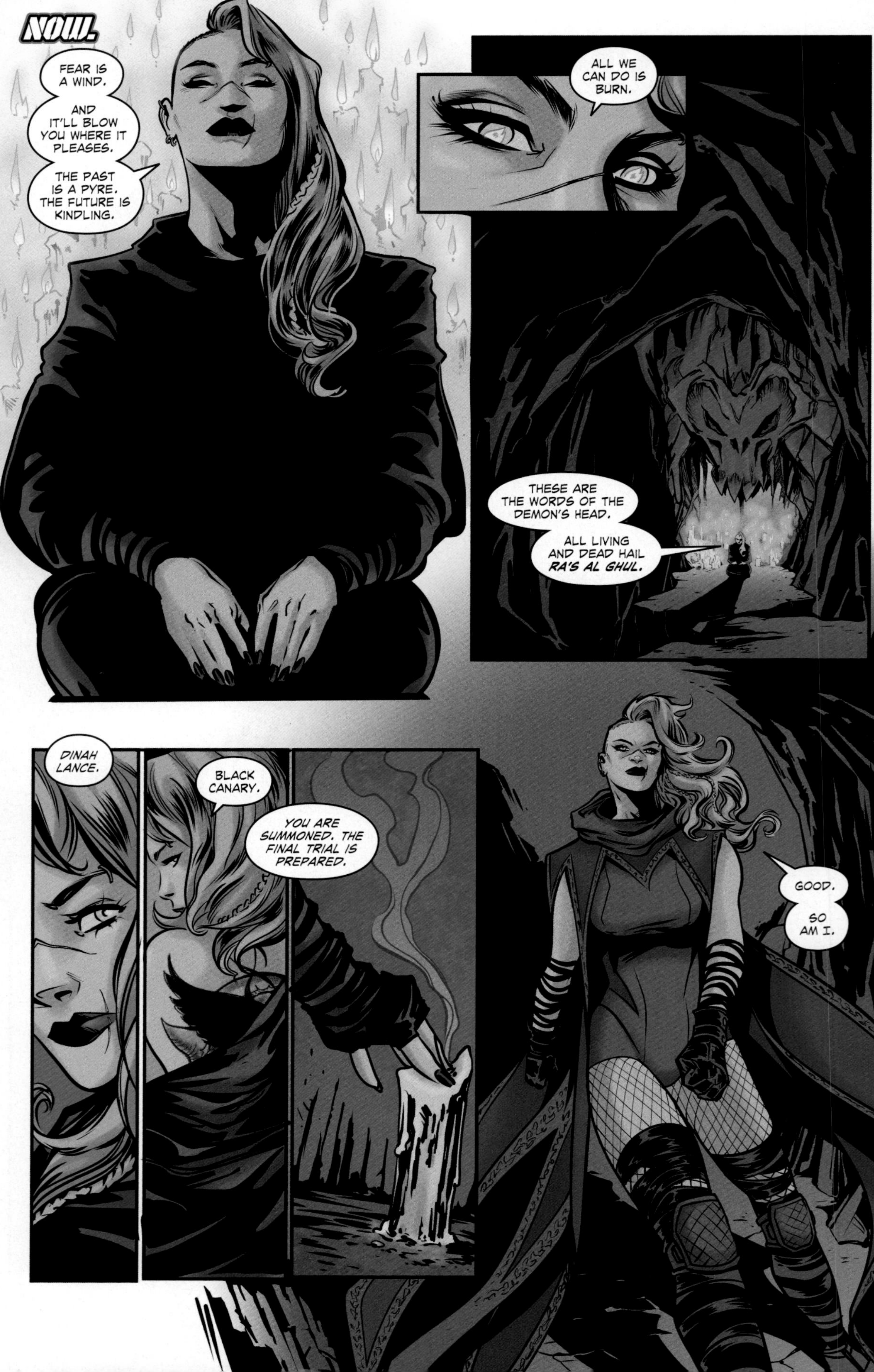
NOW.
FEAR IS A WIND.
AND IT'LL BLOW YOU WHERE IT PLEASES.
THE PAST IS A PYRE. THE FUTURE IS KINDLING.
ALL WE CAN DO IS BURN.
THESE ARE THE WORDS OF THE DEMON'S HEAD.
ALL LIVING AND DEAD HAIL *RA'S AL GHUL.*
DINAH LANCE.
BLACK CANARY.
YOU ARE SUMMONED. THE FINAL TRIAL IS PREPARED.
GOOD.
SO AM I.

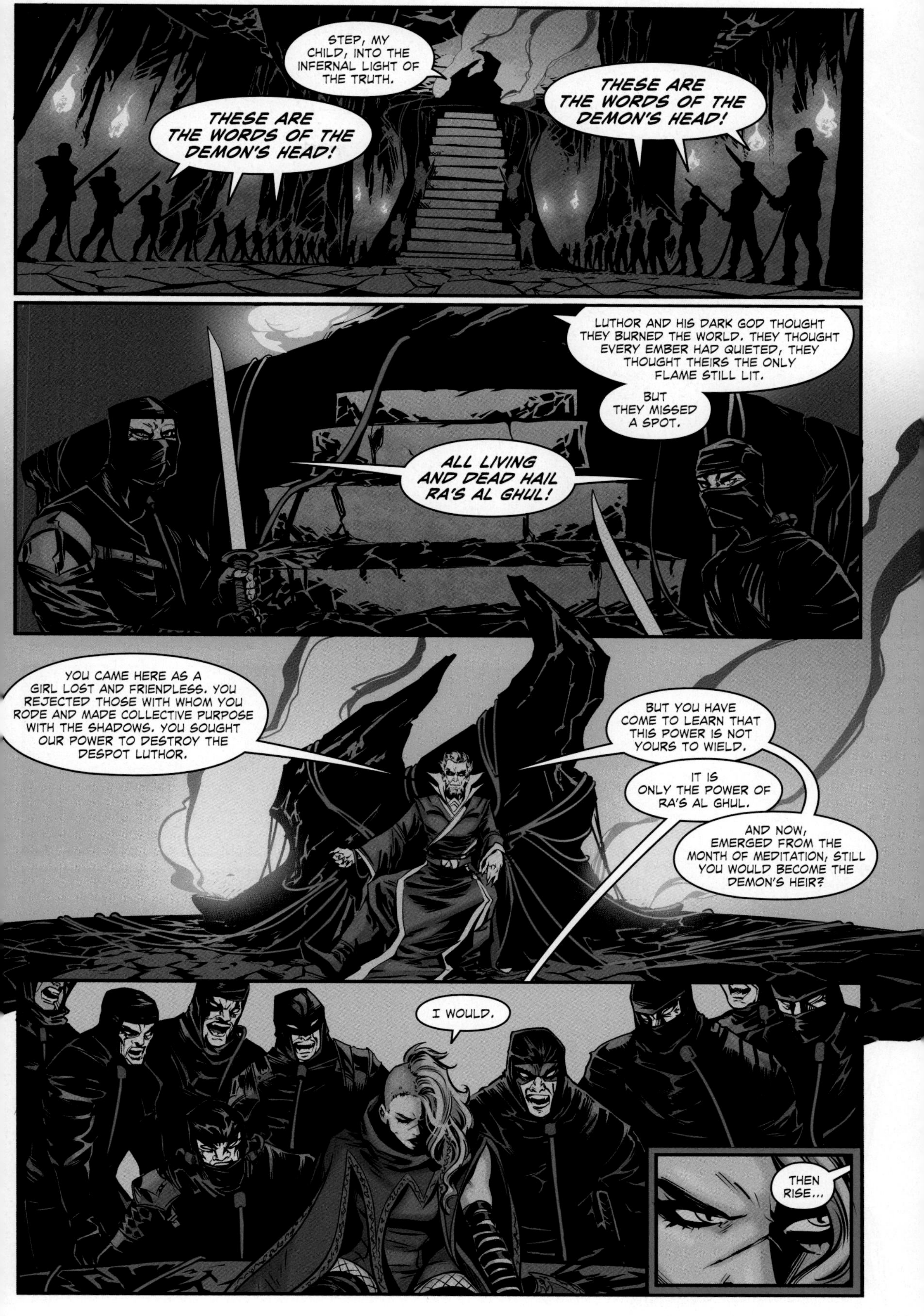
STEP, MY CHILD, INTO THE INFERNAL LIGHT OF THE TRUTH.
THESE ARE THE WORDS OF THE DEMON'S HEAD!
THESE ARE THE WORDS OF THE DEMON'S HEAD!
LUTHOR AND HIS DARK GOD THOUGHT THEY BURNED THE WORLD. THEY THOUGHT EVERY EMBER HAD QUIETED, THEY THOUGHT THEIRS THE ONLY FLAME STILL LIT.
BUT THEY MISSED A SPOT.
ALL LIVING AND DEAD HAIL RA'S AL GHUL!
YOU CAME HERE AS A GIRL LOST AND FRIENDLESS. YOU REJECTED THOSE WITH WHOM YOU RODE AND MADE COLLECTIVE PURPOSE WITH THE SHADOWS. YOU SOUGHT OUR POWER TO DESTROY THE DESPOT LUTHOR.
BUT YOU HAVE COME TO LEARN THAT THIS POWER IS NOT YOURS TO WIELD.
IT IS ONLY THE POWER OF RA'S AL GHUL.
AND NOW, EMERGED FROM THE MONTH OF MEDITATION, STILL YOU WOULD BECOME THE DEMON'S HEIR?
I WOULD.
THEN RISE...

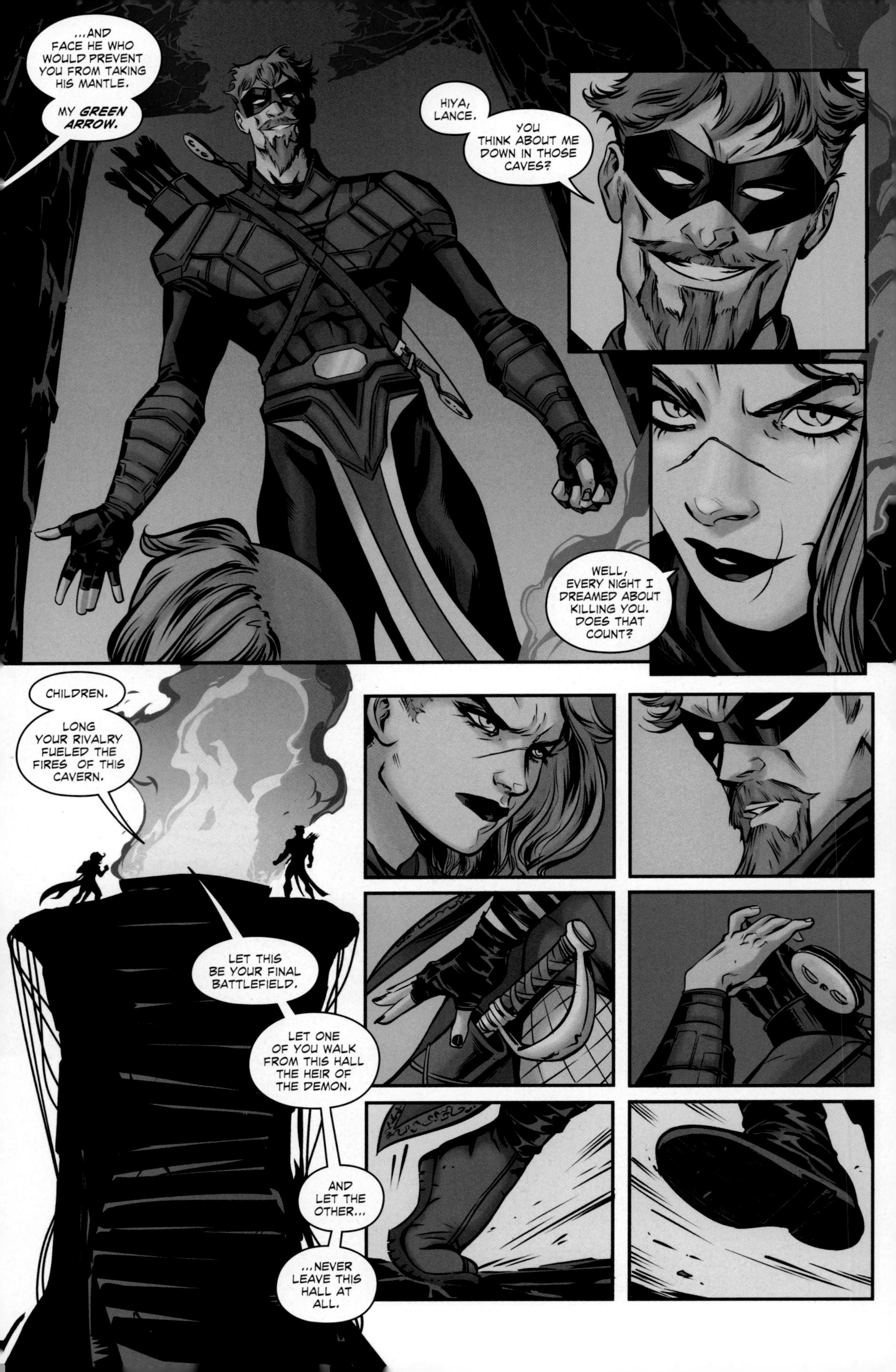

...AND FACE HE WHO WOULD PREVENT YOU FROM TAKING HIS MANTLE.
MY GREEN ARROW.
HIYA, LANCE.
YOU THINK ABOUT ME DOWN IN THOSE CAVES?
WELL, EVERY NIGHT I DREAMED ABOUT KILLING YOU. DOES THAT COUNT?
CHILDREN.
LONG YOUR RIVALRY FUELED THE FIRES OF THIS CAVERN.
LET THIS BE YOUR FINAL BATTLEFIELD.
LET ONE OF YOU WALK FROM THIS HALL THE HEIR OF THE DEMON.
AND LET THE OTHER...
...NEVER LEAVE THIS HALL AT ALL.

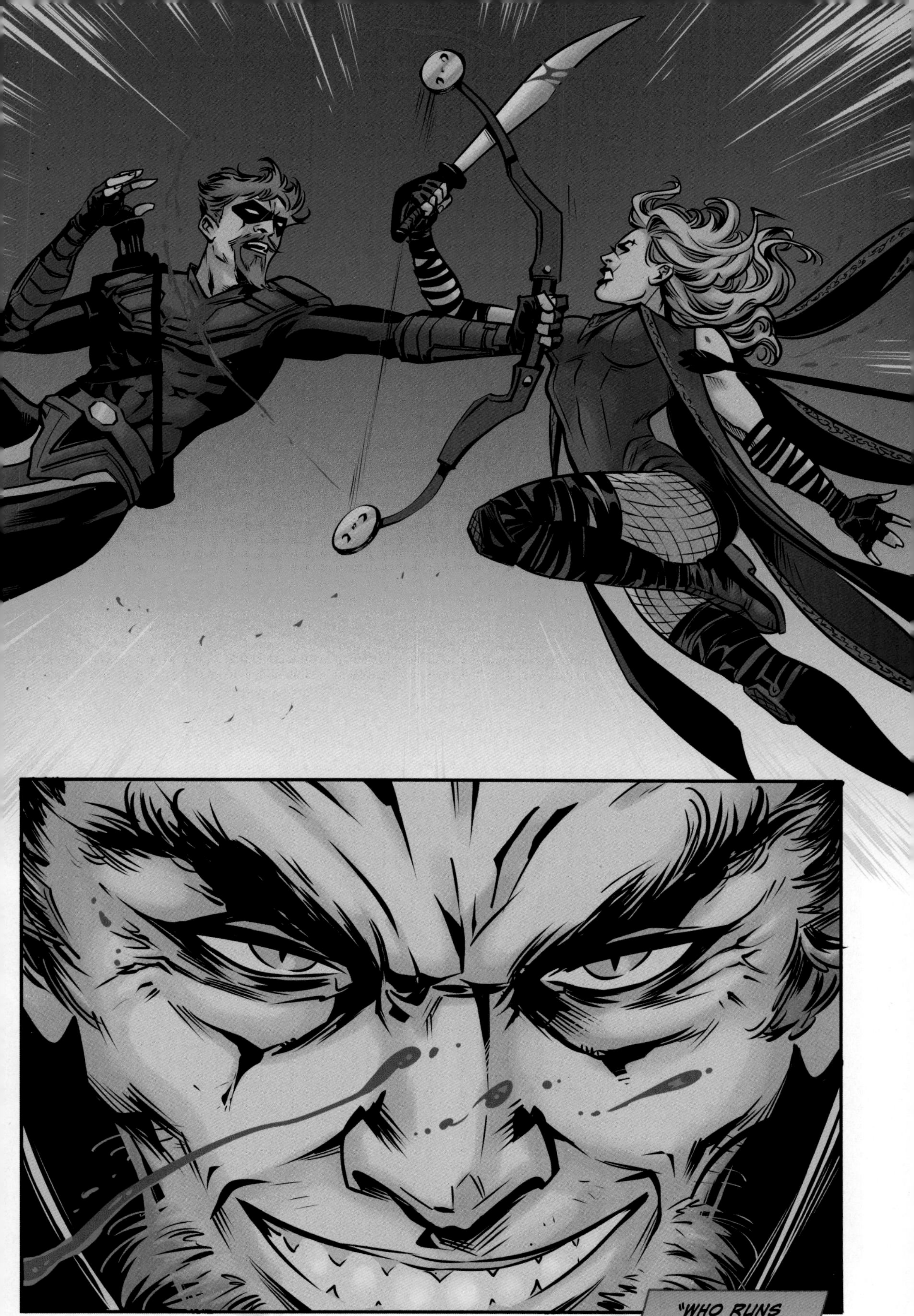
"WHO RUNS BARTERTOWN?!"

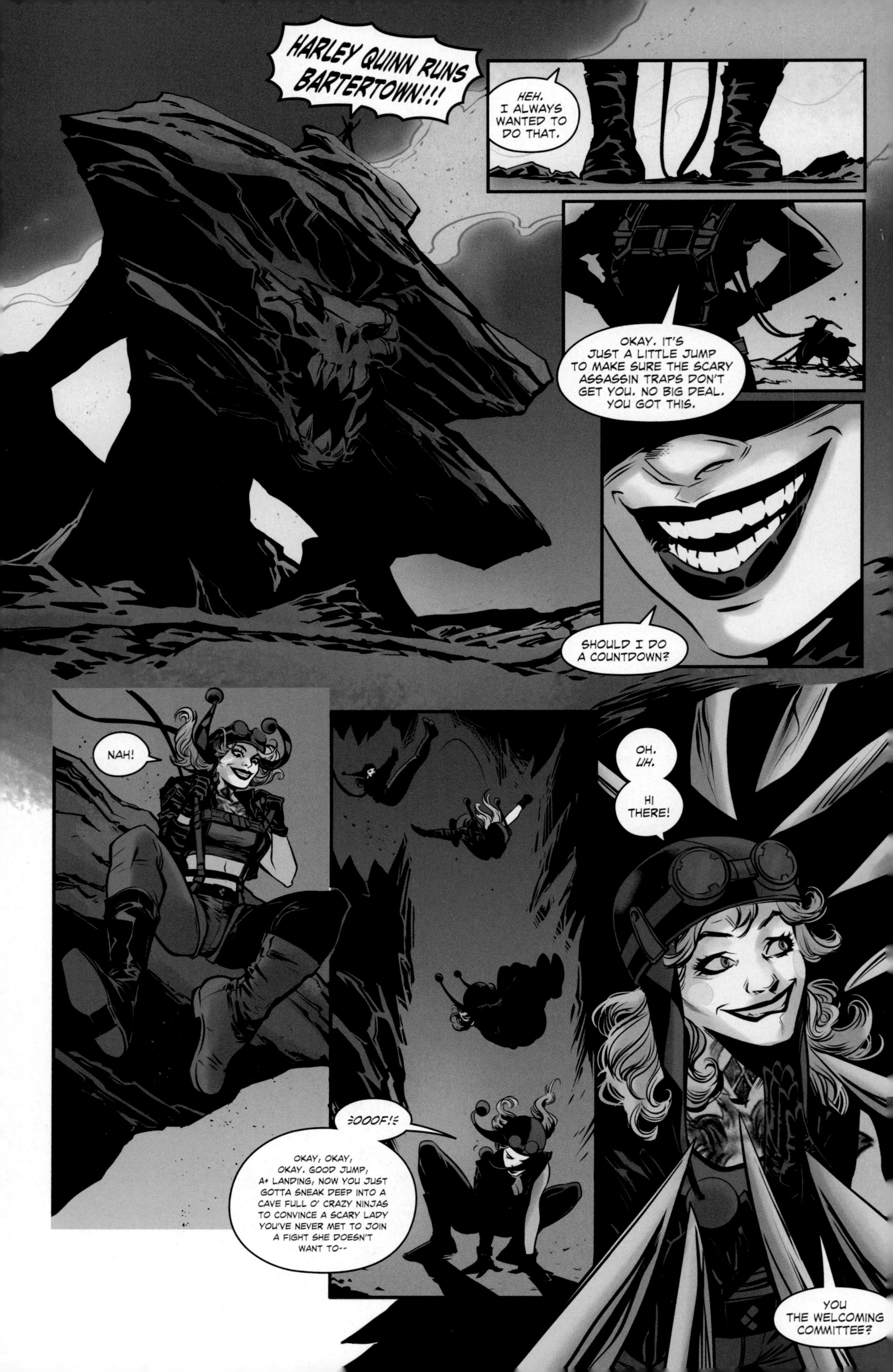
HARLEY QUINN RUNS BARTERTOWN!!!
HEH. I ALWAYS WANTED TO DO THAT.
OKAY. IT'S JUST A LITTLE JUMP TO MAKE SURE THE SCARY ASSASSIN TRAPS DON'T GET YOU. NO BIG DEAL. YOU GOT THIS.
SHOULD I DO A COUNTDOWN?
NAH!
OOOF!
OKAY, OKAY, OKAY. GOOD JUMP, A+ LANDING, NOW YOU JUST GOTTA SNEAK DEEP INTO A CAVE FULL O' CRAZY NINJAS TO CONVINCE A SCARY LADY YOU'VE NEVER MET TO JOIN A FIGHT SHE DOESN'T WANT TO--
OH. UH.
HI THERE!
YOU THE WELCOMING COMMITTEE?

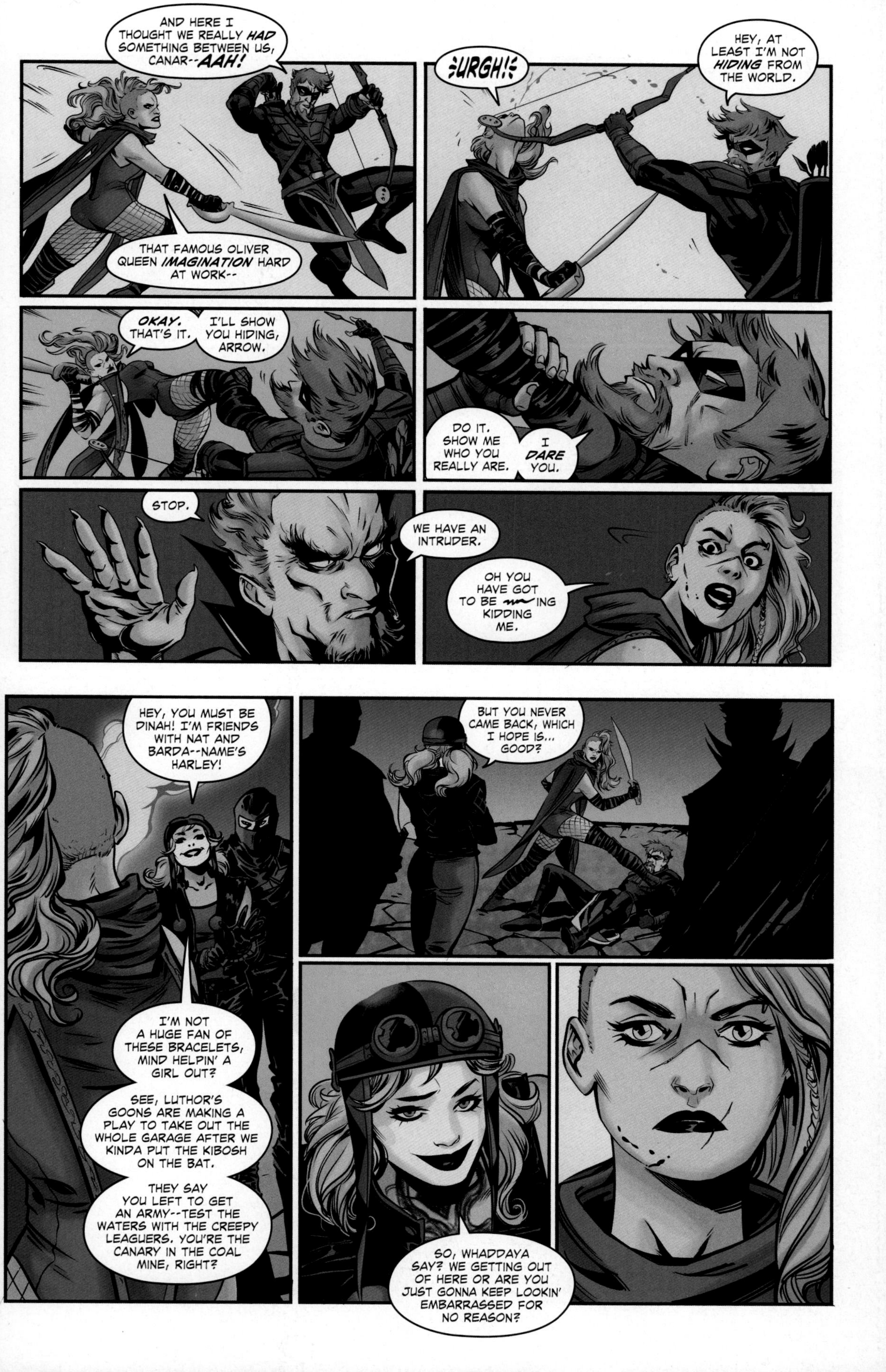
AND HERE I THOUGHT WE REALLY HAD SOMETHING BETWEEN US, CANAR--AAH!
THAT FAMOUS OLIVER QUEEN IMAGINATION HARD AT WORK--
URGH!
HEY, AT LEAST I'M NOT HIDING FROM THE WORLD.
OKAY. THAT'S IT.
I'LL SHOW YOU HIDING, ARROW.
DO IT. SHOW ME WHO YOU REALLY ARE.
I DARE YOU.
STOP.
WE HAVE AN INTRUDER.
OH YOU HAVE GOT TO BE ~~ING KIDDING ME.
HEY, YOU MUST BE DINAH! I'M FRIENDS WITH NAT AND BARDA--NAME'S HARLEY!
I'M NOT A HUGE FAN OF THESE BRACELETS, MIND HELPIN' A GIRL OUT?
SEE, LUTHOR'S GOONS ARE MAKING A PLAY TO TAKE OUT THE WHOLE GARAGE AFTER WE KINDA PUT THE KIBOSH ON THE BAT.
THEY SAY YOU LEFT TO GET AN ARMY--TEST THE WATERS WITH THE CREEPY LEAGUERS. YOU'RE THE CANARY IN THE COAL MINE, RIGHT?
BUT YOU NEVER CAME BACK, WHICH I HOPE IS... GOOD?
SO, WHADDAYA SAY? WE GETTING OUT OF HERE OR ARE YOU JUST GONNA KEEP LOOKIN' EMBARRASSED FOR NO REASON?

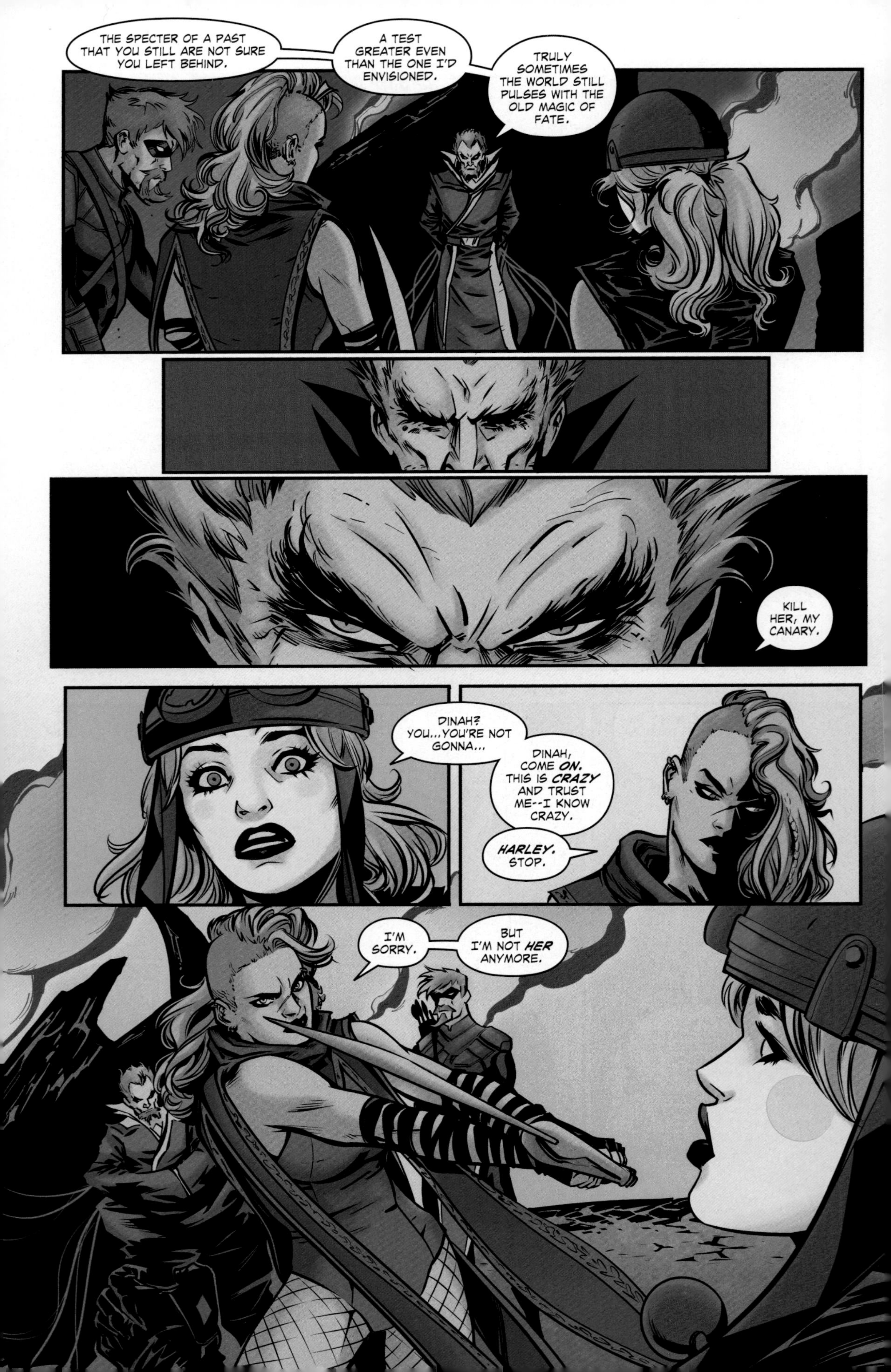
THE SPECTER OF A PAST THAT YOU STILL ARE NOT SURE YOU LEFT BEHIND.
A TEST GREATER EVEN THAN THE ONE I'D ENVISIONED.
TRULY SOMETIMES THE WORLD STILL PULSES WITH THE OLD MAGIC OF FATE.
KILL HER, MY CANARY.
DINAH? YOU...YOU'RE NOT GONNA...
DINAH, COME ON. THIS IS CRAZY AND TRUST ME--I KNOW CRAZY.
HARLEY. STOP.
I'M SORRY.
BUT I'M NOT HER ANYMORE.

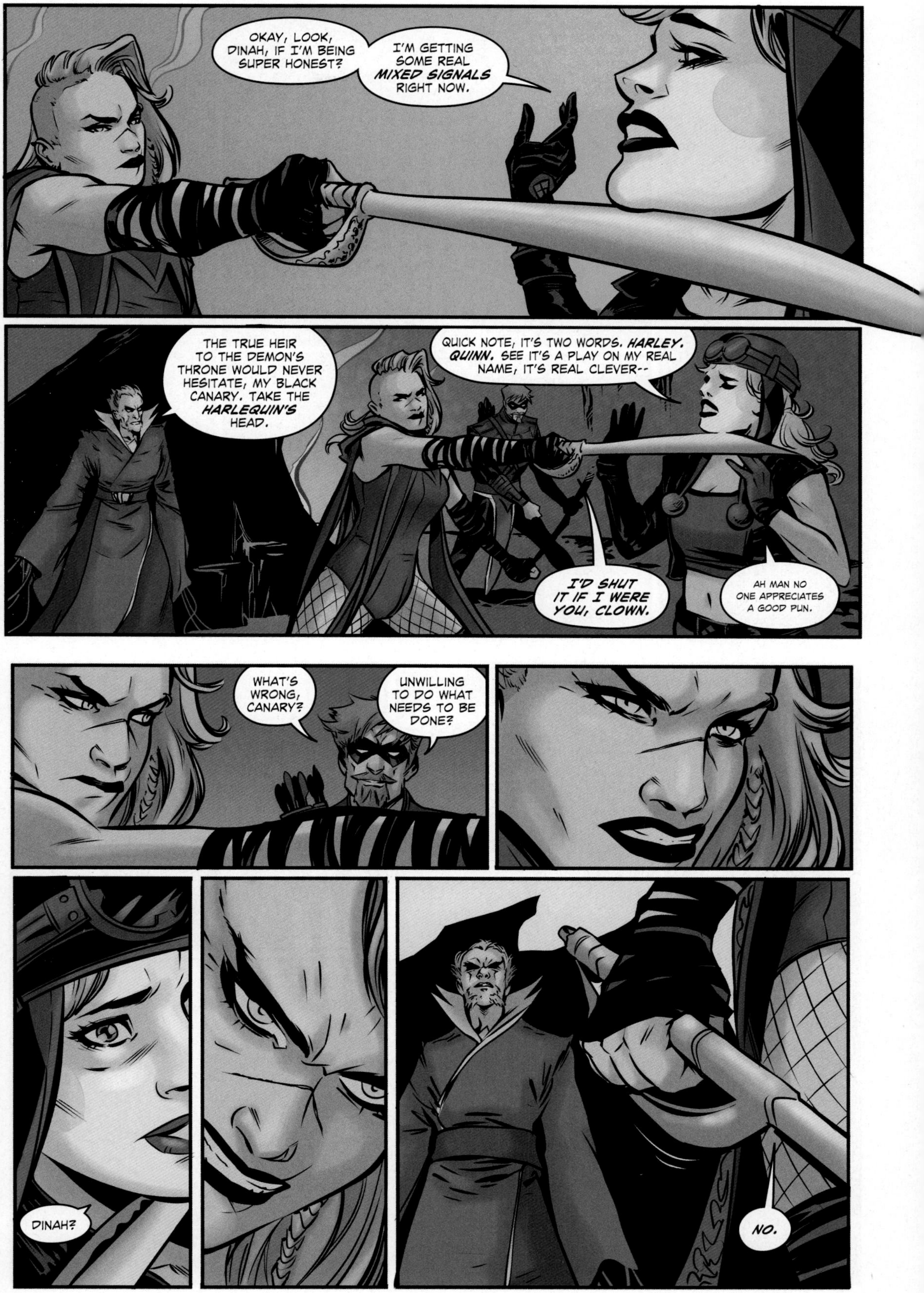

OKAY, LOOK, DINAH, IF I'M BEING SUPER HONEST?
I'M GETTING SOME REAL MIXED SIGNALS RIGHT NOW.
THE TRUE HEIR TO THE DEMON'S THRONE WOULD NEVER HESITATE, MY BLACK CANARY. TAKE THE HARLEQUIN'S HEAD.
QUICK NOTE, IT'S TWO WORDS. HARLEY. QUINN. SEE IT'S A PLAY ON MY REAL NAME, IT'S REAL CLEVER--
I'D SHUT IT IF I WERE YOU, CLOWN.
AH MAN NO ONE APPRECIATES A GOOD PUN.
WHAT'S WRONG, CANARY?
UNWILLING TO DO WHAT NEEDS TO BE DONE?
DINAH?
NO.

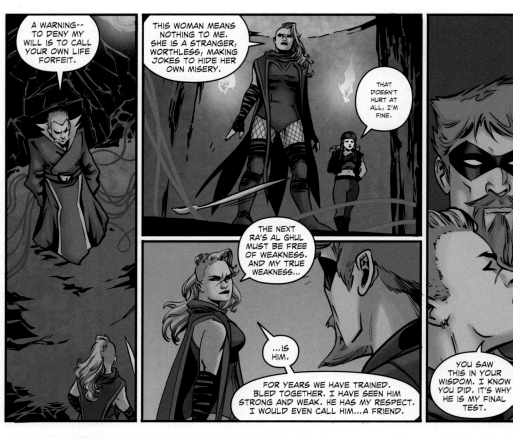

A WARNING-- TO DENY MY WILL IS TO CALL YOUR OWN LIFE FORFEIT.

THIS WOMAN MEANS NOTHING TO ME. SHE IS A STRANGER, WORTHLESS, MAKING JOKES TO HIDE HER OWN MISERY.

THAT DOESN'T HURT AT ALL, I'M FINE.

THE NEXT RA'S AL GHUL MUST BE FREE OF WEAKNESS. AND MY TRUE WEAKNESS...

...IS HIM.

FOR YEARS WE HAVE TRAINED. BLED TOGETHER. I HAVE SEEN HIM STRONG AND WEAK. HE HAS MY RESPECT. I WOULD EVEN CALL HIM...A FRIEND.

YOU SAW THIS IN YOUR WISDOM. I KNOW YOU DID. IT'S WHY HE IS MY FINAL TEST.

SO LET ME COMPLETE YOUR WILL.

...

IF WHAT SHE SAYS IS TRUE, QUEEN OF NOTHING, FREE HER FROM THIS PAIN.

IF WHAT YOU SAY IS TRUE, BLOODY LANCE...

...THEN CARVE HIM FROM YOUR HEART.

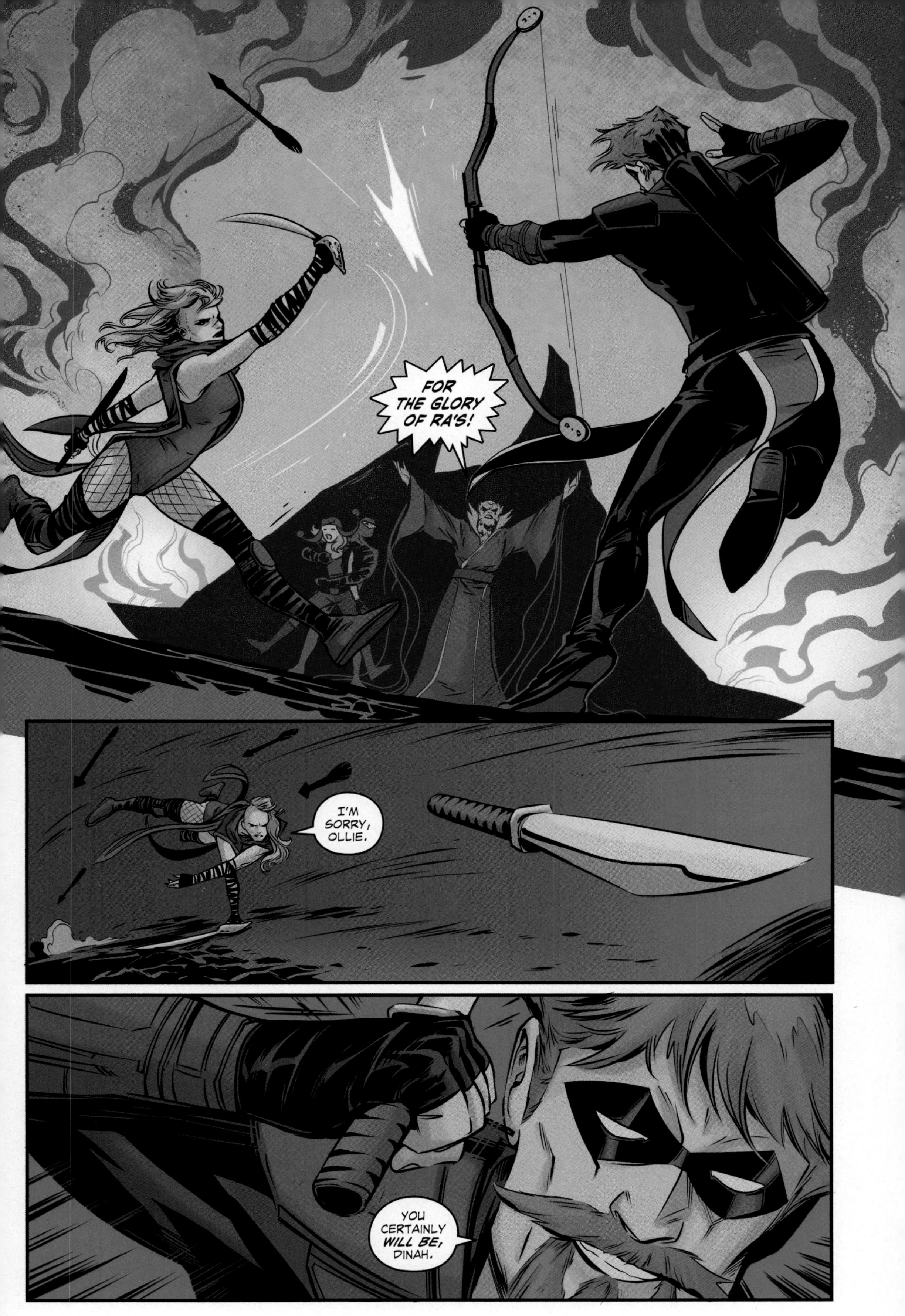
FOR THE GLORY OF RA'S!
I'M SORRY, OLLIE.
YOU CERTAINLY WILL BE, DINAH.

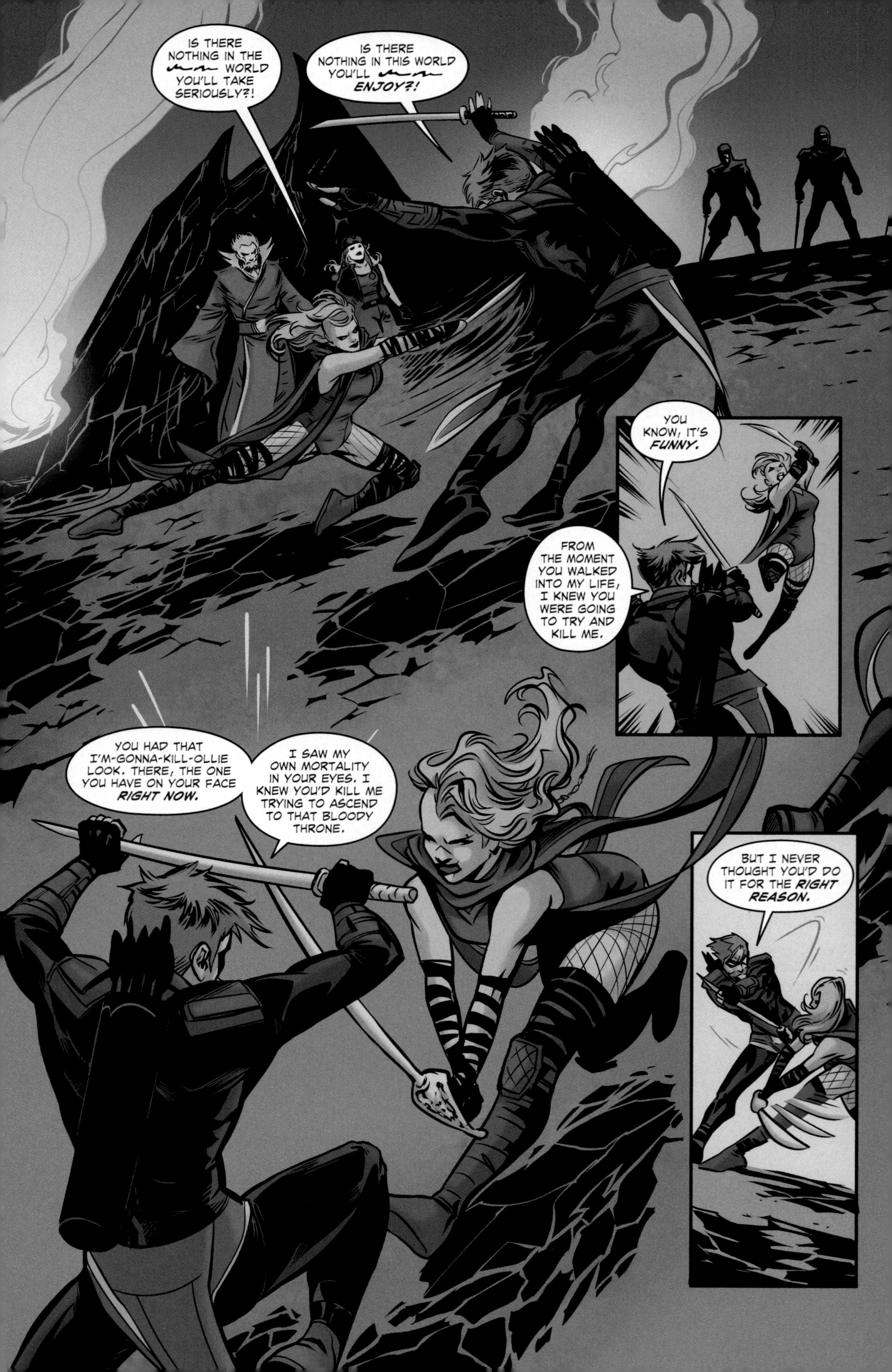
IS THERE NOTHING IN THE WORLD YOU'LL TAKE SERIOUSLY?!
IS THERE NOTHING IN THIS WORLD YOU'LL ENJOY?!
YOU KNOW, IT'S FUNNY.
FROM THE MOMENT YOU WALKED INTO MY LIFE, I KNEW YOU WERE GOING TO TRY AND KILL ME.
YOU HAD THAT I'M-GONNA-KILL-OLLIE LOOK. THERE, THE ONE YOU HAVE ON YOUR FACE RIGHT NOW.
I SAW MY OWN MORTALITY IN YOUR EYES. I KNEW YOU'D KILL ME TRYING TO ASCEND TO THAT BLOODY THRONE.
BUT I NEVER THOUGHT YOU'D DO IT FOR THE RIGHT REASON.

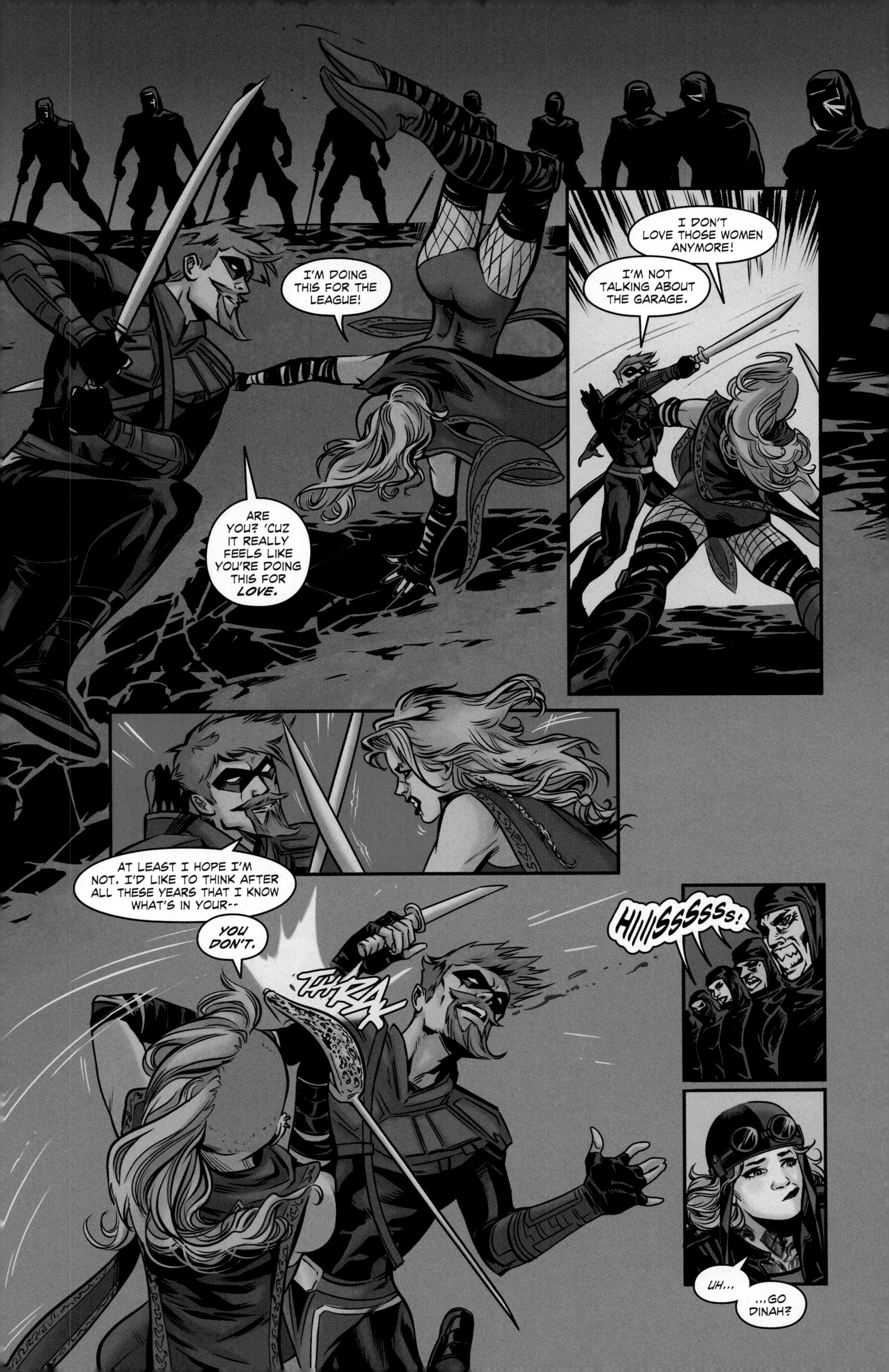
I'M DOING THIS FOR THE LEAGUE!
ARE YOU? 'CUZ IT REALLY FEELS LIKE YOU'RE DOING THIS FOR LOVE.
I DON'T LOVE THOSE WOMEN ANYMORE!
I'M NOT TALKING ABOUT THE GARAGE.
AT LEAST I HOPE I'M NOT. I'D LIKE TO THINK AFTER ALL THESE YEARS THAT I KNOW WHAT'S IN YOUR--
YOU DON'T.
THKA
HIIIISSSSSs!
UH...
...GO DINAH?

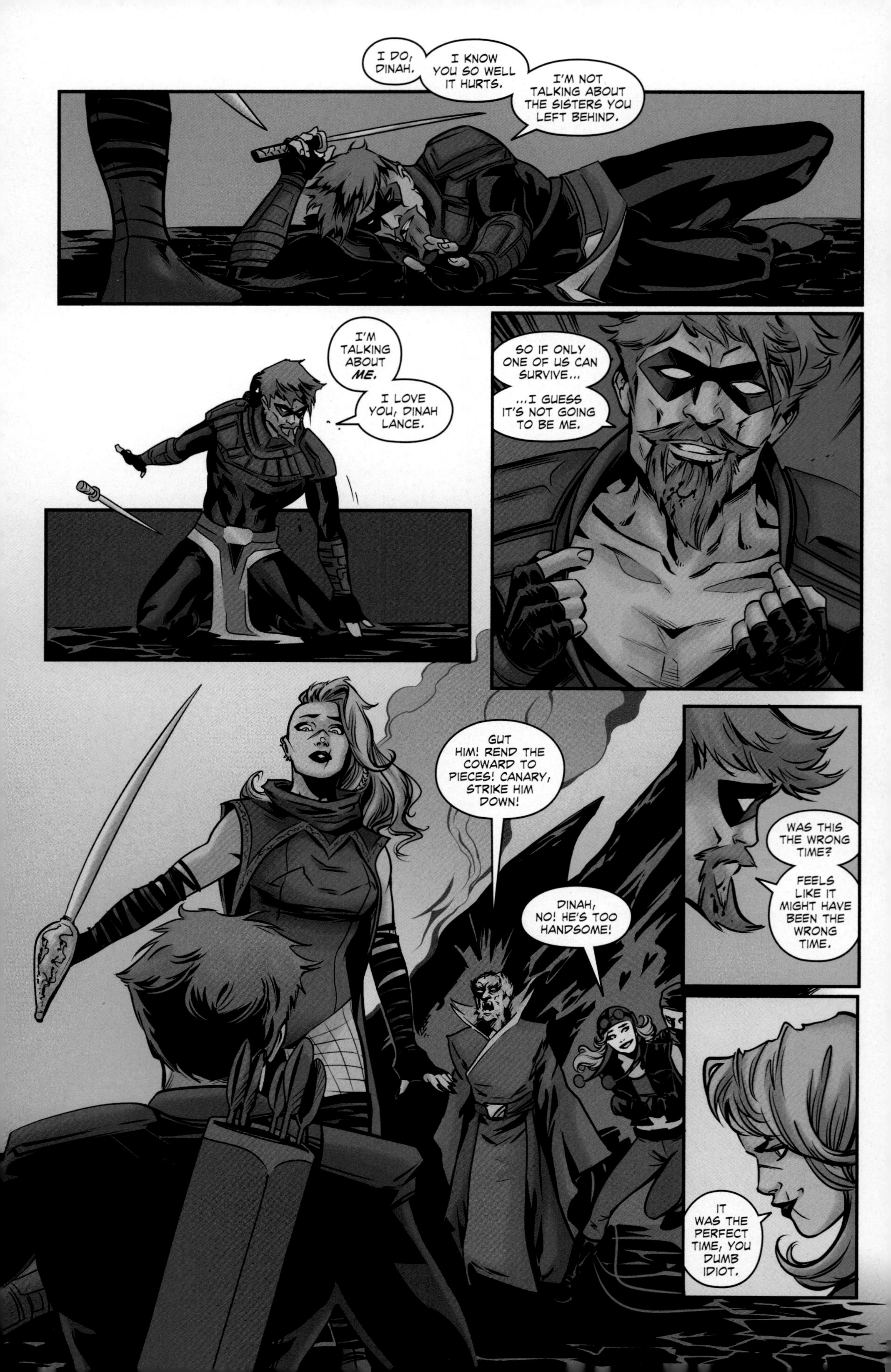
I DO, DINAH.
I KNOW YOU SO WELL IT HURTS.
I'M NOT TALKING ABOUT THE SISTERS YOU LEFT BEHIND.
I'M TALKING ABOUT *ME.*
I LOVE YOU, DINAH LANCE.
SO IF ONLY ONE OF US CAN SURVIVE...
...I GUESS IT'S NOT GOING TO BE ME.
GUT HIM! REND THE COWARD TO PIECES! CANARY, STRIKE HIM DOWN!
DINAH, NO! HE'S TOO HANDSOME!
WAS THIS THE WRONG TIME?
FEELS LIKE IT MIGHT HAVE BEEN THE WRONG TIME.
IT WAS THE PERFECT TIME, YOU DUMB IDIOT.

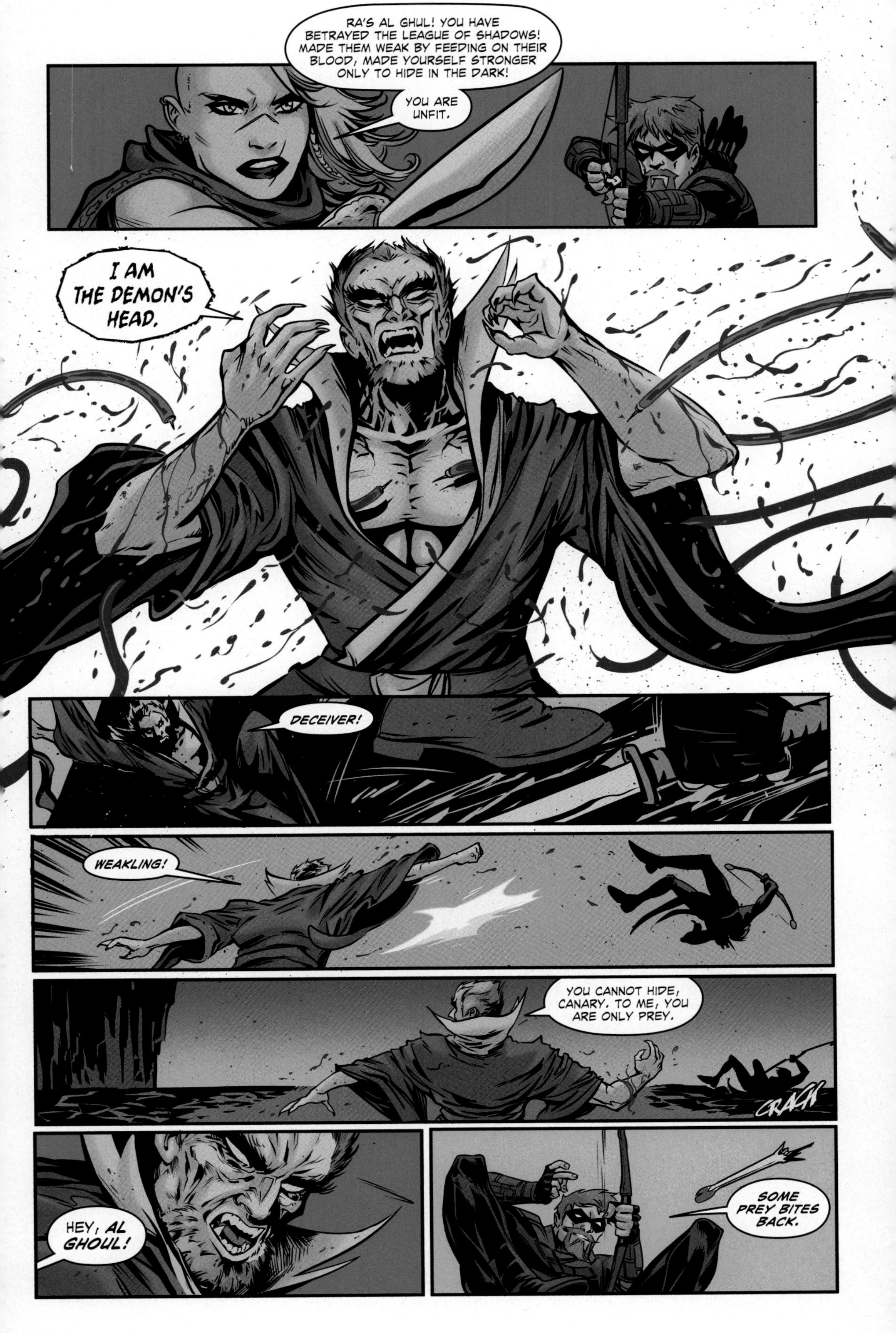
RA'S AL GHUL! YOU HAVE BETRAYED THE LEAGUE OF SHADOWS! MADE THEM WEAK BY FEEDING ON THEIR BLOOD, MADE YOURSELF STRONGER ONLY TO HIDE IN THE DARK!
YOU ARE UNFIT.
I AM THE DEMON'S HEAD.
DECEIVER!
WEAKLING!
YOU CANNOT HIDE, CANARY. TO ME, YOU ARE ONLY PREY.
CRACK
HEY, AL GHOUL!
SOME PREY BITES BACK.

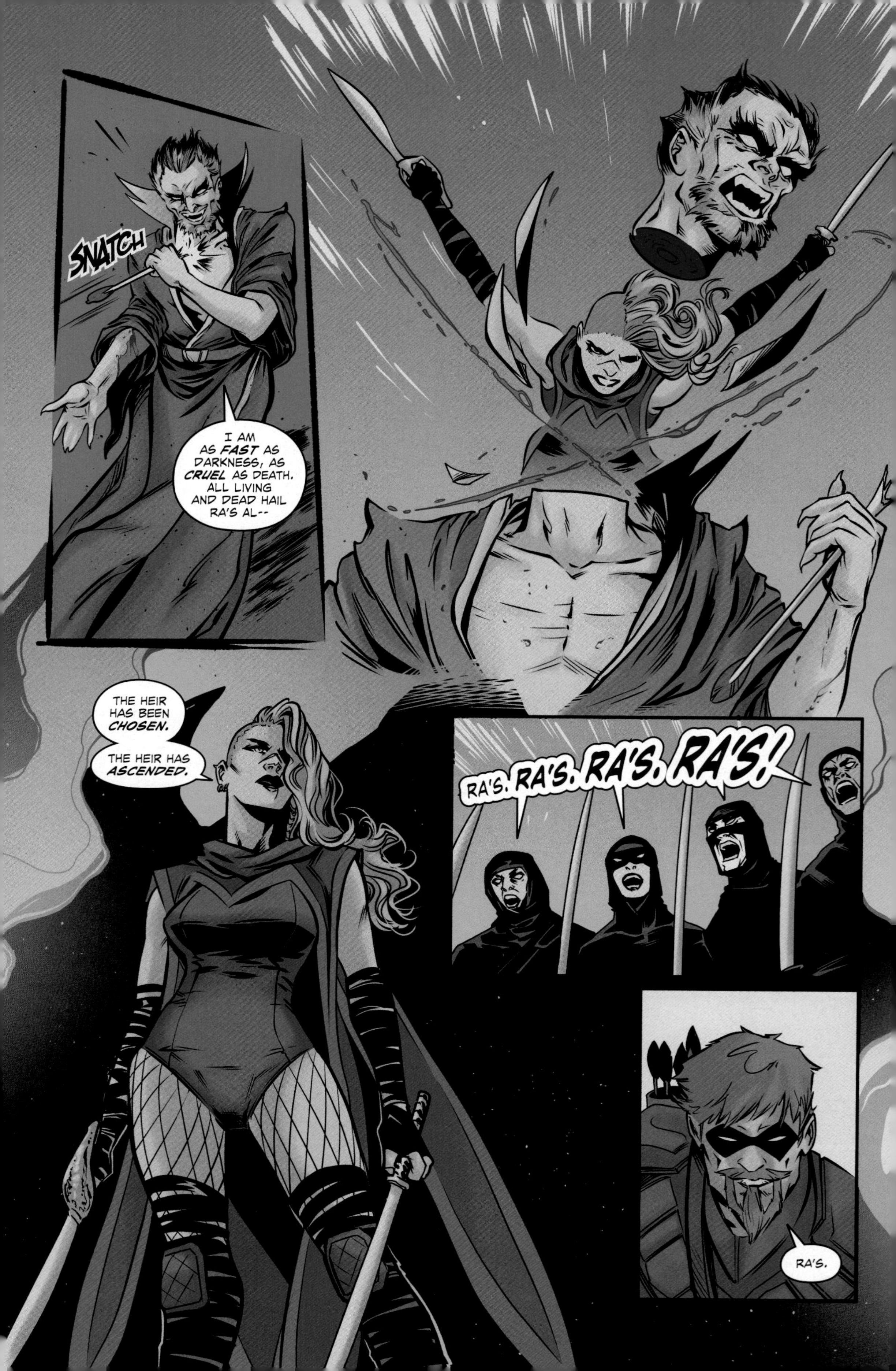
SNATCH
I AM AS *FAST* AS DARKNESS, AS *CRUEL* AS DEATH. ALL LIVING AND DEAD HAIL RA'S AL--
THE HEIR HAS BEEN *CHOSEN.*
THE HEIR HAS *ASCENDED.*
RA'S. RA'S. RA'S. RA'S!
RA'S.

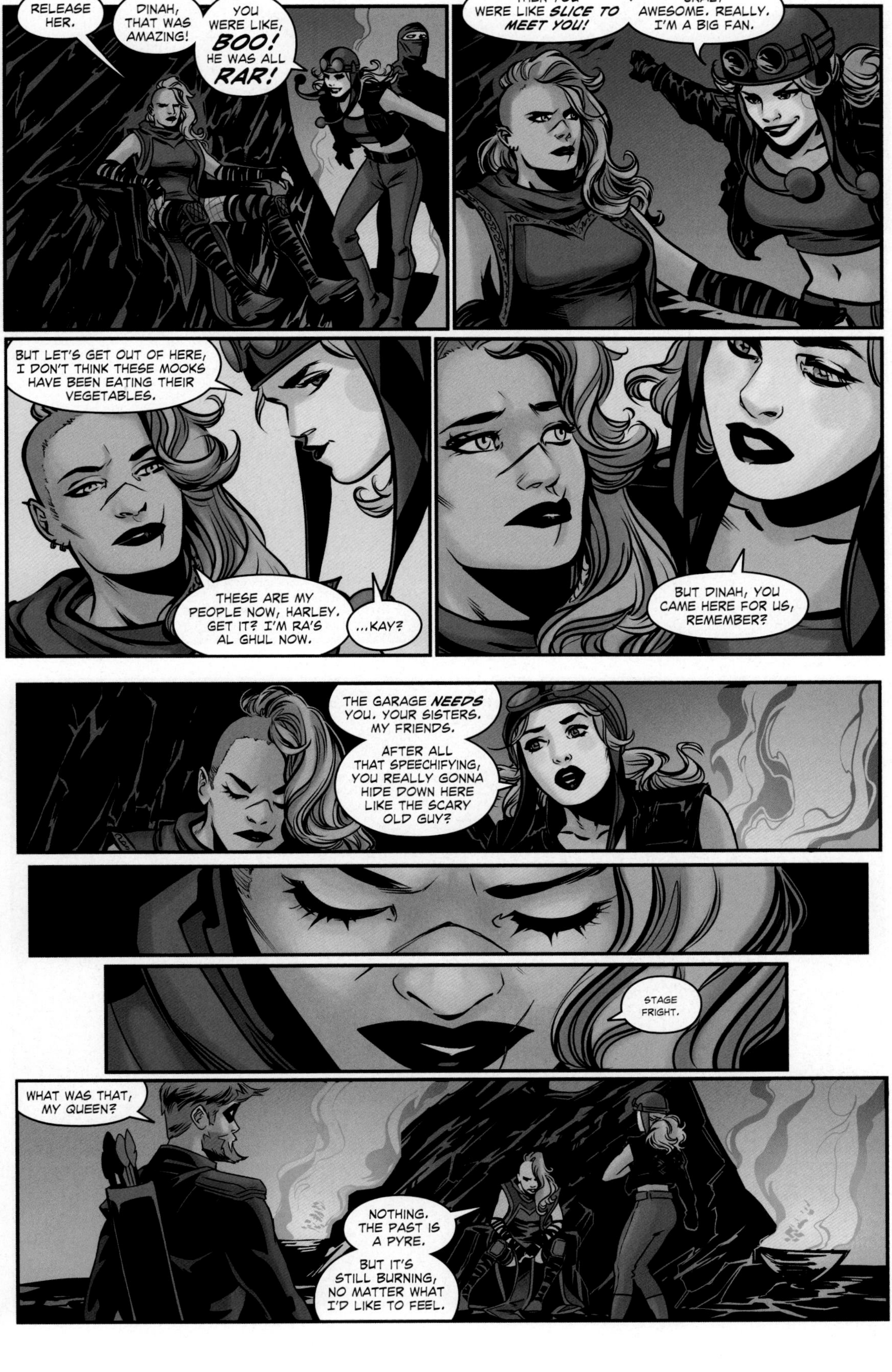

RELEASE HER.
DINAH, THAT WAS AMAZING!
YOU WERE LIKE, **BOO!** HE WAS ALL **RAR!**
THEN YOU WERE LIKE ***SLICE TO MEET YOU!***
CRAZY AWESOME. REALLY. I'M A BIG FAN.
BUT LET'S GET OUT OF HERE, I DON'T THINK THESE MOOKS HAVE BEEN EATING THEIR VEGETABLES.
THESE ARE MY PEOPLE NOW, HARLEY. GET IT? I'M RA'S AL GHUL NOW.
...KAY?
BUT DINAH, YOU CAME HERE FOR US, REMEMBER?
THE GARAGE ***NEEDS*** YOU. YOUR SISTERS. MY FRIENDS.
AFTER ALL THAT SPEECHIFYING, YOU REALLY GONNA HIDE DOWN HERE LIKE THE SCARY OLD GUY?
STAGE FRIGHT.
WHAT WAS THAT, MY QUEEN?
NOTHING. THE PAST IS A PYRE.
BUT IT'S STILL BURNING, NO MATTER WHAT I'D LIKE TO FEEL.

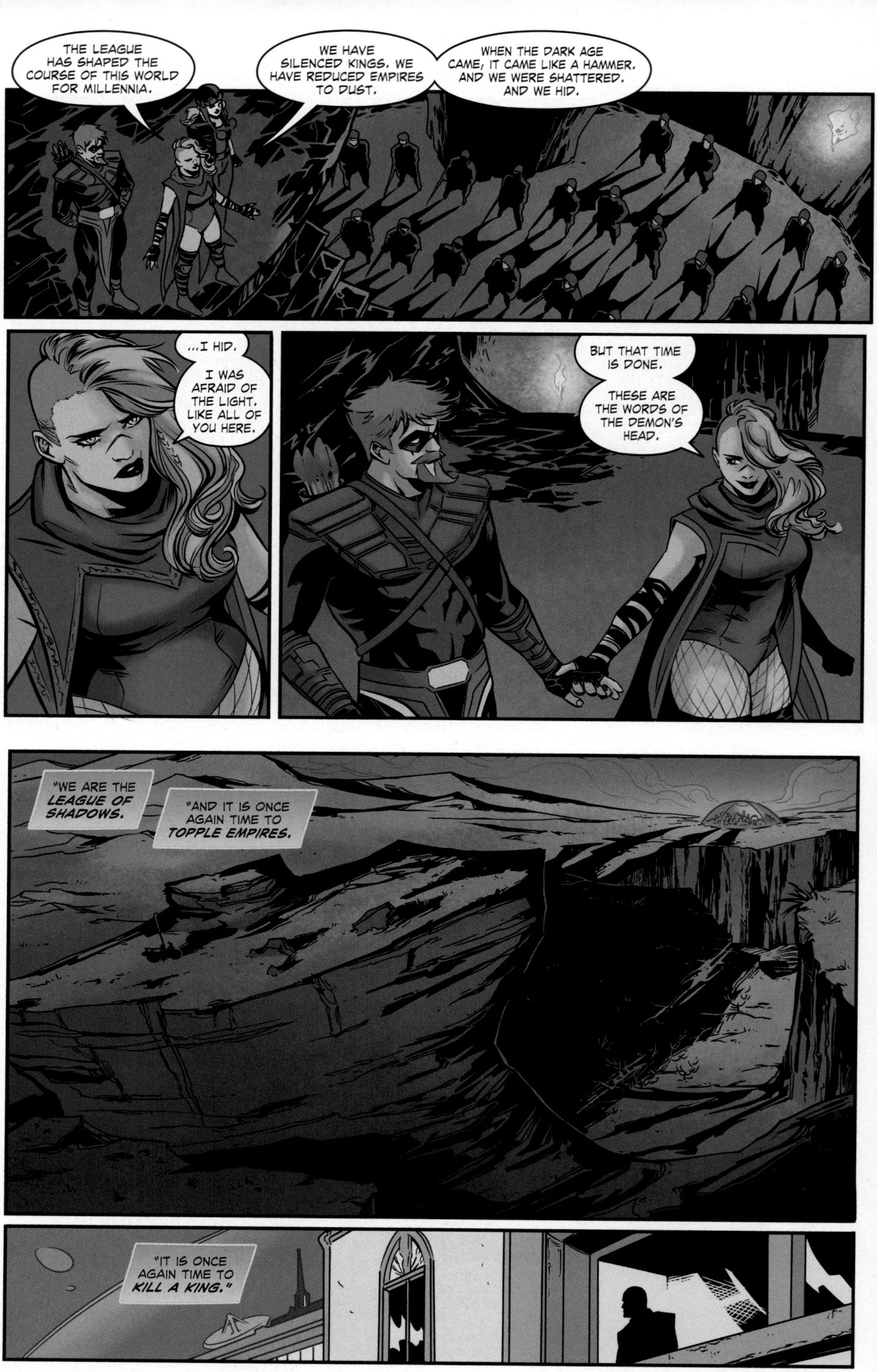
THE LEAGUE HAS SHAPED THE COURSE OF THIS WORLD FOR MILLENNIA.
WE HAVE SILENCED KINGS. WE HAVE REDUCED EMPIRES TO DUST.
WHEN THE DARK AGE CAME, IT CAME LIKE A HAMMER. AND WE WERE SHATTERED. AND WE HID.
...I HID.
I WAS AFRAID OF THE LIGHT. LIKE ALL OF YOU HERE.
BUT THAT TIME IS DONE.
THESE ARE THE WORDS OF THE DEMON'S HEAD.
"WE ARE THE *LEAGUE OF SHADOWS.*
"AND IT IS ONCE AGAIN TIME TO *TOPPLE EMPIRES.*
"IT IS ONCE AGAIN TIME TO *KILL A KING.*"

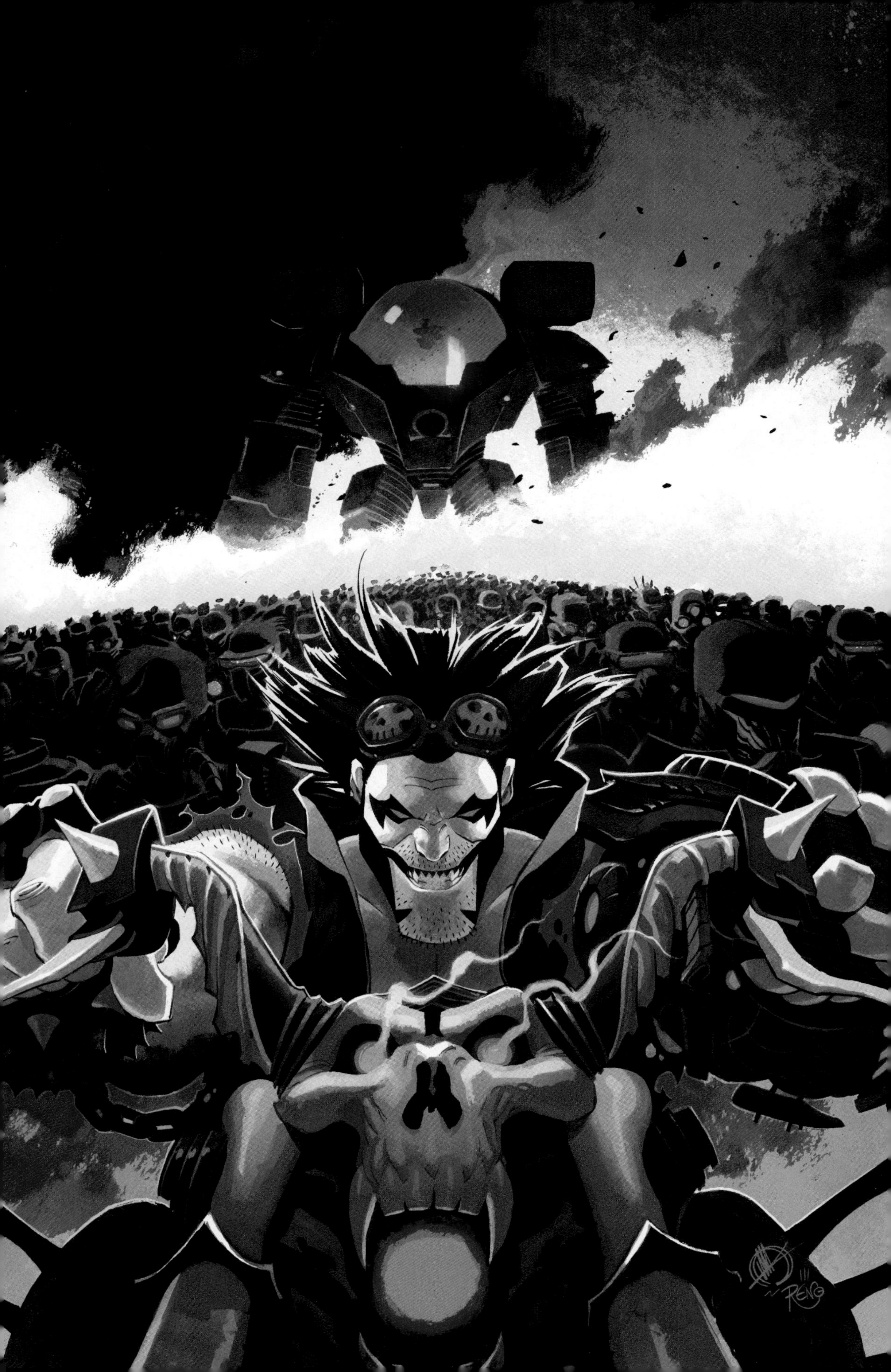

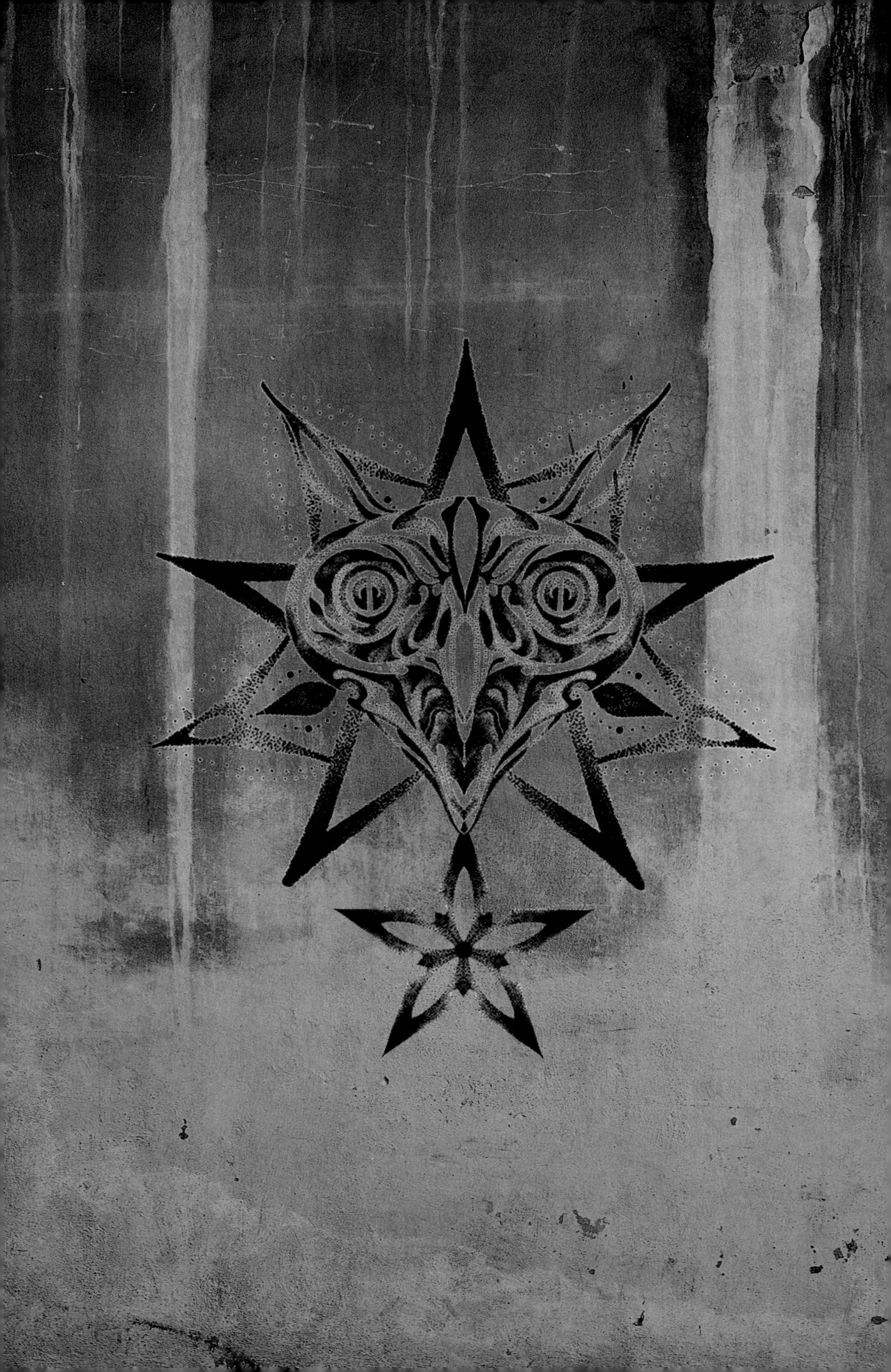

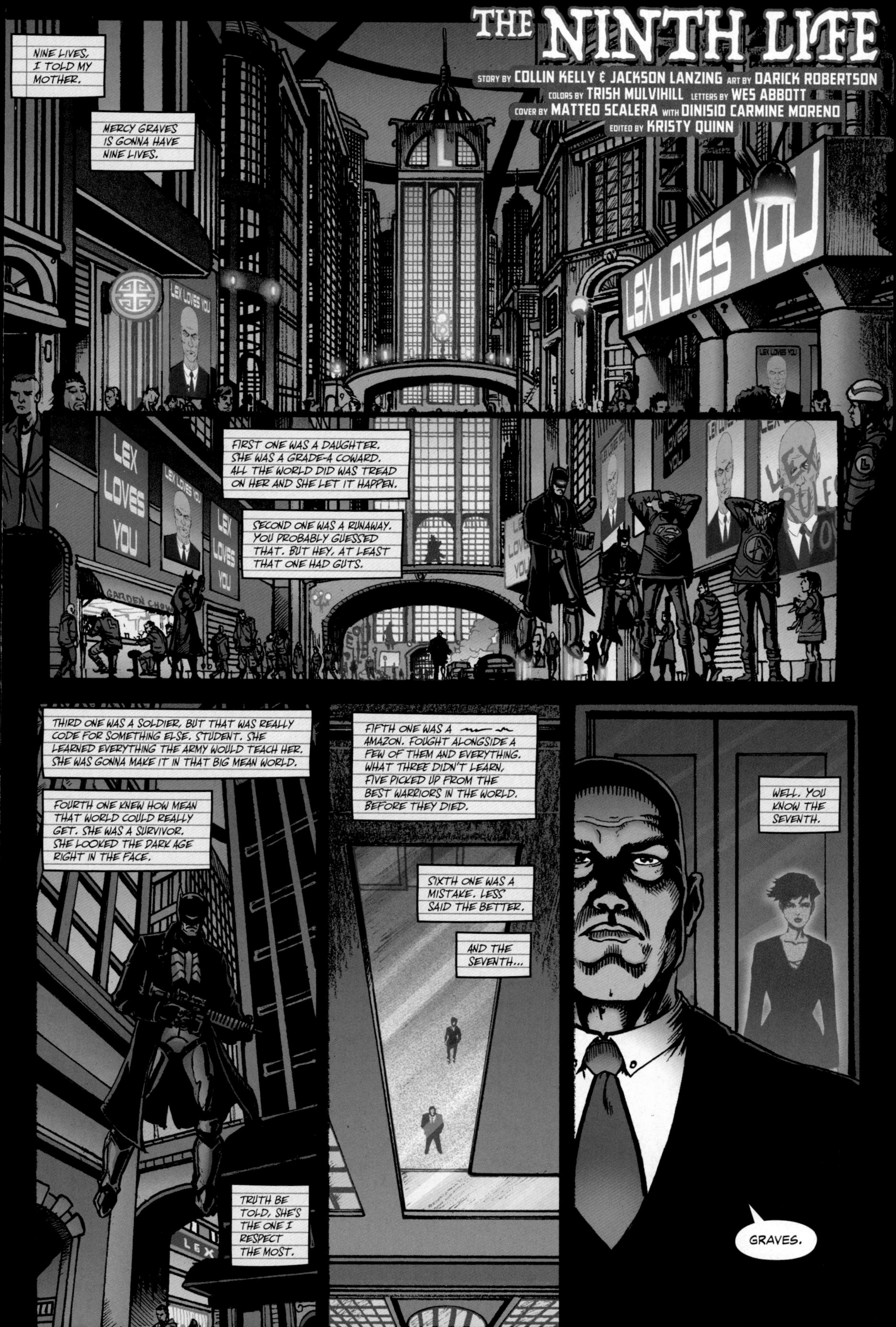
THE NINTH LIFE
STORY BY COLLIN KELLY & JACKSON LANZING ART BY DARICK ROBERTSON
COLORS BY TRISH MULVIHILL LETTERS BY WES ABBOTT
COVER BY MATTEO SCALERA WITH DINISIO CARMINE MORENO
EDITED BY KRISTY QUINN
NINE LIVES, I TOLD MY MOTHER.
MERCY GRAVES IS GONNA HAVE NINE LIVES.
LEX LOVES YOU
FIRST ONE WAS A DAUGHTER. SHE WAS A GRADE-A COWARD. ALL THE WORLD DID WAS TREAD ON HER AND SHE LET IT HAPPEN.
SECOND ONE WAS A RUNAWAY. YOU PROBABLY GUESSED THAT. BUT HEY, AT LEAST THAT ONE HAD GUTS.
LEX LOVES YOU
THIRD ONE WAS A SOLDIER, BUT THAT WAS REALLY CODE FOR SOMETHING ELSE. STUDENT. SHE LEARNED EVERYTHING THE ARMY WOULD TEACH HER. SHE WAS GONNA MAKE IT IN THAT BIG MEAN WORLD.
FOURTH ONE KNEW HOW MEAN THAT WORLD COULD REALLY GET. SHE WAS A SURVIVOR. SHE LOOKED THE DARK AGE RIGHT IN THE FACE.
TRUTH BE TOLD, SHE'S THE ONE I RESPECT THE MOST.
FIFTH ONE WAS A AMAZON. FOUGHT ALONGSIDE A FEW OF THEM AND EVERYTHING. WHAT THREE DIDN'T LEARN, FIVE PICKED UP FROM THE BEST WARRIORS IN THE WORLD. BEFORE THEY DIED.
SIXTH ONE WAS A MISTAKE. LESS SAID THE BETTER.
AND THE SEVENTH...
WELL. YOU KNOW THE SEVENTH.
GRAVES.

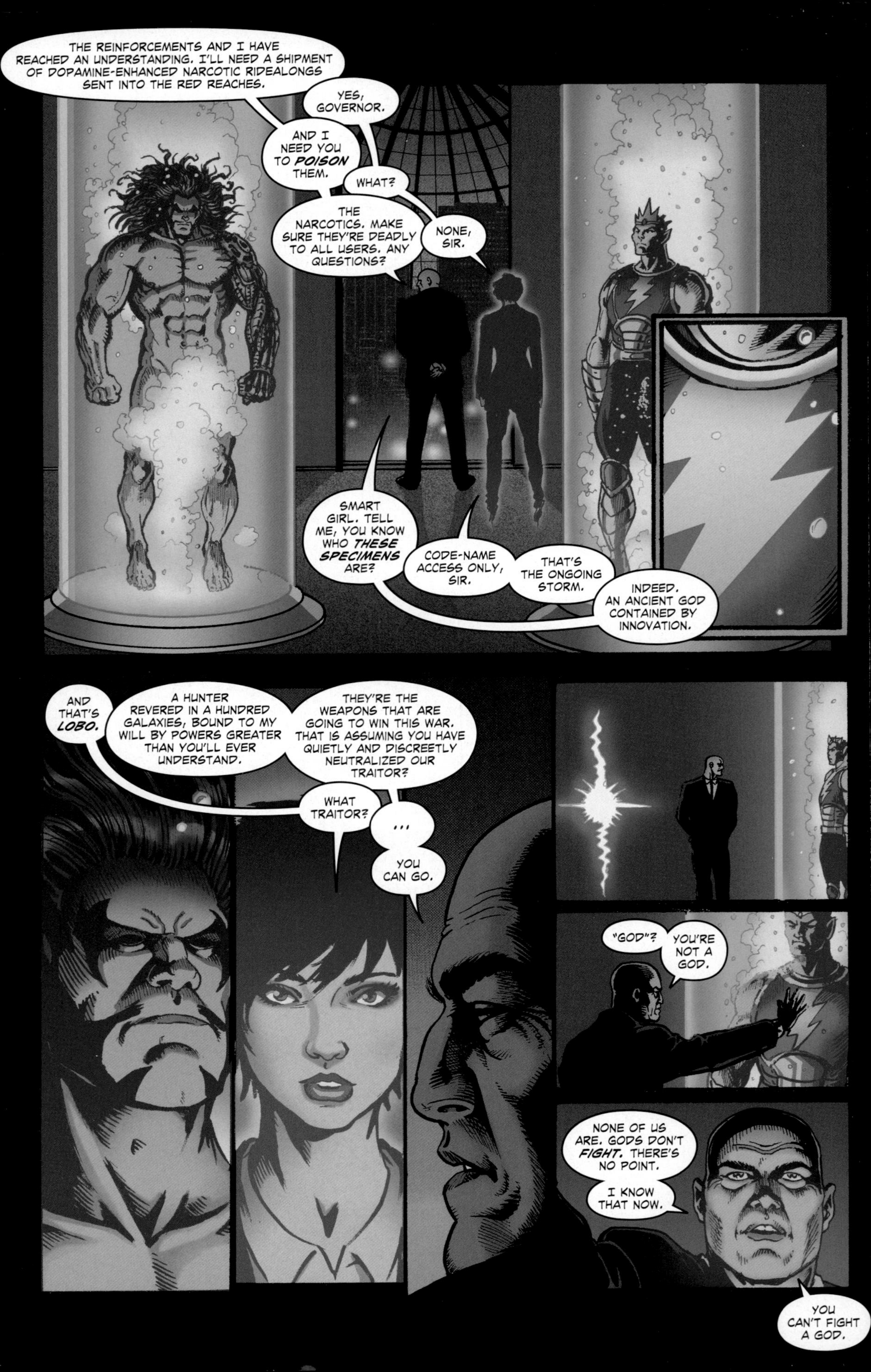
THE REINFORCEMENTS AND I HAVE REACHED AN UNDERSTANDING. I'LL NEED A SHIPMENT OF DOPAMINE-ENHANCED NARCOTIC RIDEALONGS SENT INTO THE RED REACHES.
YES, GOVERNOR.
AND I NEED YOU TO POISON THEM.
WHAT?
THE NARCOTICS. MAKE SURE THEY'RE DEADLY TO ALL USERS. ANY QUESTIONS?
NONE, SIR.
SMART GIRL. TELL ME, YOU KNOW WHO THESE SPECIMENS ARE?
CODE-NAME ACCESS ONLY, SIR.
THAT'S THE ONGOING STORM.
INDEED. AN ANCIENT GOD CONTAINED BY INNOVATION.
AND THAT'S LOBO.
A HUNTER REVERED IN A HUNDRED GALAXIES, BOUND TO MY WILL BY POWERS GREATER THAN YOU'LL EVER UNDERSTAND.
THEY'RE THE WEAPONS THAT ARE GOING TO WIN THIS WAR. THAT IS ASSUMING YOU HAVE QUIETLY AND DISCREETLY NEUTRALIZED OUR TRAITOR?
WHAT TRAITOR?
...
YOU CAN GO.
"GOD"?
YOU'RE NOT A GOD.
NONE OF US ARE. GODS DON'T FIGHT. THERE'S NO POINT.
I KNOW THAT NOW.
YOU CAN'T FIGHT A GOD.

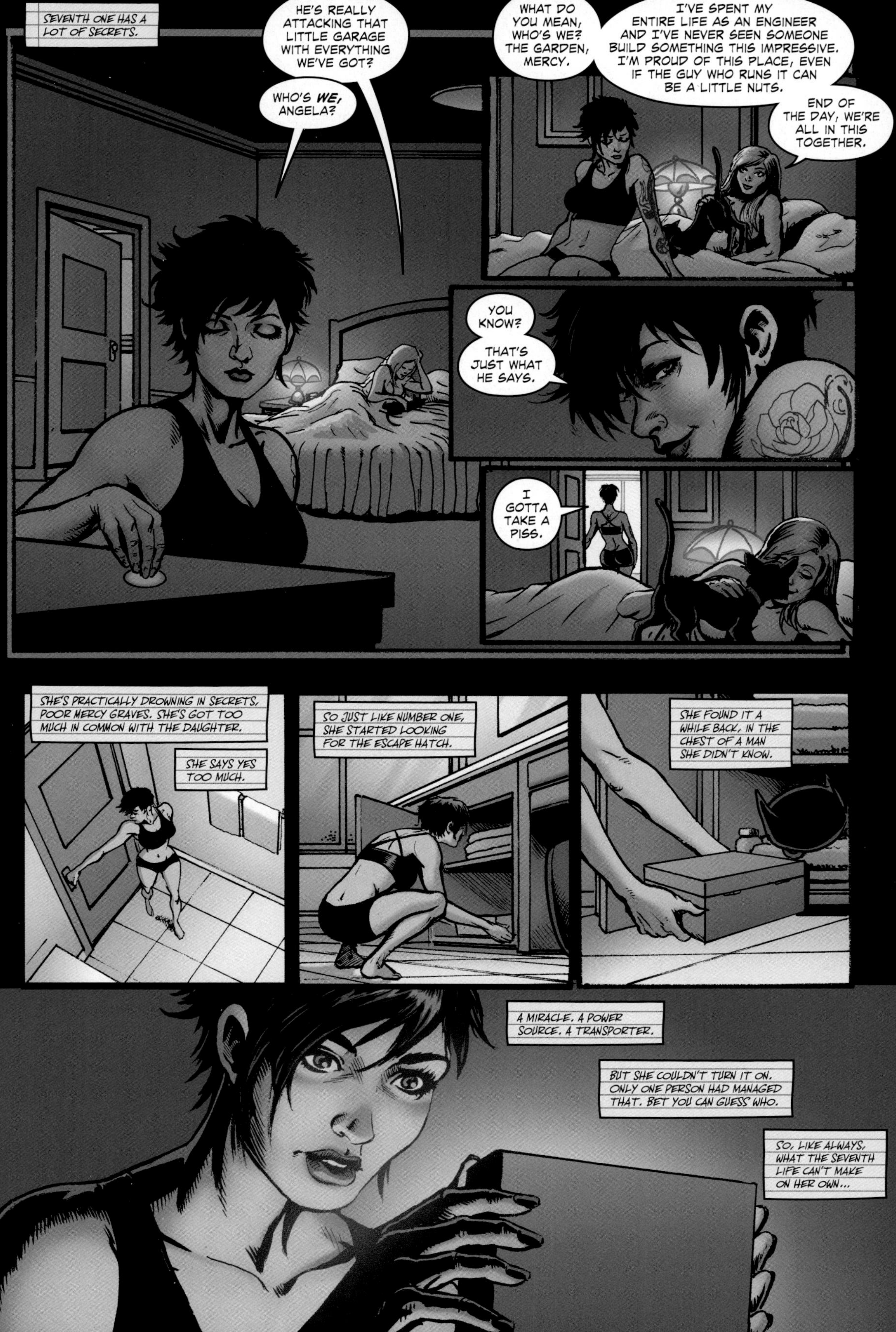
SEVENTH ONE HAS A LOT OF SECRETS.
HE'S REALLY ATTACKING THAT LITTLE GARAGE WITH EVERYTHING WE'VE GOT?
WHO'S WE, ANGELA?
WHAT DO YOU MEAN, WHO'S WE? THE GARDEN, MERCY.
I'VE SPENT MY ENTIRE LIFE AS AN ENGINEER AND I'VE NEVER SEEN SOMEONE BUILD SOMETHING THIS IMPRESSIVE. I'M PROUD OF THIS PLACE, EVEN IF THE GUY WHO RUNS IT CAN BE A LITTLE NUTS.
END OF THE DAY, WE'RE ALL IN THIS TOGETHER.
YOU KNOW?
THAT'S JUST WHAT HE SAYS.
I GOTTA TAKE A PISS.
SHE'S PRACTICALLY DROWNING IN SECRETS, POOR MERCY GRAVES. SHE'S GOT TOO MUCH IN COMMON WITH THE DAUGHTER.
SHE SAYS YES TOO MUCH.
SO JUST LIKE NUMBER ONE, SHE STARTED LOOKING FOR THE ESCAPE HATCH.
SHE FOUND IT A WHILE BACK, IN THE CHEST OF A MAN SHE DIDN'T KNOW.
A MIRACLE. A POWER SOURCE. A TRANSPORTER.
BUT SHE COULDN'T TURN IT ON. ONLY ONE PERSON HAD MANAGED THAT. BET YOU CAN GUESS WHO.
SO, LIKE ALWAYS, WHAT THE SEVENTH LIFE CAN'T MAKE ON HER OWN...

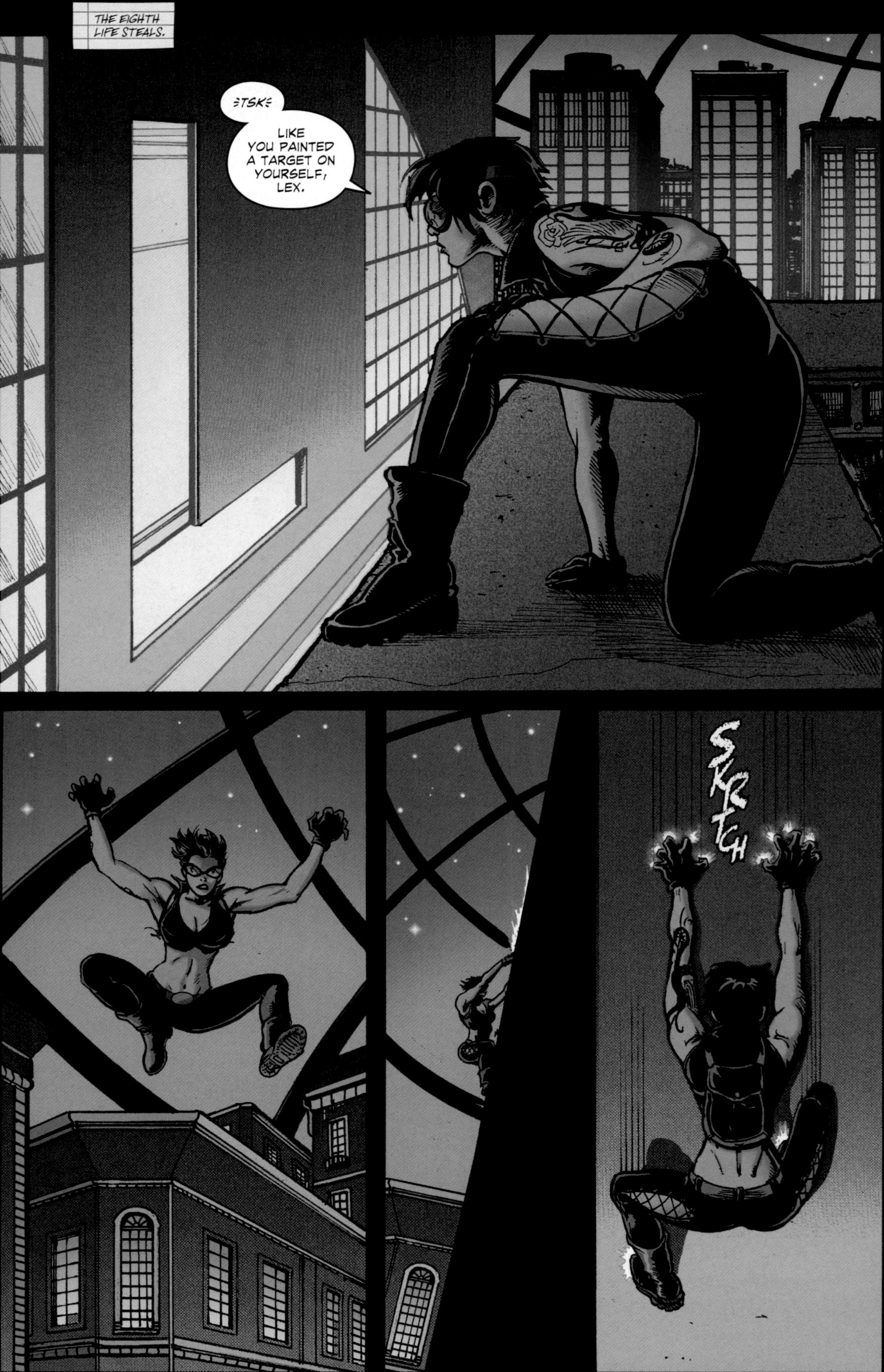
THE EIGHTH LIFE STEALS.
TSK
LIKE YOU PAINTED A TARGET ON YOURSELF, LEX.
SKRTCH

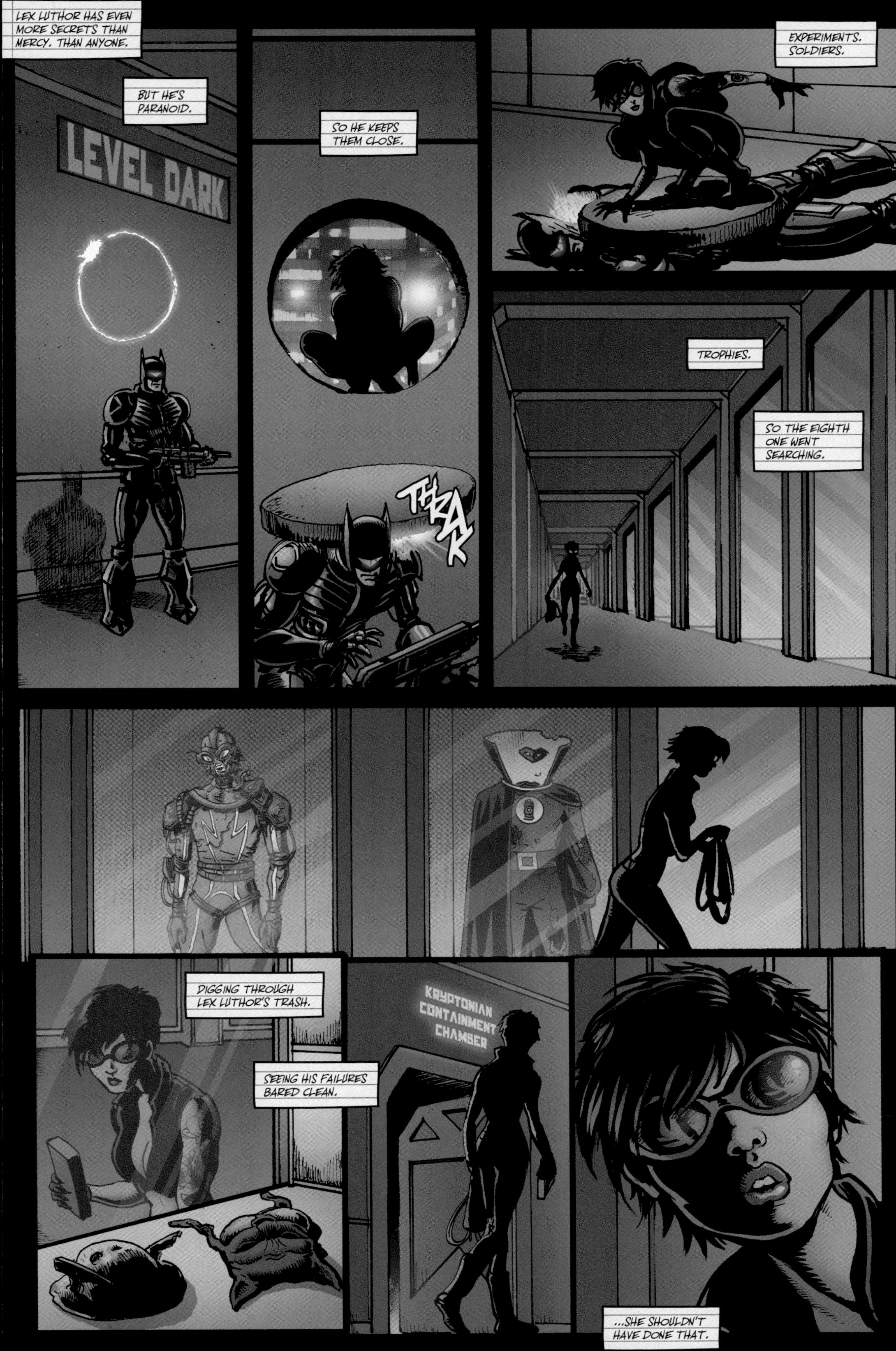
LEX LUTHOR HAS EVEN MORE SECRETS THAN MERCY. THAN ANYONE.
BUT HE'S PARANOID.
LEVEL DARK
SO HE KEEPS THEM CLOSE.
THRAK
EXPERIMENTS. SOLDIERS.
TROPHIES.
SO THE EIGHTH ONE WENT SEARCHING.
DIGGING THROUGH LEX LUTHOR'S TRASH.
SEEING HIS FAILURES BARED CLEAN.
KRYPTONIAN CONTAINMENT CHAMBER
...SHE SHOULDN'T HAVE DONE THAT.

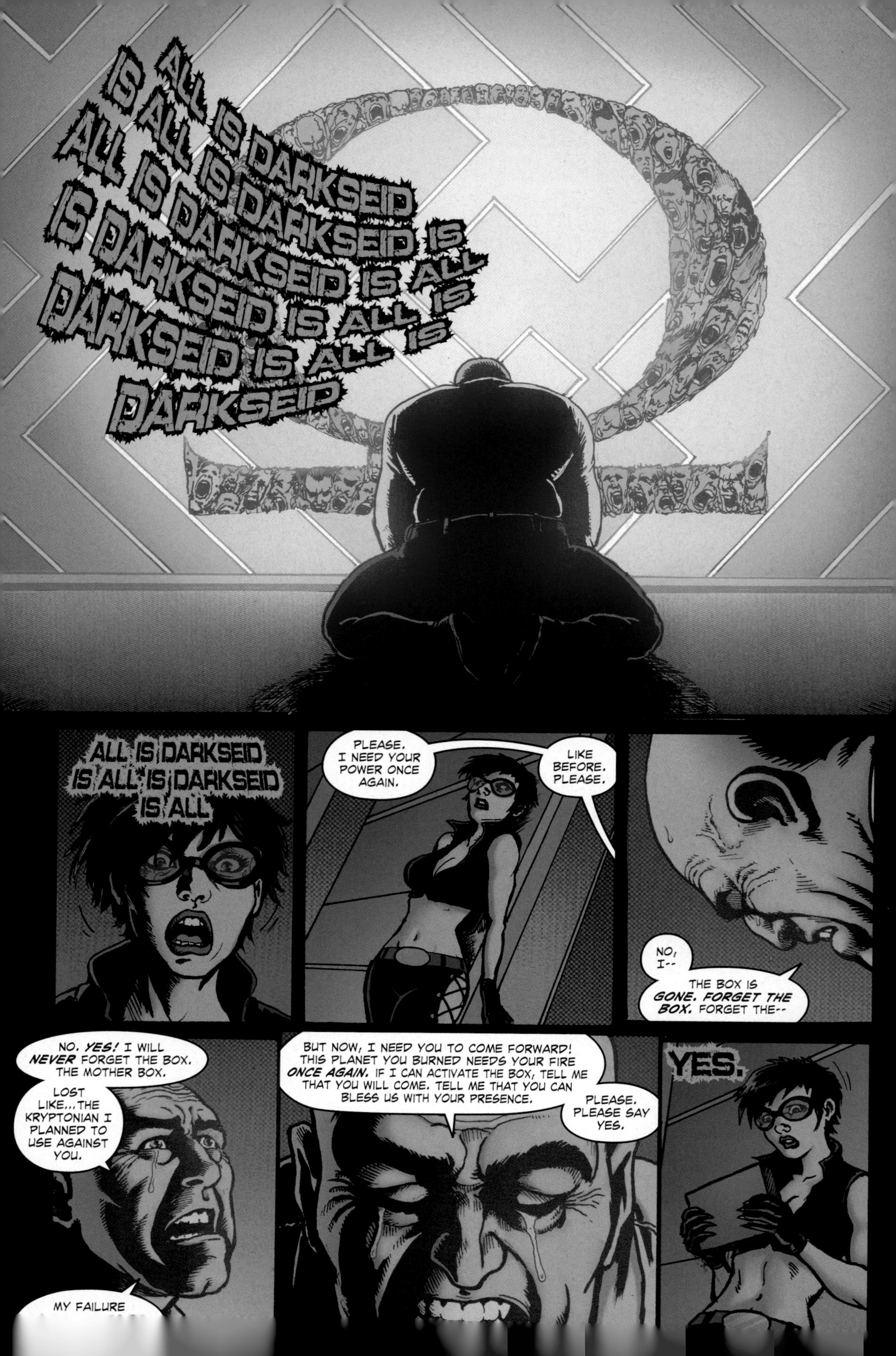

ALL IS DARKSEID IS ALL IS DARKSEID IS ALL IS DARKSEID IS ALL IS DARKSEID IS ALL IS DARKSEID IS ALL IS DARKSEID
ALL IS DARKSEID IS ALL IS DARKSEID IS ALL
PLEASE. I NEED YOUR POWER ONCE AGAIN.
LIKE BEFORE. PLEASE.
NO, I--
THE BOX IS GONE. FORGET THE BOX. FORGET THE--
NO. YES! I WILL NEVER FORGET THE BOX. THE MOTHER BOX.
LOST LIKE...THE KRYPTONIAN I PLANNED TO USE AGAINST YOU.
MY FAILURE
BUT NOW, I NEED YOU TO COME FORWARD! THIS PLANET YOU BURNED NEEDS YOUR FIRE ONCE AGAIN. IF I CAN ACTIVATE THE BOX, TELL ME THAT YOU WILL COME. TELL ME THAT YOU CAN BLESS US WITH YOUR PRESENCE.
PLEASE. PLEASE SAY YES.
YES.

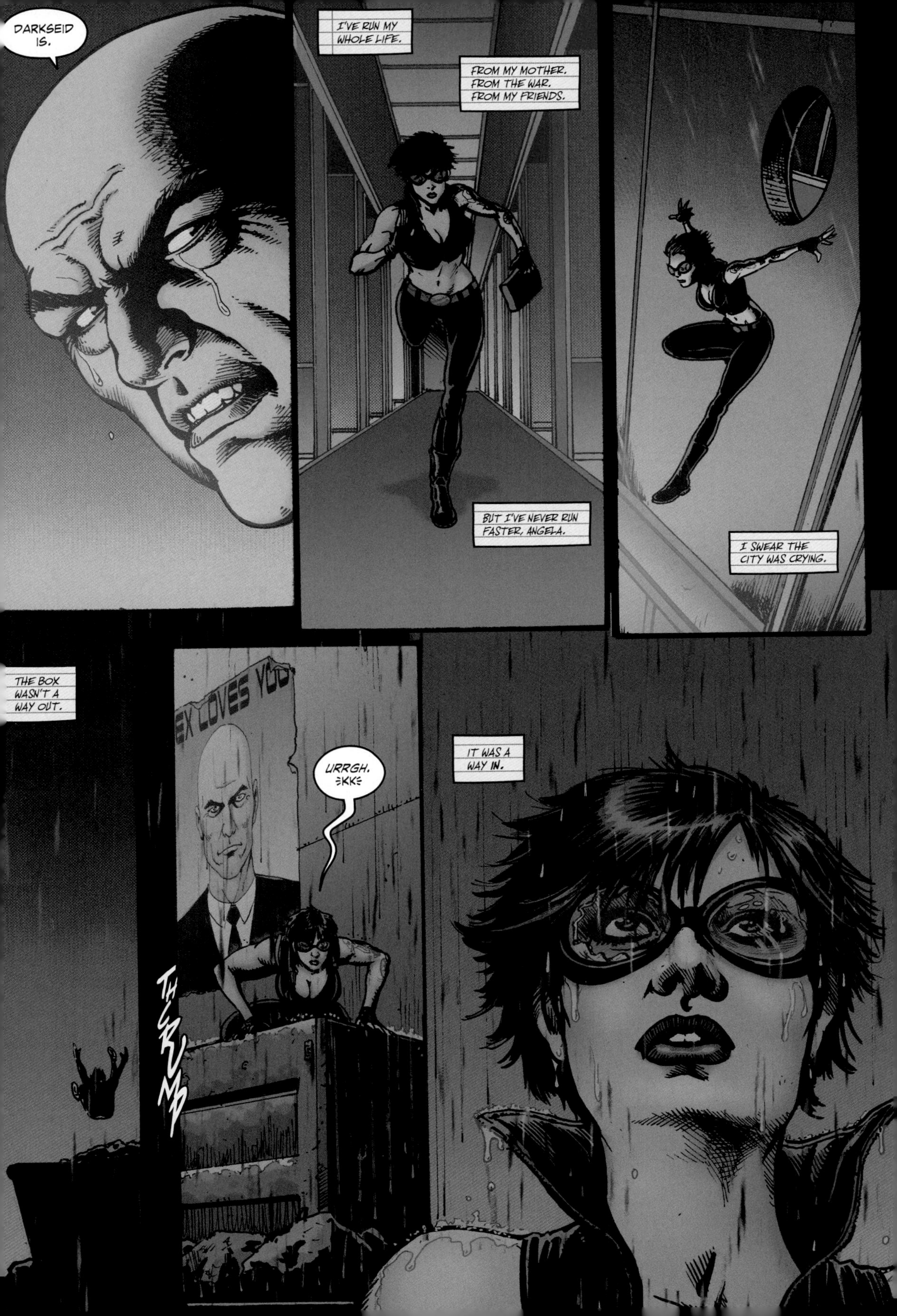
DARKSEID IS.
I'VE RUN MY WHOLE LIFE.
FROM MY MOTHER. FROM THE WAR. FROM MY FRIENDS.
BUT I'VE NEVER RUN FASTER, ANGELA.
I SWEAR THE CITY WAS CRYING.
THE BOX WASN'T A WAY OUT.
EX LOVES YOU
URRGH. KK
THRUMP
IT WAS A WAY IN.

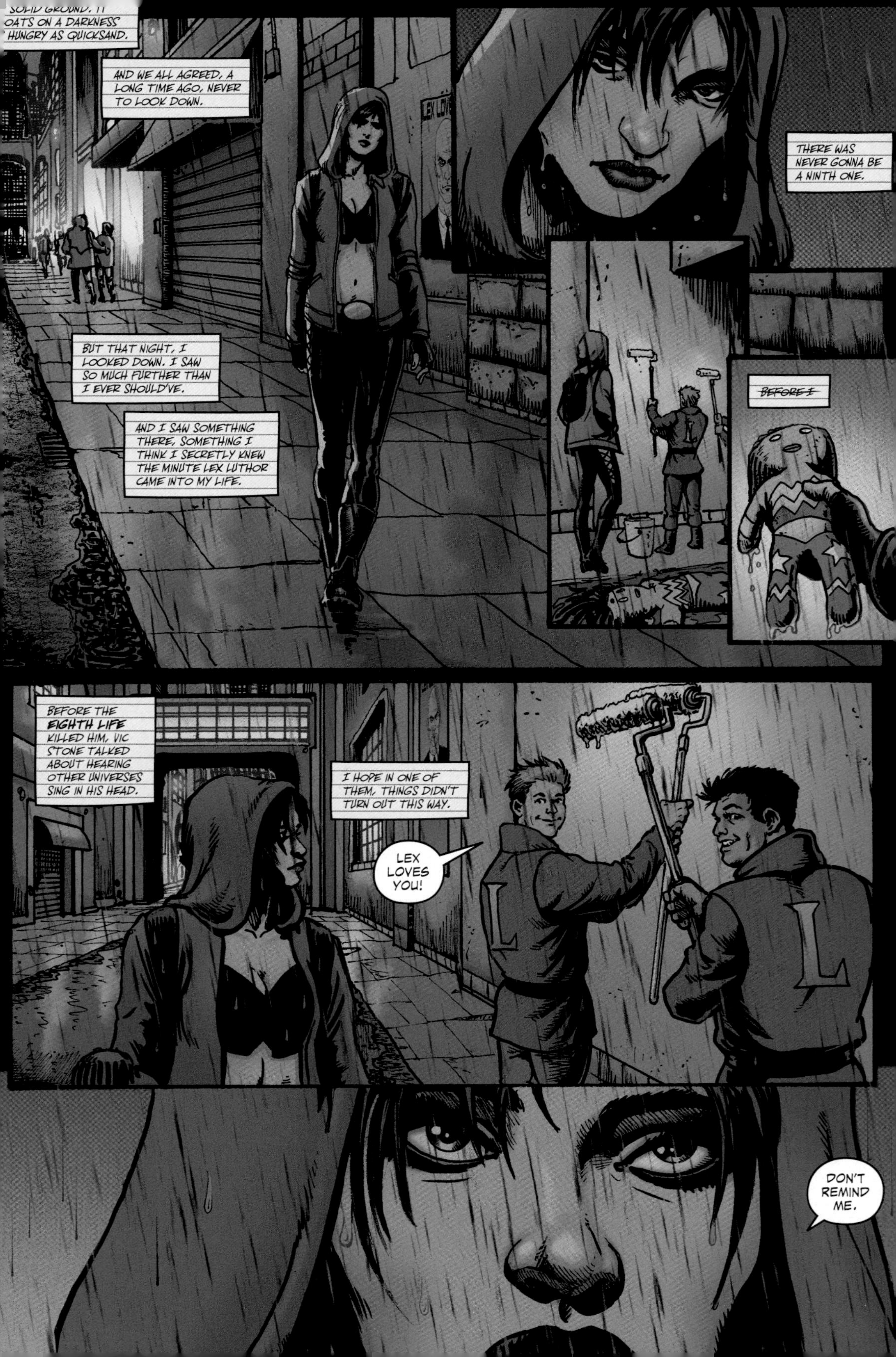
SOLID GROUND. IT
OATS ON A DARKNESS
HUNGRY AS QUICKSAND.
AND WE ALL AGREED, A LONG TIME AGO, NEVER TO LOOK DOWN.
BUT THAT NIGHT, I LOOKED DOWN. I SAW SO MUCH FURTHER THAN I EVER SHOULD'VE.
AND I SAW SOMETHING THERE, SOMETHING I THINK I SECRETLY KNEW THE MINUTE LEX LUTHOR CAME INTO MY LIFE.
THERE WAS NEVER GONNA BE A NINTH ONE.
BEFORE I
BEFORE THE **EIGHTH LIFE** KILLED HIM, VIC STONE TALKED ABOUT HEARING OTHER UNIVERSES SING IN HIS HEAD.
I HOPE IN ONE OF THEM, THINGS DIDN'T TURN OUT THIS WAY.
LEX LOVES YOU!
DON'T REMIND ME.

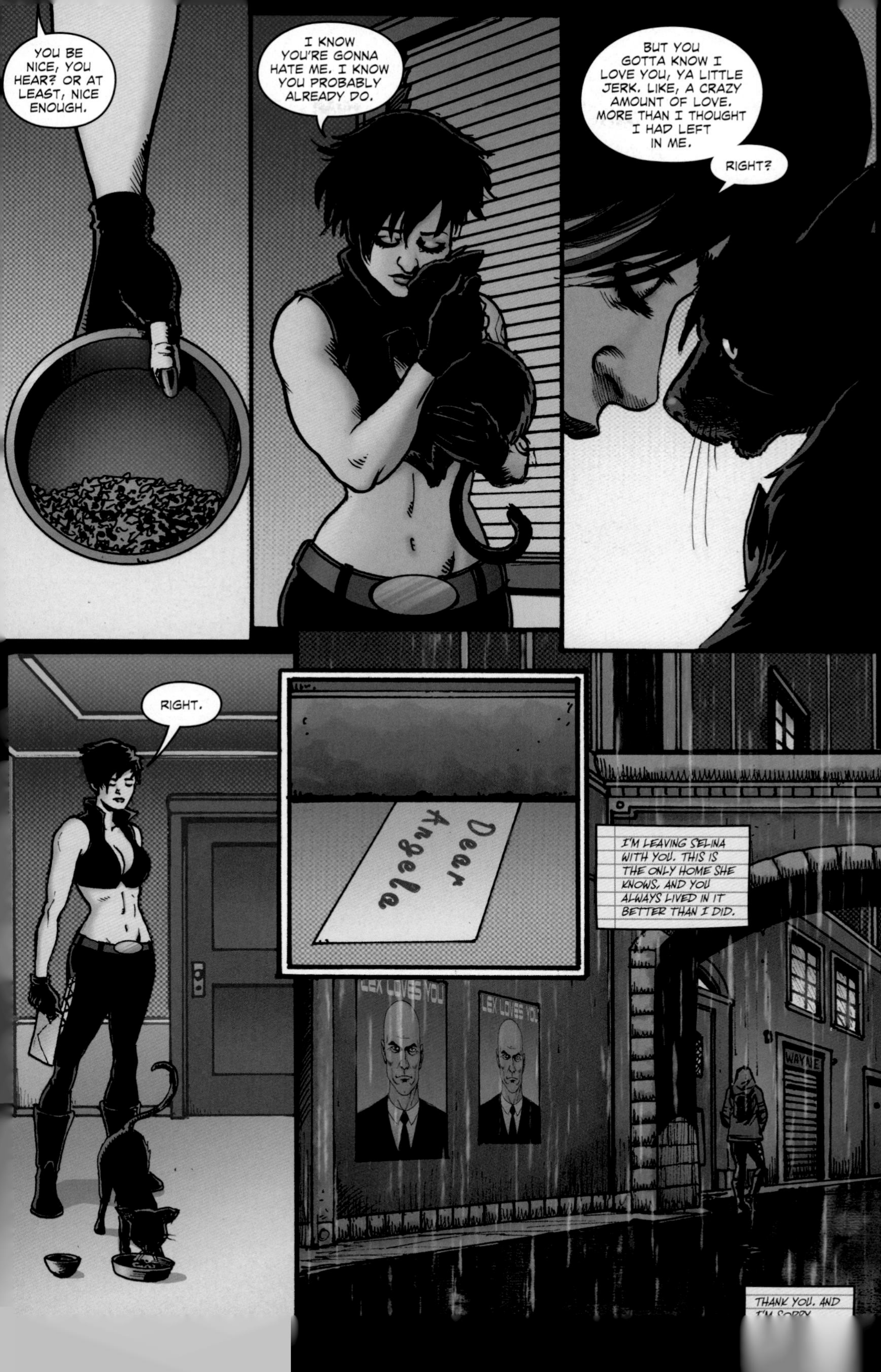
YOU BE NICE, YOU HEAR? OR AT LEAST, NICE ENOUGH.
I KNOW YOU'RE GONNA HATE ME. I KNOW YOU PROBABLY ALREADY DO.
BUT YOU GOTTA KNOW I LOVE YOU, YA LITTLE JERK. LIKE, A CRAZY AMOUNT OF LOVE. MORE THAN I THOUGHT I HAD LEFT IN ME.
RIGHT?
RIGHT.
Dear Angela
I'M LEAVING SELINA WITH YOU. THIS IS THE ONLY HOME SHE KNOWS, AND YOU ALWAYS LIVED IN IT BETTER THAN I DID.
LEX LOVES YOU
LEX LOVES YOU
WAYNE
THANK YOU. AND

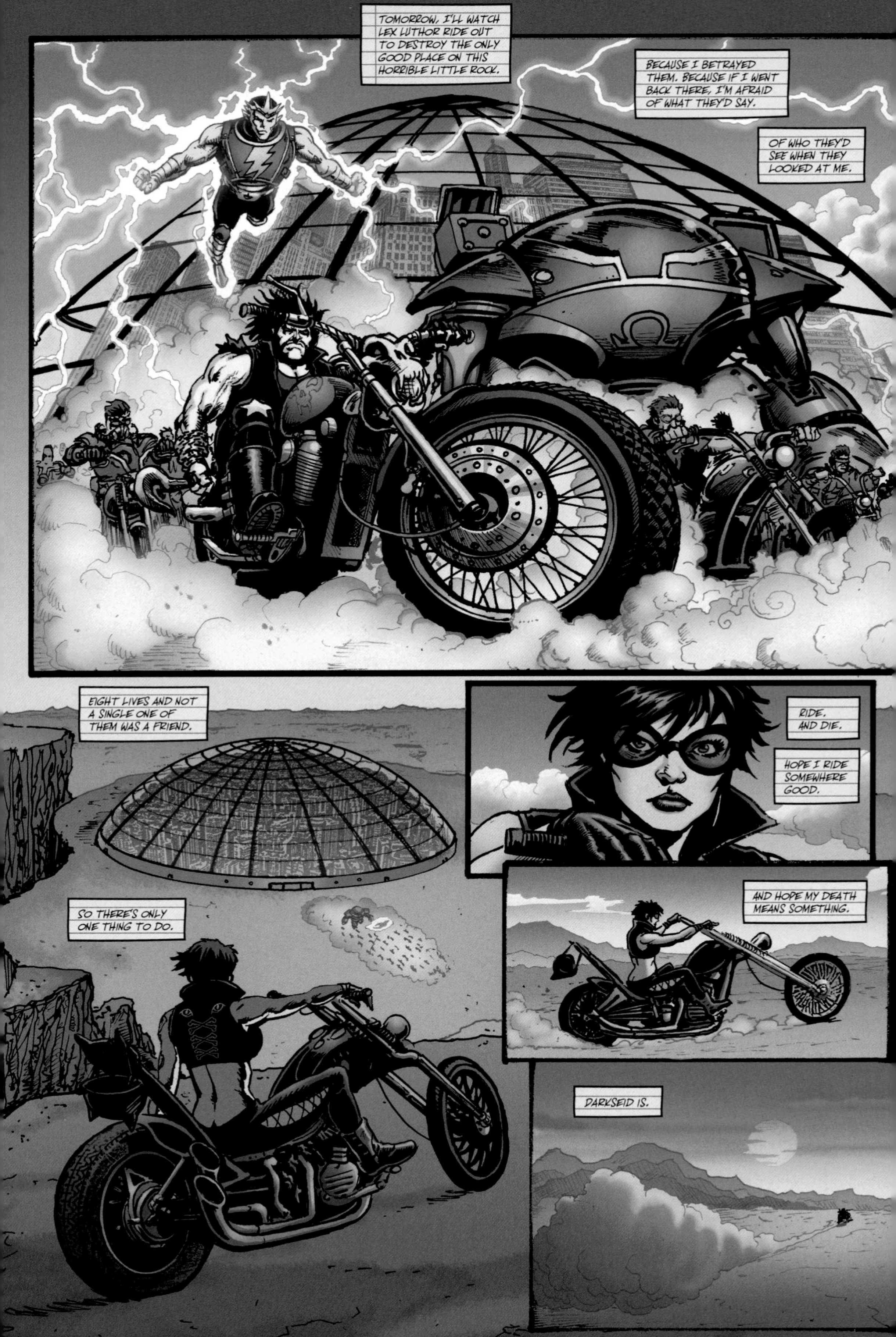
TOMORROW, I'LL WATCH LEX LUTHOR RIDE OUT TO DESTROY THE ONLY GOOD PLACE ON THIS HORRIBLE LITTLE ROCK.
BECAUSE I BETRAYED THEM. BECAUSE IF I WENT BACK THERE, I'M AFRAID OF WHAT THEY'D SAY.
OF WHO THEY'D SEE WHEN THEY LOOKED AT ME.
EIGHT LIVES AND NOT A SINGLE ONE OF THEM WAS A FRIEND.
SO THERE'S ONLY ONE THING TO DO.
RIDE. AND DIE.
HOPE I RIDE SOMEWHERE GOOD.
AND HOPE MY DEATH MEANS SOMETHING.
DARKSEID IS.

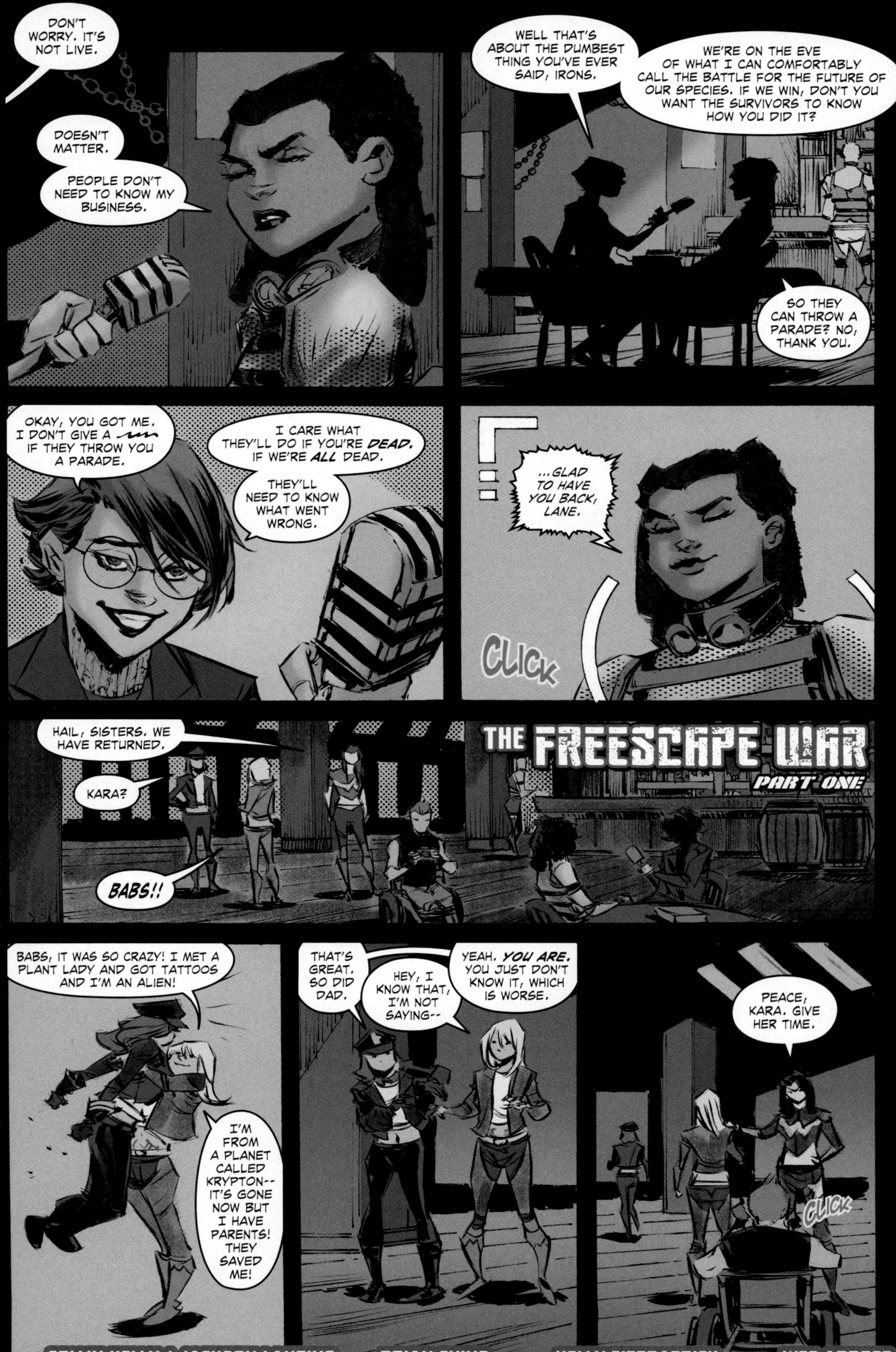
DON'T WORRY. IT'S NOT LIVE.
DOESN'T MATTER.
PEOPLE DON'T NEED TO KNOW MY BUSINESS.
WELL THAT'S ABOUT THE DUMBEST THING YOU'VE EVER SAID, IRONS.
WE'RE ON THE EVE OF WHAT I CAN COMFORTABLY CALL THE BATTLE FOR THE FUTURE OF OUR SPECIES. IF WE WIN, DON'T YOU WANT THE SURVIVORS TO KNOW HOW YOU DID IT?
SO THEY CAN THROW A PARADE? NO, THANK YOU.
OKAY, YOU GOT ME. I DON'T GIVE A ~~ IF THEY THROW YOU A PARADE.
I CARE WHAT THEY'LL DO IF YOU'RE DEAD. IF WE'RE ALL DEAD.
THEY'LL NEED TO KNOW WHAT WENT WRONG.
...GLAD TO HAVE YOU BACK, LANE.
CLICK
HAIL, SISTERS. WE HAVE RETURNED.
KARA?
BABS!!
THE FREESCAPE WAR
PART ONE
BABS, IT WAS SO CRAZY! I MET A PLANT LADY AND GOT TATTOOS AND I'M AN ALIEN!
I'M FROM A PLANET CALLED KRYPTON-- IT'S GONE NOW BUT I HAVE PARENTS! THEY SAVED ME!
THAT'S GREAT. SO DID DAD.
HEY, I KNOW THAT, I'M NOT SAYING--
YEAH. YOU ARE. YOU JUST DON'T KNOW IT, WHICH IS WORSE.
PEACE, KARA. GIVE HER TIME.
CLICK

STORY BY COLLIN KELLY & JACKSON LANZING ART BY BRIAN CHING COLORS BY KELLY FITZPATRICK LETTERS BY WES ABBOTT
EDITED BY KRISTY QUINN

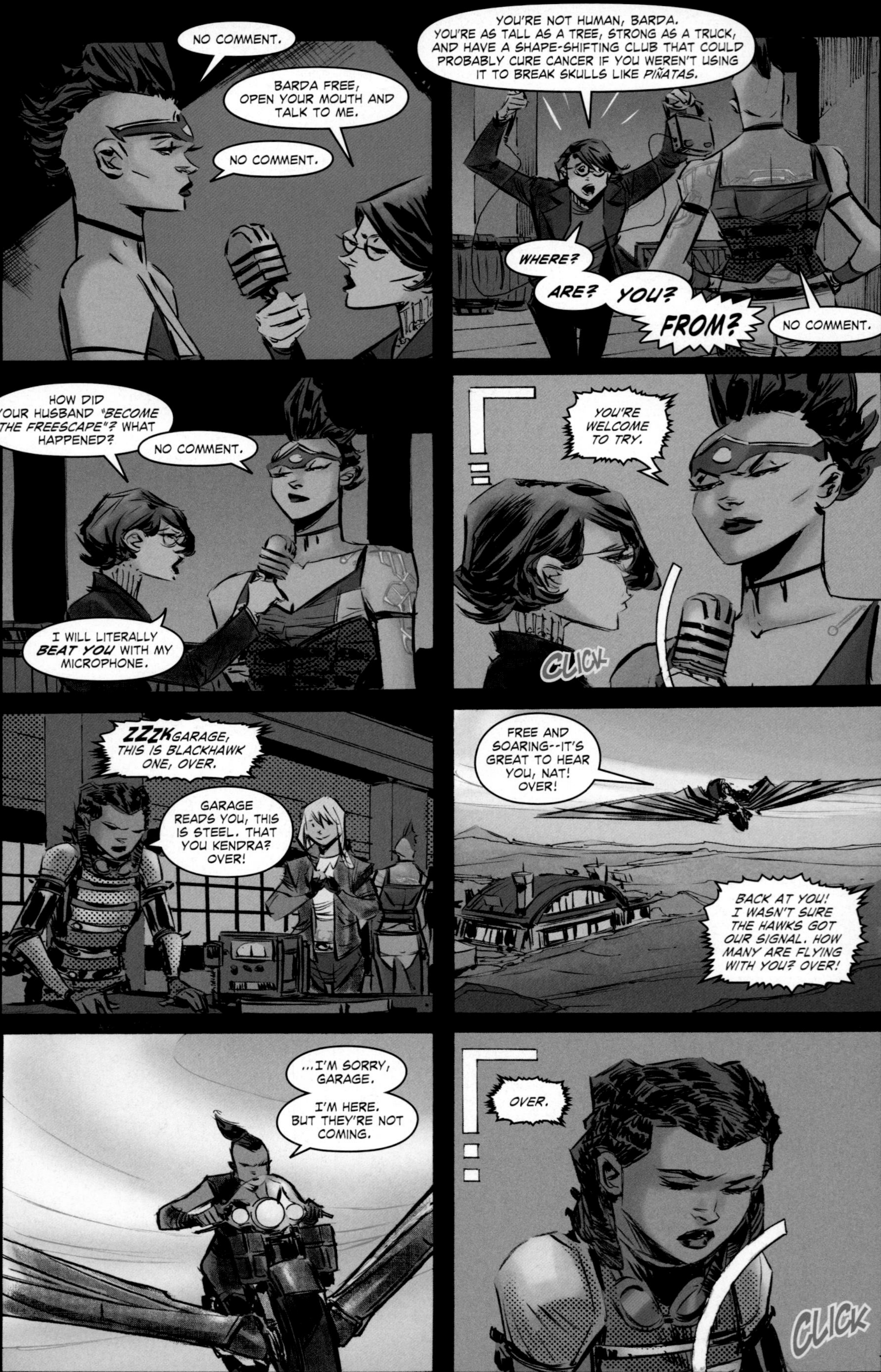
NO COMMENT.
BARDA FREE, OPEN YOUR MOUTH AND TALK TO ME.
NO COMMENT.
YOU'RE NOT HUMAN, BARDA. YOU'RE AS TALL AS A TREE, STRONG AS A TRUCK, AND HAVE A SHAPE-SHIFTING CLUB THAT COULD PROBABLY CURE CANCER IF YOU WEREN'T USING IT TO BREAK SKULLS LIKE PIÑATAS.
WHERE?
ARE?
YOU?
FROM?
NO COMMENT.
HOW DID YOUR HUSBAND "BECOME THE FREESCAPE"? WHAT HAPPENED?
NO COMMENT.
I WILL LITERALLY BEAT YOU WITH MY MICROPHONE.
YOU'RE WELCOME TO TRY.
CLICK
ZZZK GARAGE, THIS IS BLACKHAWK ONE, OVER.
GARAGE READS YOU, THIS IS STEEL. THAT YOU KENDRA? OVER!
FREE AND SOARING--IT'S GREAT TO HEAR YOU, NAT! OVER!
BACK AT YOU! I WASN'T SURE THE HAWKS GOT OUR SIGNAL. HOW MANY ARE FLYING WITH YOU? OVER!
...I'M SORRY, GARAGE.
I'M HERE. BUT THEY'RE NOT COMING.
OVER.
CLICK

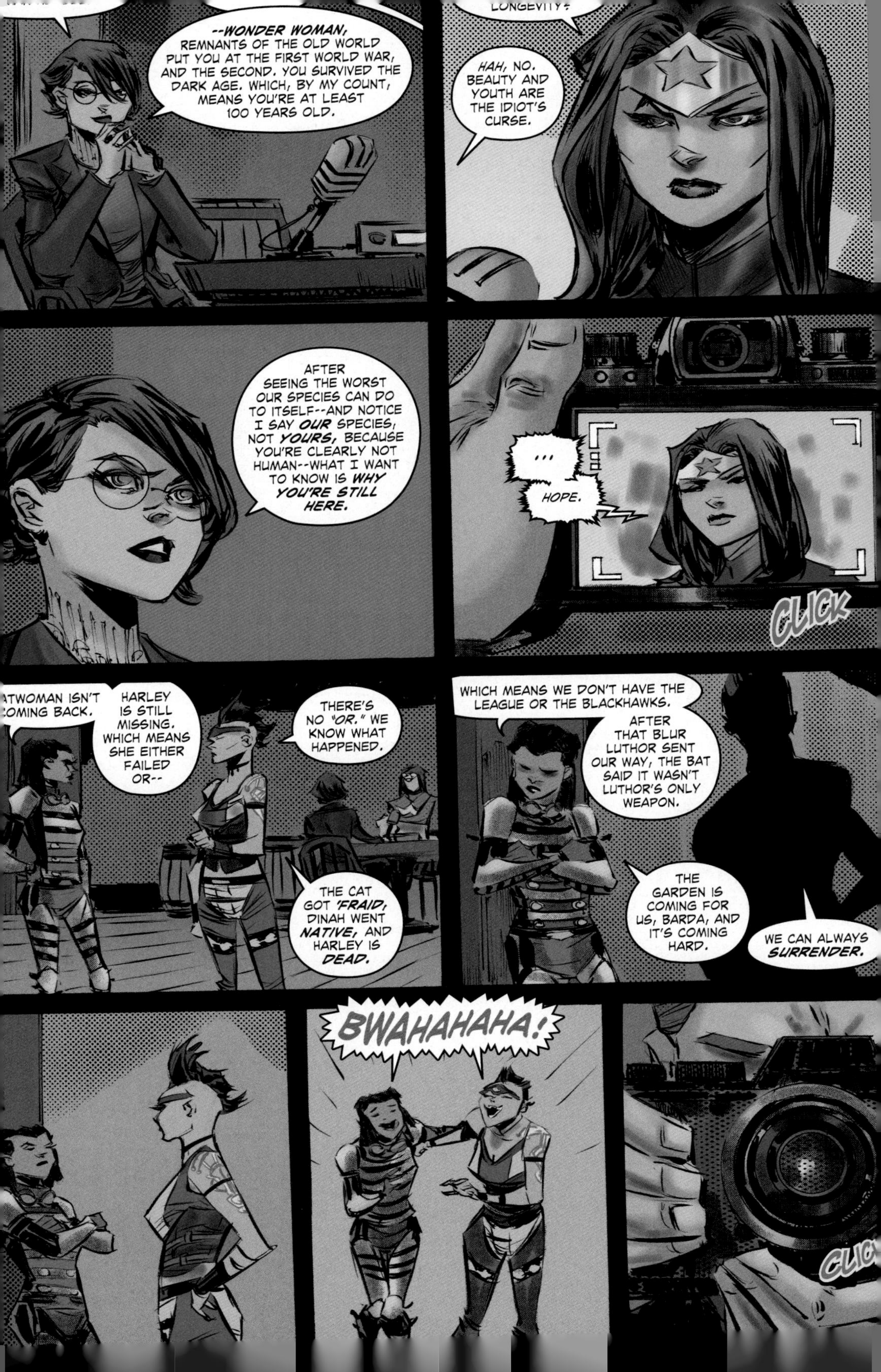

LONGEVITY?
--WONDER WOMAN, REMNANTS OF THE OLD WORLD PUT YOU AT THE FIRST WORLD WAR, AND THE SECOND. YOU SURVIVED THE DARK AGE. WHICH, BY MY COUNT, MEANS YOU'RE AT LEAST 100 YEARS OLD.
HAH, NO. BEAUTY AND YOUTH ARE THE IDIOT'S CURSE.
AFTER SEEING THE WORST OUR SPECIES CAN DO TO ITSELF--AND NOTICE I SAY OUR SPECIES, NOT YOURS, BECAUSE YOU'RE CLEARLY NOT HUMAN--WHAT I WANT TO KNOW IS WHY YOU'RE STILL HERE.
...
HOPE.
CLICK
ATWOMAN ISN'T COMING BACK.
HARLEY IS STILL MISSING. WHICH MEANS SHE EITHER FAILED OR--
THERE'S NO "OR." WE KNOW WHAT HAPPENED.
THE CAT GOT 'FRAID, DINAH WENT NATIVE, AND HARLEY IS DEAD.
WHICH MEANS WE DON'T HAVE THE LEAGUE OR THE BLACKHAWKS.
AFTER THAT BLUR LUTHOR SENT OUR WAY, THE BAT SAID IT WASN'T LUTHOR'S ONLY WEAPON.
THE GARDEN IS COMING FOR US, BARDA, AND IT'S COMING HARD.
WE CAN ALWAYS SURRENDER.
BWAHAHAHA!
CLIC

YOU REALLY THINK THEY'LL THROW A PARADE?

WHO CAN SAY?

I DON'T THINK PEOPLE WILL BE IN THE MOOD. WITH THE RIDEALONGS DEACTIVATED, THE PEOPLE WILL BE...I MEAN, SOME OF THEM HAVEN'T THOUGHT FOR THEMSELVES IN *YEARS. DECADES.*

DO YOU THIN DOCTORS V REMEMBER TO HEAL? ENGINEER HOW TO BUILD?

WHAT WILL YOU DO IF, IN WINNING, YOU DAMN OUR SPECIES TO ITS OWN OUROBOROS OF IGNORANCE AND STARVATION, COLLAPSING UNDER THE WEIGHT OF THAT WHICH WE DO NOT KNOW?

THEN THEY'LL DIE *FREE.*

ALSO, WE *WON'T* LET THAT HAPPEN.

ALSO?! YOU'VE GOT A REAL *NEGATIVE ATTITUDE!*

THIS INTERVIEW IS SO *OVER.*

ЭHRM€

SMART KID.

JIMMY, DON'T YO *DARE* TA A PICTURE

CLIC

YOU PLANNING ON SHOOTING WITH THAT WHEN THE FIGHTING HAPPENS?

I'LL SHOOT WITH WHATEVER YOU'VE GOT FOR ME.

WHAT I LIKE TO HEAR. A FEW YEARS BACK, BANSHEE TOOK A FALL. BOTH LEGS BROKEN. DIDN'T SEE WHY THAT SHOULD SLOW HER DOWN.

YOU'RE CLEARLY GOOD ON YOUR WHEELS.

HOW ABOUT WE GIVE YOU SOME HORSEPOWER?

CLICK.

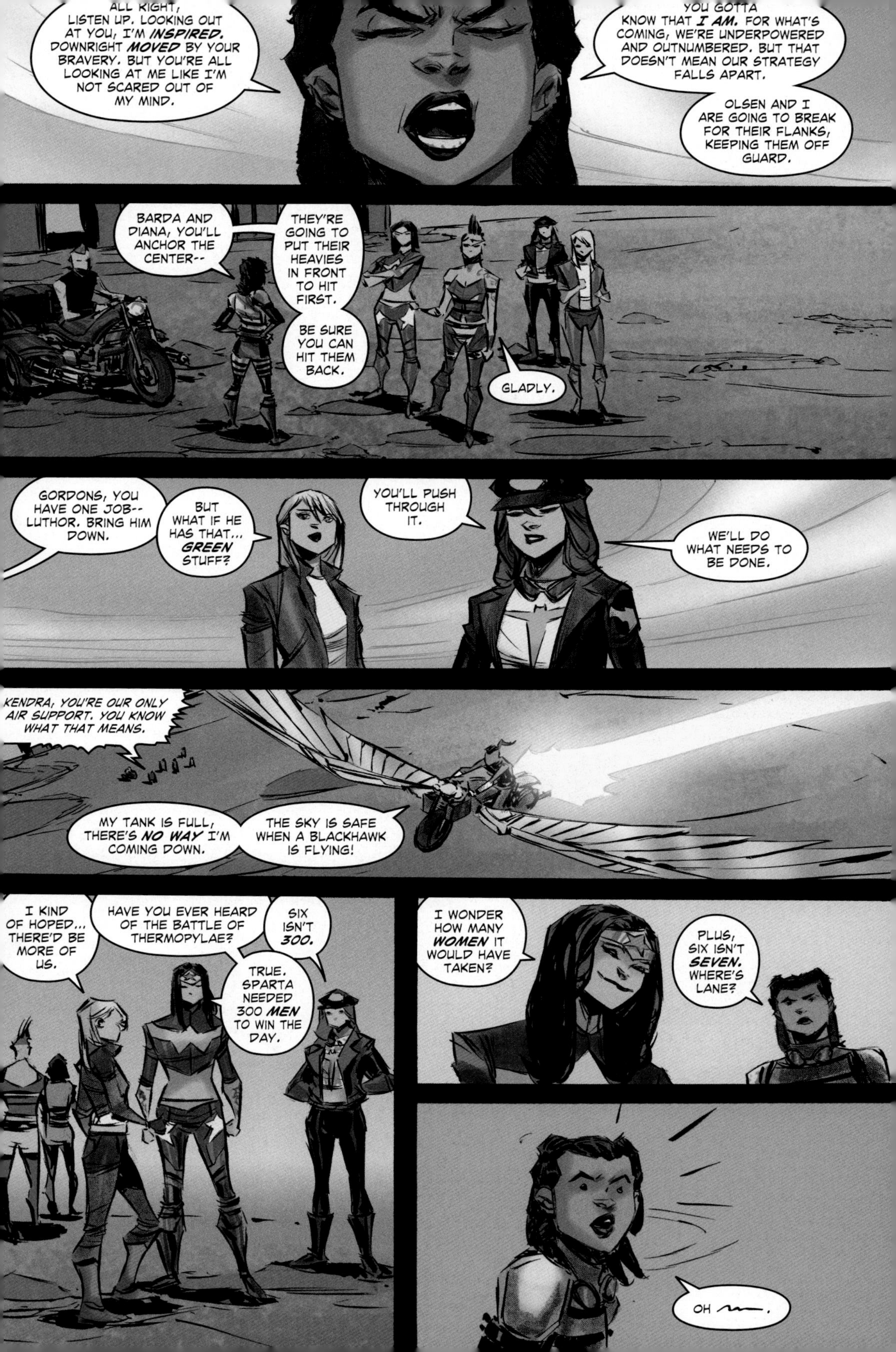

ALL RIGHT, LISTEN UP. LOOKING OUT AT YOU, I'M *INSPIRED.* DOWNRIGHT *MOVED* BY YOUR BRAVERY. BUT YOU'RE ALL LOOKING AT ME LIKE I'M NOT SCARED OUT OF MY MIND.
YOU GOTTA KNOW THAT *I AM.* FOR WHAT'S COMING, WE'RE UNDERPOWERED AND OUTNUMBERED. BUT THAT DOESN'T MEAN OUR STRATEGY FALLS APART.
OLSEN AND I ARE GOING TO BREAK FOR THEIR FLANKS, KEEPING THEM OFF GUARD.
BARDA AND DIANA, YOU'LL ANCHOR THE CENTER--
THEY'RE GOING TO PUT THEIR HEAVIES IN FRONT TO HIT FIRST.
BE SURE YOU CAN HIT THEM BACK.
GLADLY.
GORDONS, YOU HAVE ONE JOB-- LUTHOR. BRING HIM DOWN.
BUT WHAT IF HE HAS THAT... *GREEN* STUFF?
YOU'LL PUSH THROUGH IT.
WE'LL DO WHAT NEEDS TO BE DONE.
KENDRA, YOU'RE OUR ONLY AIR SUPPORT. YOU KNOW WHAT THAT MEANS.
MY TANK IS FULL, THERE'S *NO WAY* I'M COMING DOWN.
THE SKY IS SAFE WHEN A BLACKHAWK IS FLYING!
I KIND OF HOPED... THERE'D BE MORE OF US.
HAVE YOU EVER HEARD OF THE BATTLE OF THERMOPYLAE?
SIX ISN'T *300.*
TRUE. SPARTA NEEDED 300 *MEN* TO WIN THE DAY.
I WONDER HOW MANY *WOMEN* IT WOULD HAVE TAKEN?
PLUS, SIX ISN'T *SEVEN.* WHERE'S LANE?
OH ~~.

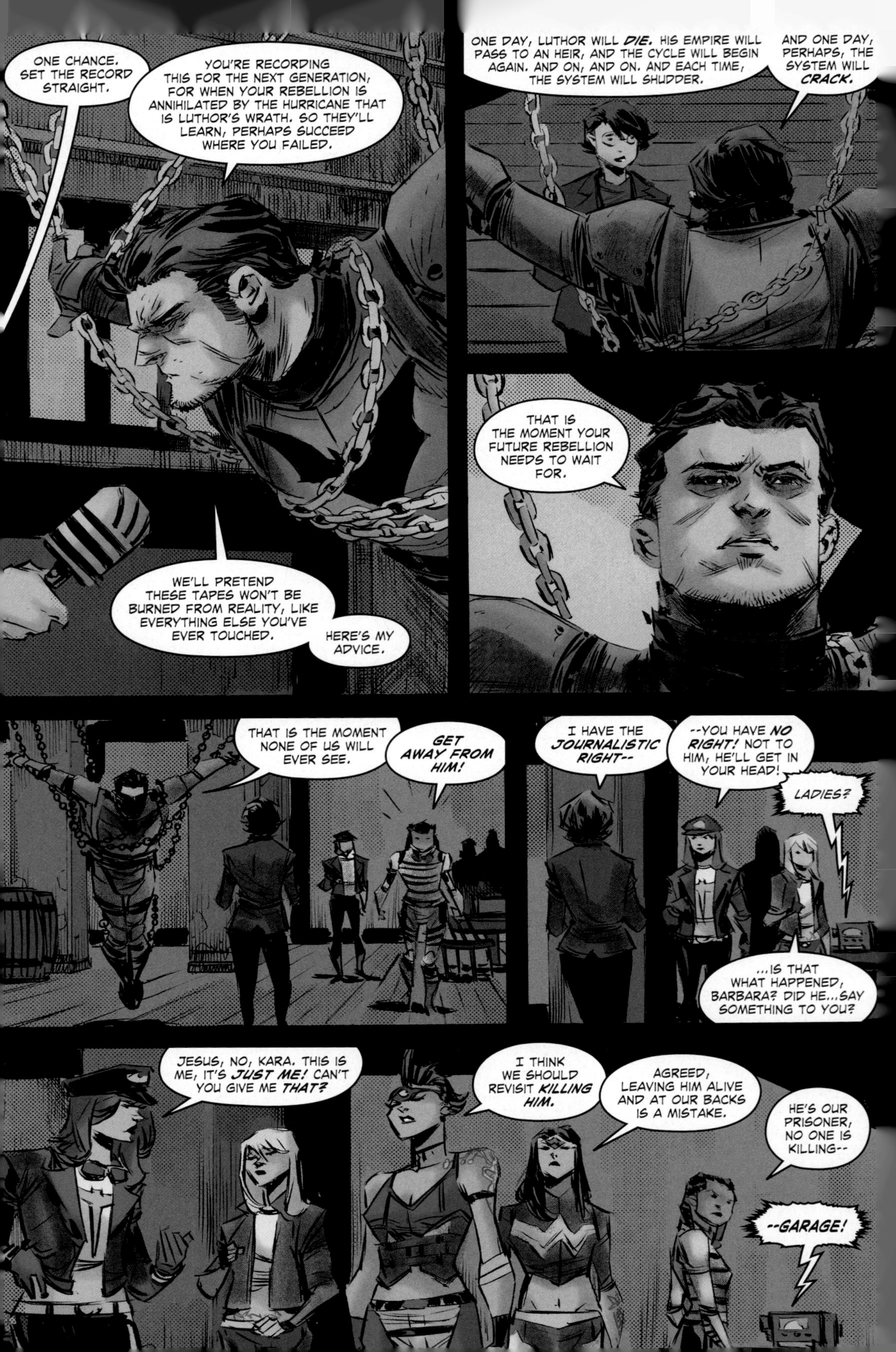
ONE CHANCE. SET THE RECORD STRAIGHT.
YOU'RE RECORDING THIS FOR THE NEXT GENERATION, FOR WHEN YOUR REBELLION IS ANNIHILATED BY THE HURRICANE THAT IS LUTHOR'S WRATH. SO THEY'LL LEARN, PERHAPS SUCCEED WHERE YOU FAILED.
WE'LL PRETEND THESE TAPES WON'T BE BURNED FROM REALITY, LIKE EVERYTHING ELSE YOU'VE EVER TOUCHED.
HERE'S MY ADVICE.
ONE DAY, LUTHOR WILL *DIE.* HIS EMPIRE WILL PASS TO AN HEIR, AND THE CYCLE WILL BEGIN AGAIN. AND ON, AND ON. AND EACH TIME, THE SYSTEM WILL SHUDDER.
AND ONE DAY, PERHAPS, THE SYSTEM WILL *CRACK.*
THAT IS THE MOMENT YOUR FUTURE REBELLION NEEDS TO WAIT FOR.
THAT IS THE MOMENT NONE OF US WILL EVER SEE.
GET AWAY FROM HIM!
I HAVE THE *JOURNALISTIC RIGHT--*
--YOU HAVE *NO RIGHT!* NOT TO HIM, HE'LL GET IN YOUR HEAD!
LADIES?
...IS THAT WHAT HAPPENED, BARBARA? DID HE...SAY SOMETHING TO YOU?
JESUS, NO, KARA. THIS IS ME, IT'S *JUST ME!* CAN'T YOU GIVE ME *THAT?*
I THINK WE SHOULD REVISIT *KILLING HIM.*
AGREED, LEAVING HIM ALIVE AND AT OUR BACKS IS A MISTAKE.
HE'S OUR PRISONER, NO ONE IS KILLING--
--GARAGE!

WE'VE GOT INCOMING!

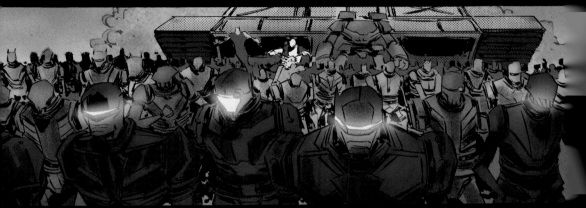

IS IT TIME, LUTHOR?

OH, YES.

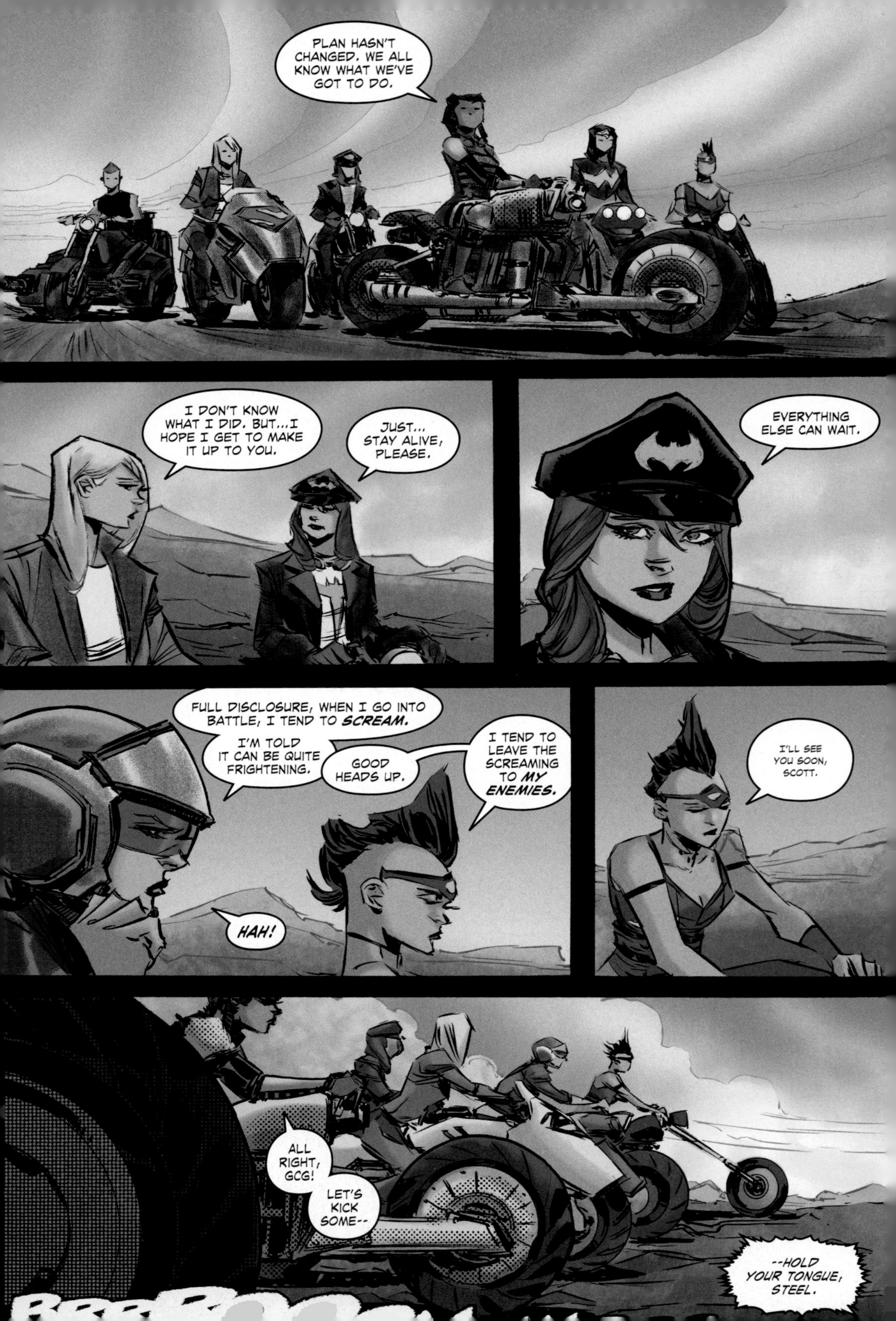
PLAN HASN'T CHANGED. WE ALL KNOW WHAT WE'VE GOT TO DO.
I DON'T KNOW WHAT I DID. BUT...I HOPE I GET TO MAKE IT UP TO YOU.
JUST... STAY ALIVE, PLEASE.
EVERYTHING ELSE CAN WAIT.
FULL DISCLOSURE, WHEN I GO INTO BATTLE, I TEND TO *SCREAM.*
I'M TOLD IT CAN BE QUITE FRIGHTENING.
GOOD HEADS UP.
I TEND TO LEAVE THE SCREAMING TO *MY ENEMIES.*
HAH!
I'LL SEE YOU SOON, SCOTT.
ALL RIGHT, GCG!
LET'S KICK SOME--
--HOLD YOUR TONGUE, STEEL.

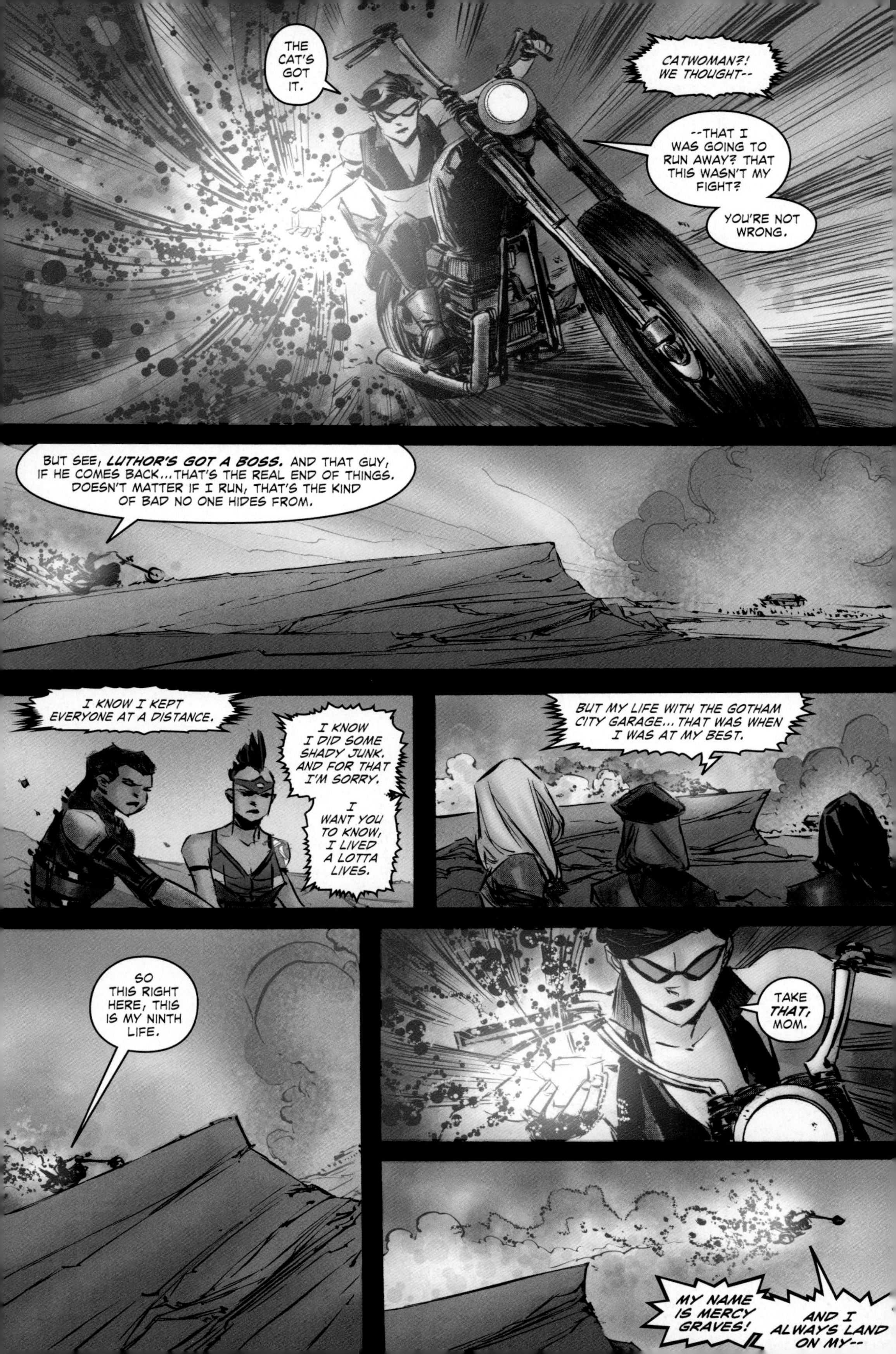
THE CAT'S GOT IT.
CATWOMAN?! WE THOUGHT--
--THAT I WAS GOING TO RUN AWAY? THAT THIS WASN'T MY FIGHT?
YOU'RE NOT WRONG.
BUT SEE, LUTHOR'S GOT A BOSS. AND THAT GUY, IF HE COMES BACK...THAT'S THE REAL END OF THINGS. DOESN'T MATTER IF I RUN, THAT'S THE KIND OF BAD NO ONE HIDES FROM.
I KNOW I KEPT EVERYONE AT A DISTANCE.
I KNOW I DID SOME SHADY JUNK. AND FOR THAT I'M SORRY.
I WANT YOU TO KNOW, I LIVED A LOTTA LIVES.
BUT MY LIFE WITH THE GOTHAM CITY GARAGE... THAT WAS WHEN I WAS AT MY BEST.
SO THIS RIGHT HERE, THIS IS MY NINTH LIFE.
TAKE THAT, MOM.
MY NAME IS MERCY GRAVES!
AND I ALWAYS LAND ON MY--

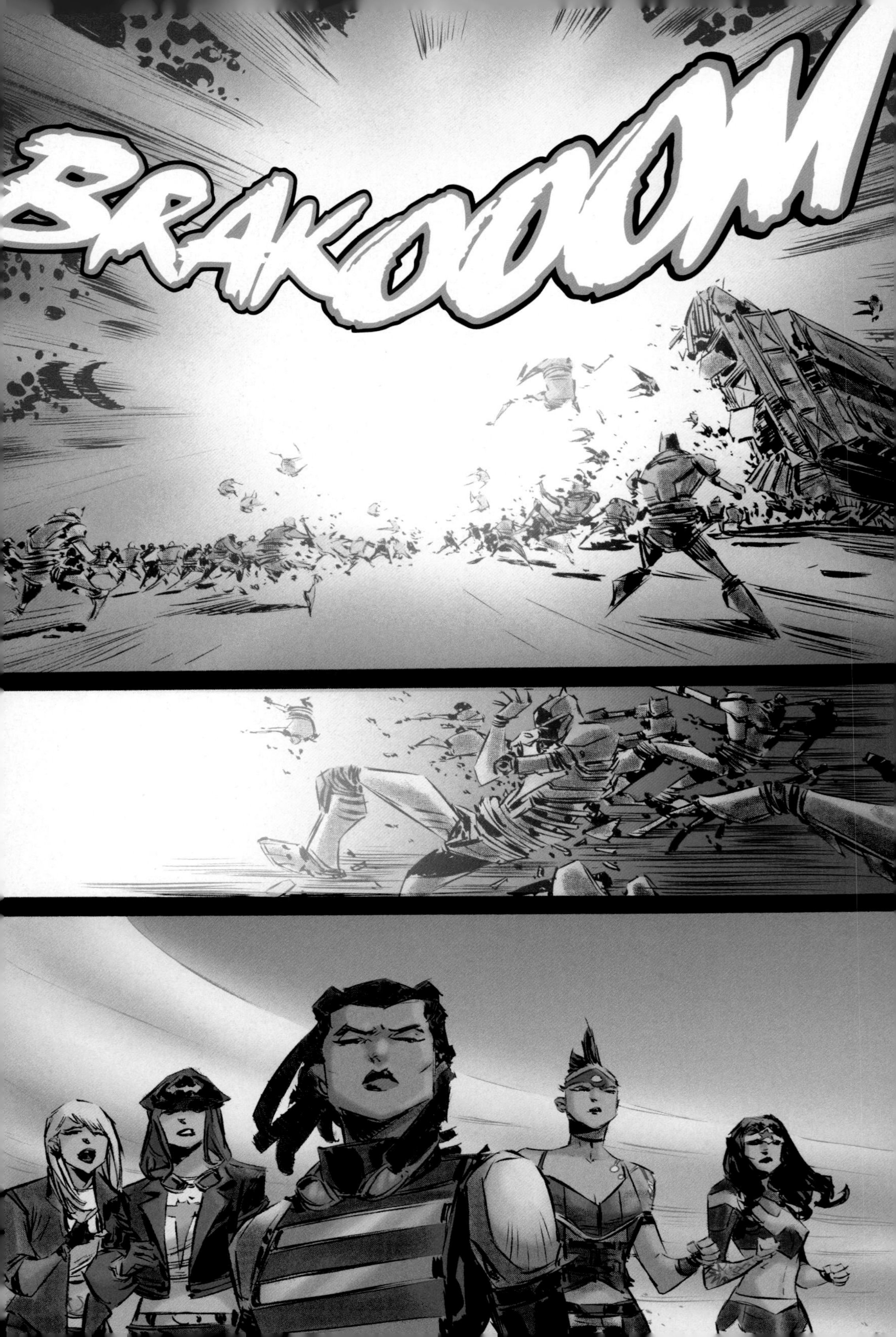
BRAKOOOM

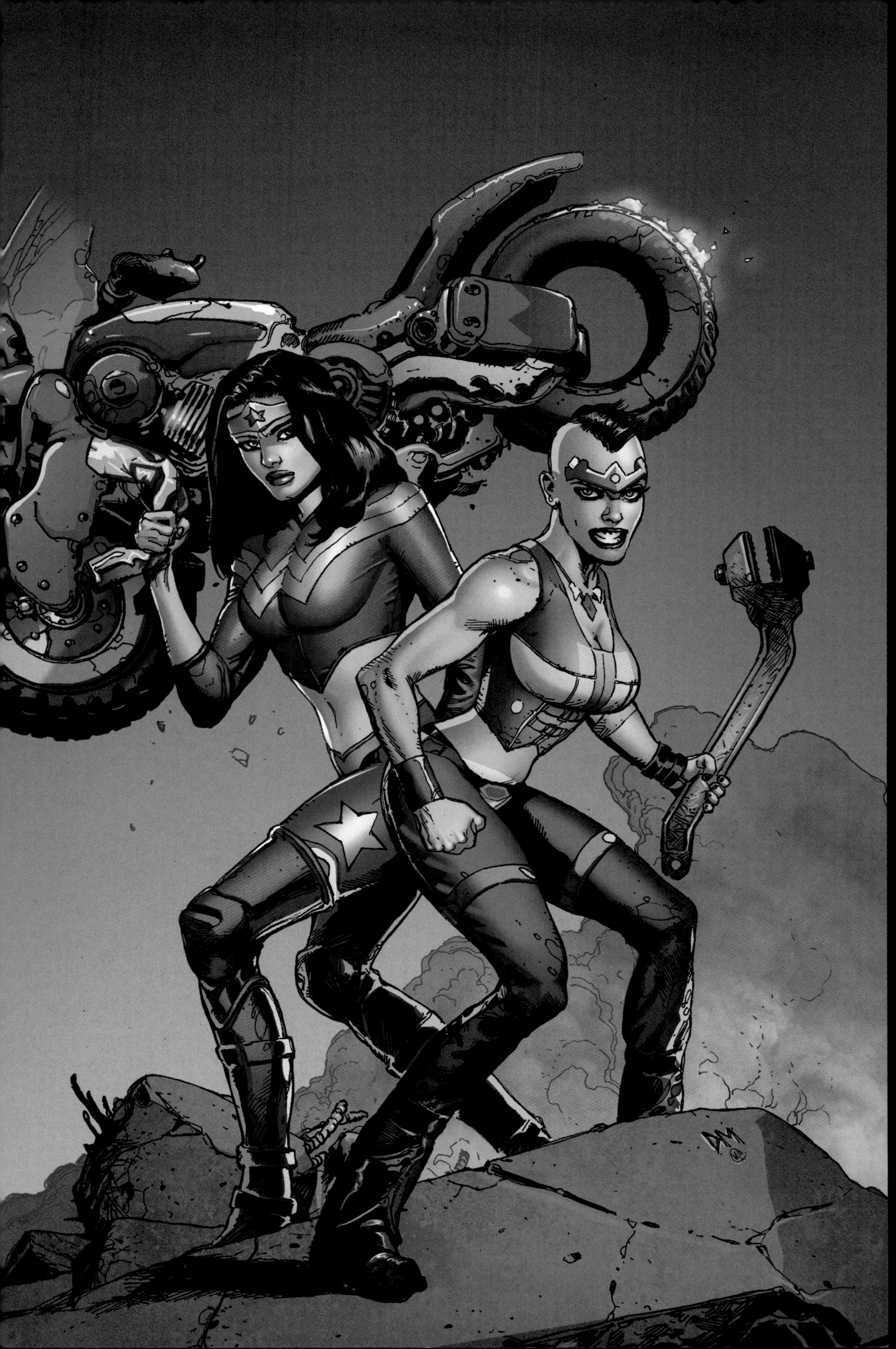

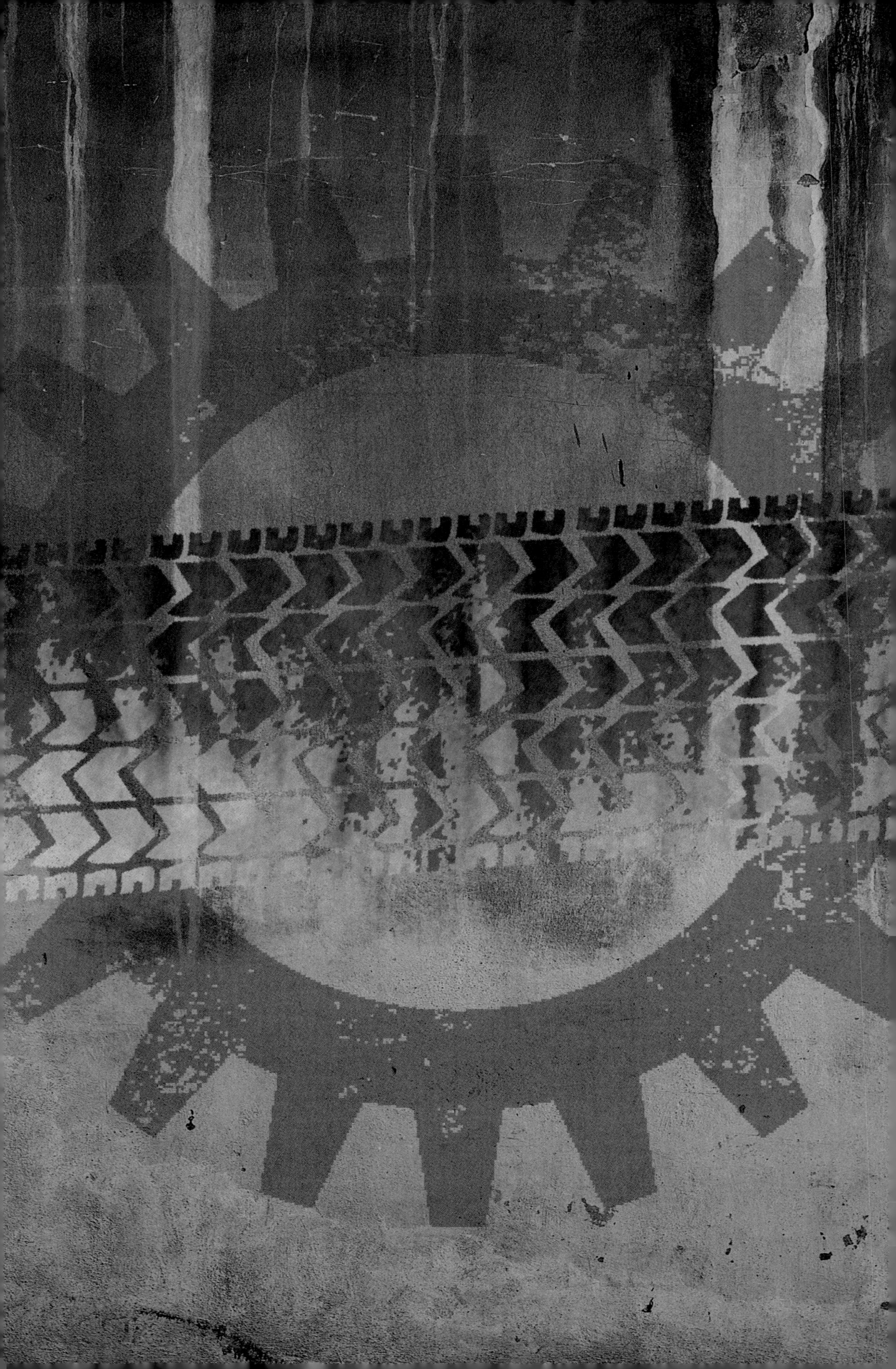

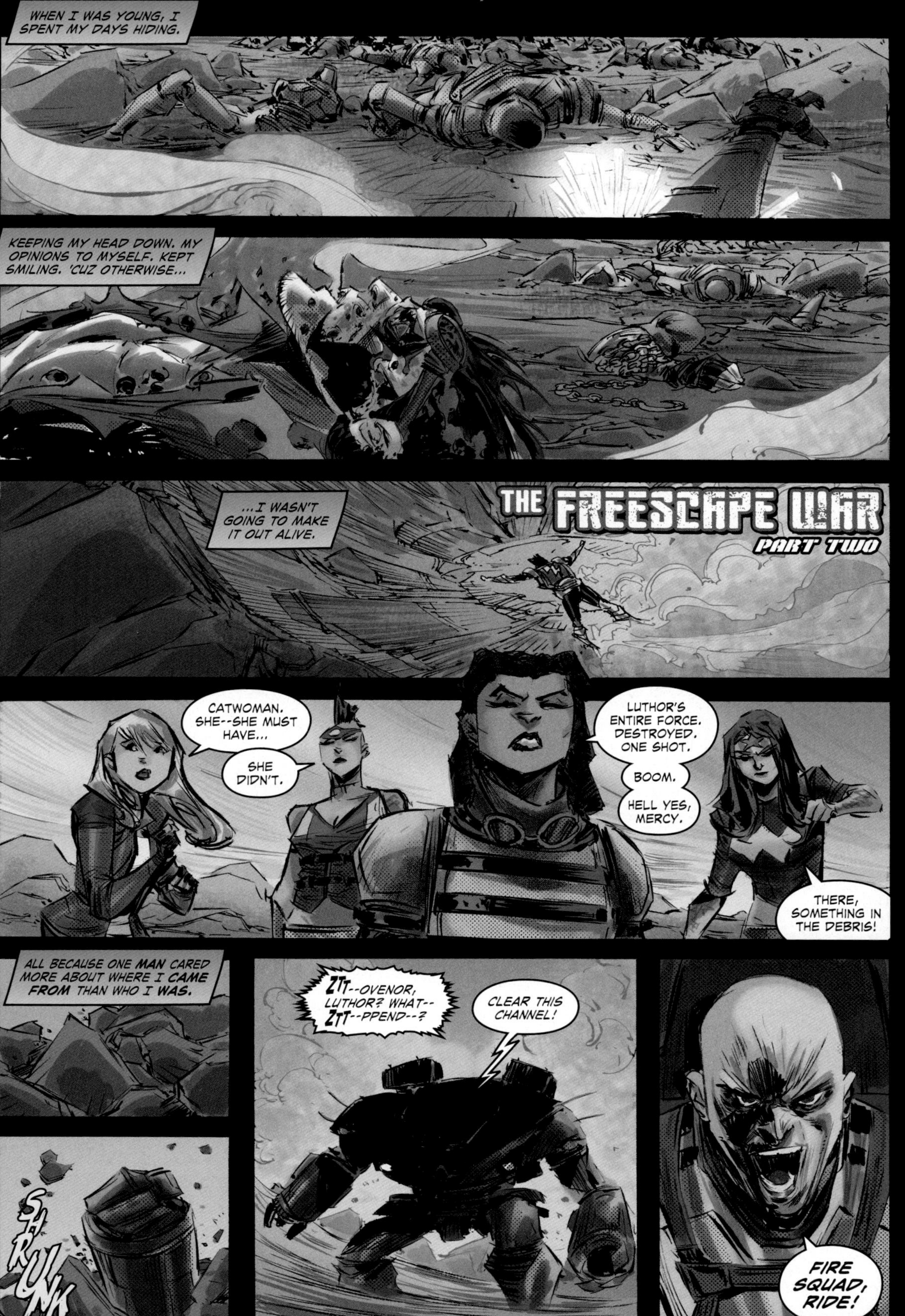
WHEN I WAS YOUNG, I SPENT MY DAYS HIDING.
KEEPING MY HEAD DOWN. MY OPINIONS TO MYSELF. KEPT SMILING. 'CUZ OTHERWISE...
...I WASN'T GOING TO MAKE IT OUT ALIVE.
THE FREESCAPE WAR
PART TWO
CATWOMAN. SHE--SHE MUST HAVE...
SHE DIDN'T.
LUTHOR'S ENTIRE FORCE. DESTROYED. ONE SHOT.
BOOM.
HELL YES, MERCY.
THERE, SOMETHING IN THE DEBRIS!
ALL BECAUSE ONE MAN CARED MORE ABOUT WHERE I CAME FROM THAN WHO I WAS.
SHRUNK
ZTT--OVENOR, LUTHOR? WHAT-- ZTT--PPEND--?
CLEAR THIS CHANNEL!
FIRE SQUAD, RIDE!

TORY BY COLLIN KELLY & JACKSON LANZING ART BY BRIAN CHING COLORS BY KELLY FITZPATRICK LETTERS BY WES ABBOTT

EDITED BY KRISTY QUINN

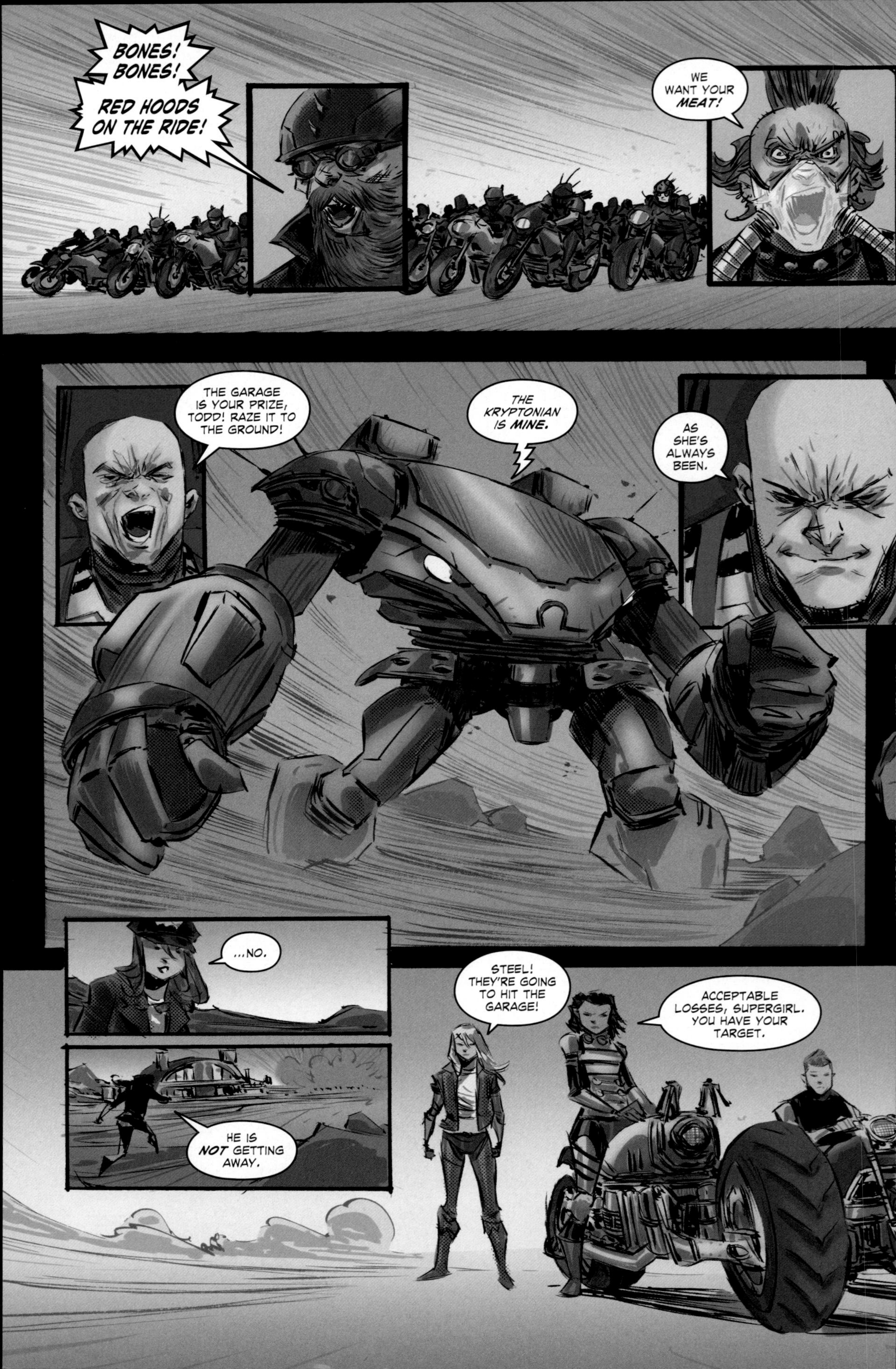
BONES! BONES!
RED HOODS ON THE RIDE!
WE WANT YOUR MEAT!
THE GARAGE IS YOUR PRIZE, TODD! RAZE IT TO THE GROUND!
THE KRYPTONIAN IS MINE.
AS SHE'S ALWAYS BEEN.
...NO.
HE IS NOT GETTING AWAY.
STEEL! THEY'RE GOING TO HIT THE GARAGE!
ACCEPTABLE LOSSES, SUPERGIRL. YOU HAVE YOUR TARGET.

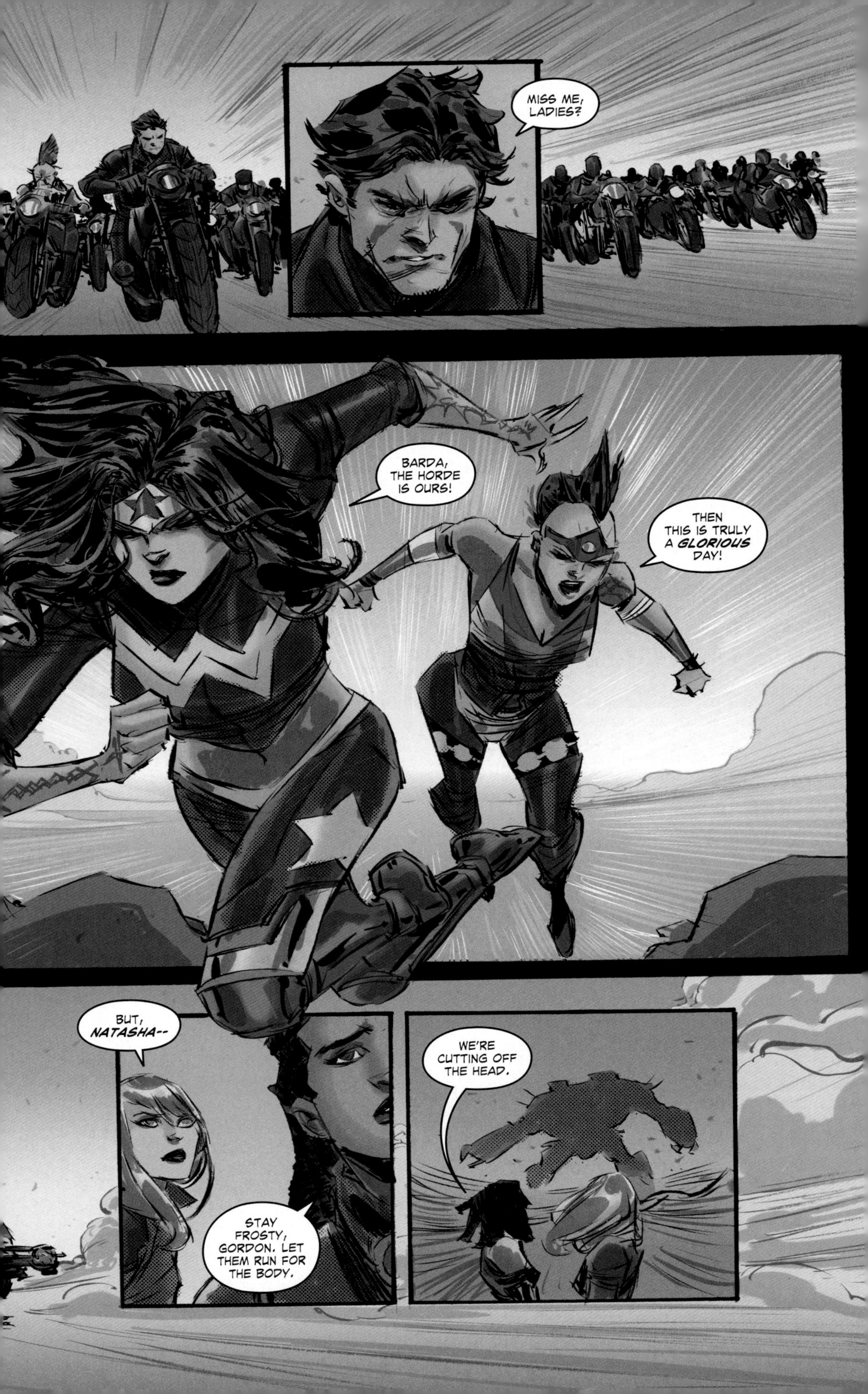
MISS ME, LADIES?
BARDA, THE HORDE IS OURS!
THEN THIS IS TRULY A GLORIOUS DAY!
BUT, NATASHA--
STAY FROSTY, GORDON. LET THEM RUN FOR THE BODY.
WE'RE CUTTING OFF THE HEAD.

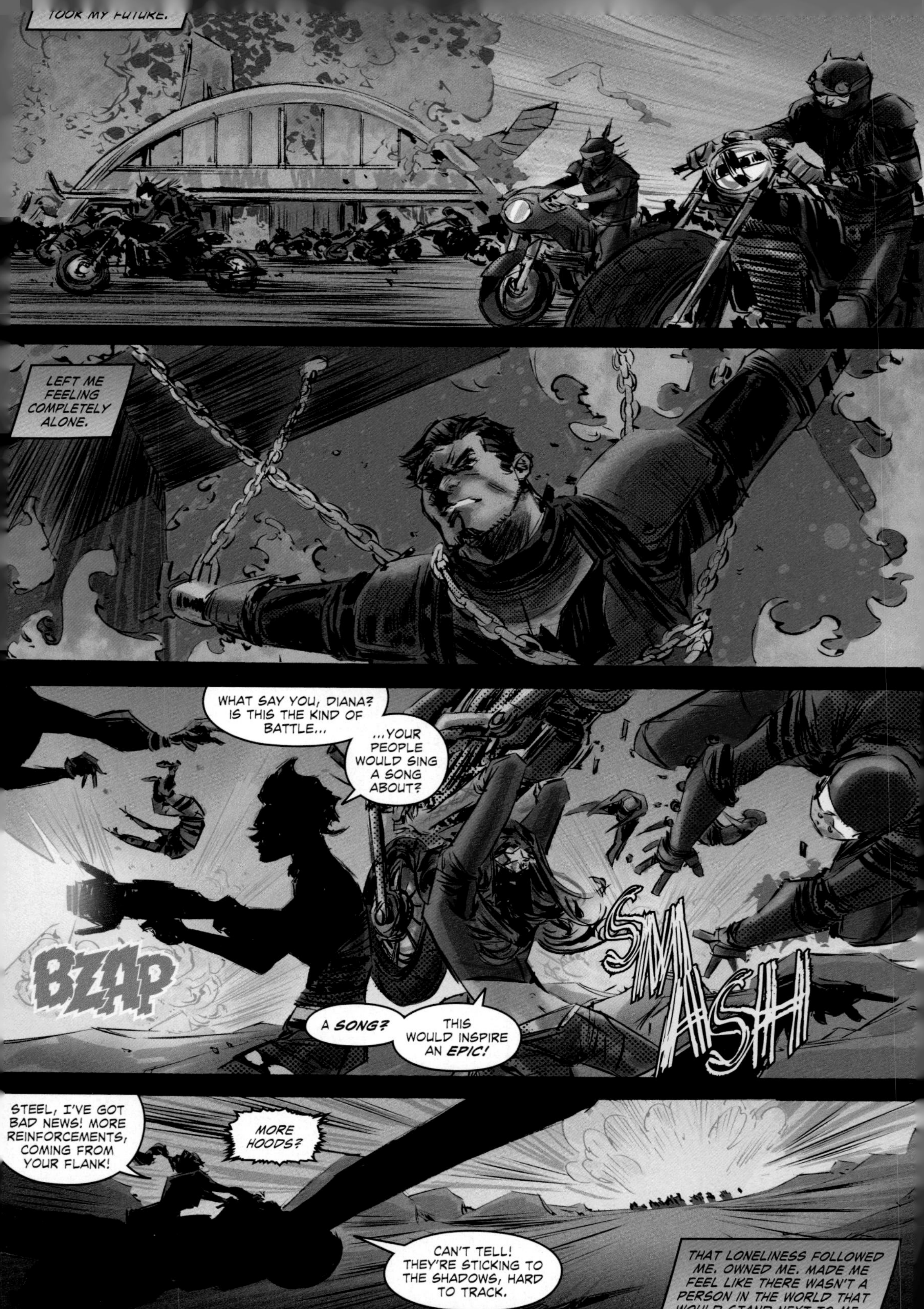
TOOK MY FUTURE.
LEFT ME FEELING COMPLETELY ALONE.
WHAT SAY YOU, DIANA? IS THIS THE KIND OF BATTLE...
...YOUR PEOPLE WOULD SING A SONG ABOUT?
BZAP
SMASH
A SONG?
THIS WOULD INSPIRE AN EPIC!
STEEL, I'VE GOT BAD NEWS! MORE REINFORCEMENTS, COMING FROM YOUR FLANK!
MORE HOODS?
CAN'T TELL! THEY'RE STICKING TO THE SHADOWS, HARD TO TRACK.
THAT LONELINESS FOLLOWED ME. OWNED ME. MADE ME FEEL LIKE THERE WASN'T A PERSON IN THE WORLD THAT WOULD STAND NEXT TO ME.

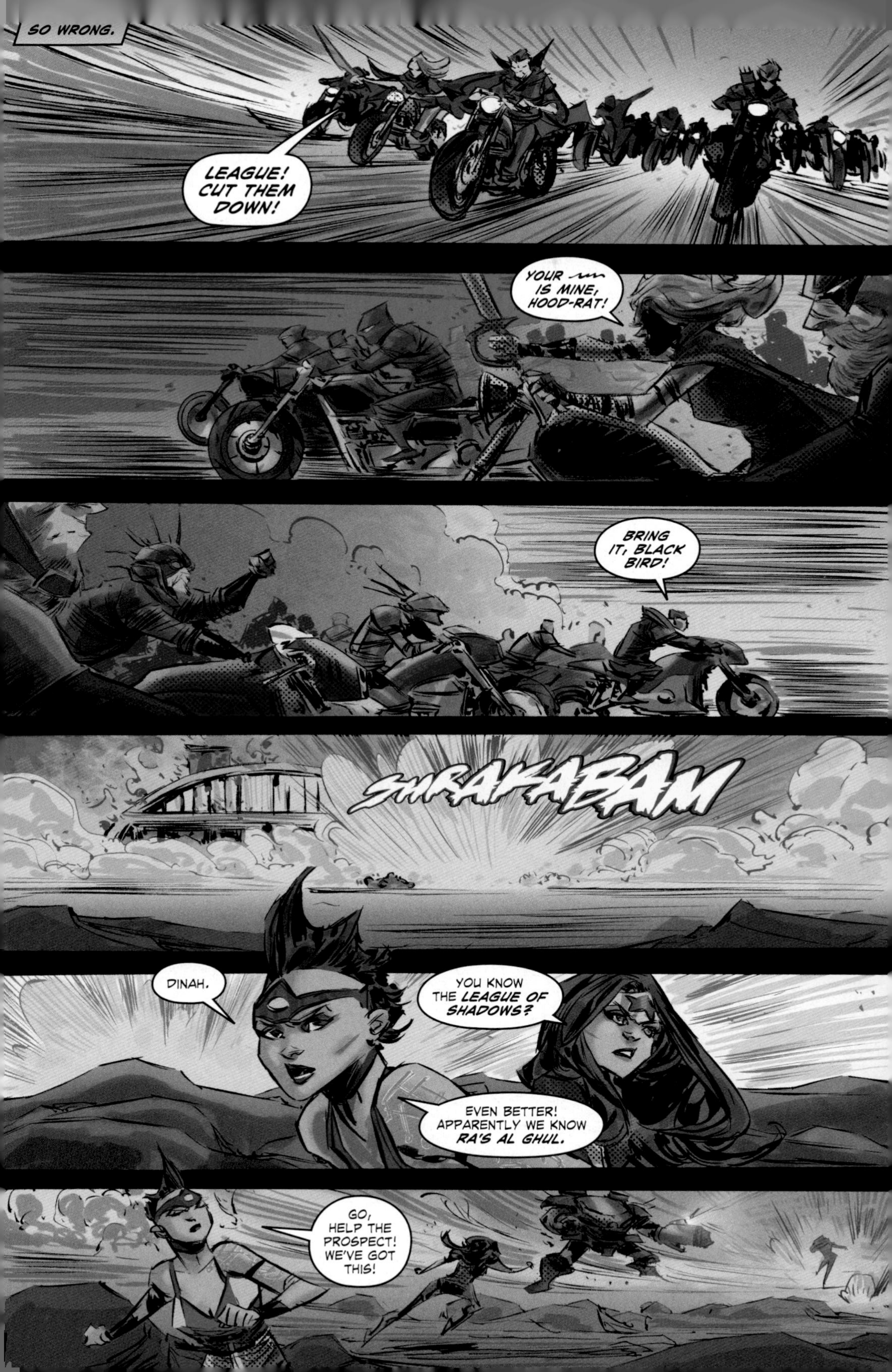

SO WRONG.
LEAGUE! CUT THEM DOWN!
YOUR ~~~ IS MINE, HOOD-RAT!
BRING IT, BLACK BIRD!
SHRAKABAM
DINAH.
YOU KNOW THE LEAGUE OF SHADOWS?
EVEN BETTER! APPARENTLY WE KNOW RA'S AL GHUL.
GO, HELP THE PROSPECT! WE'VE GOT THIS!

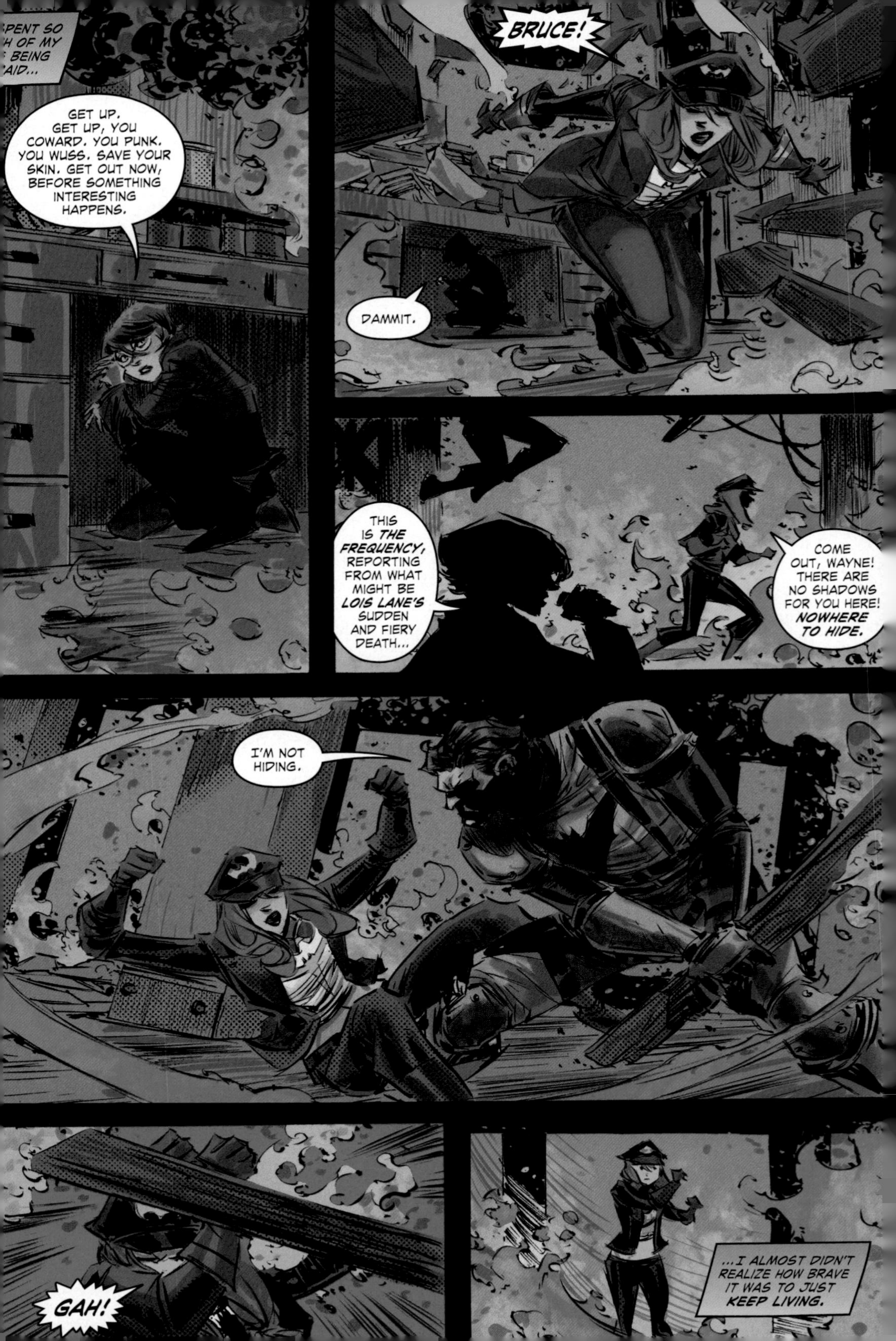
SPENT SO
H OF MY
BEING
AID...
GET UP. GET UP, YOU COWARD. YOU PUNK. YOU WUSS. SAVE YOUR SKIN. GET OUT NOW, BEFORE SOMETHING INTERESTING HAPPENS.
BRUCE!
DAMMIT.
THIS IS THE FREQUENCY, REPORTING FROM WHAT MIGHT BE LOIS LANE'S SUDDEN AND FIERY DEATH...
COME OUT, WAYNE! THERE ARE NO SHADOWS FOR YOU HERE! NOWHERE TO HIDE.
I'M NOT HIDING.
GAH!
...I ALMOST DIDN'T REALIZE HOW BRAVE IT WAS TO JUST KEEP LIVING.

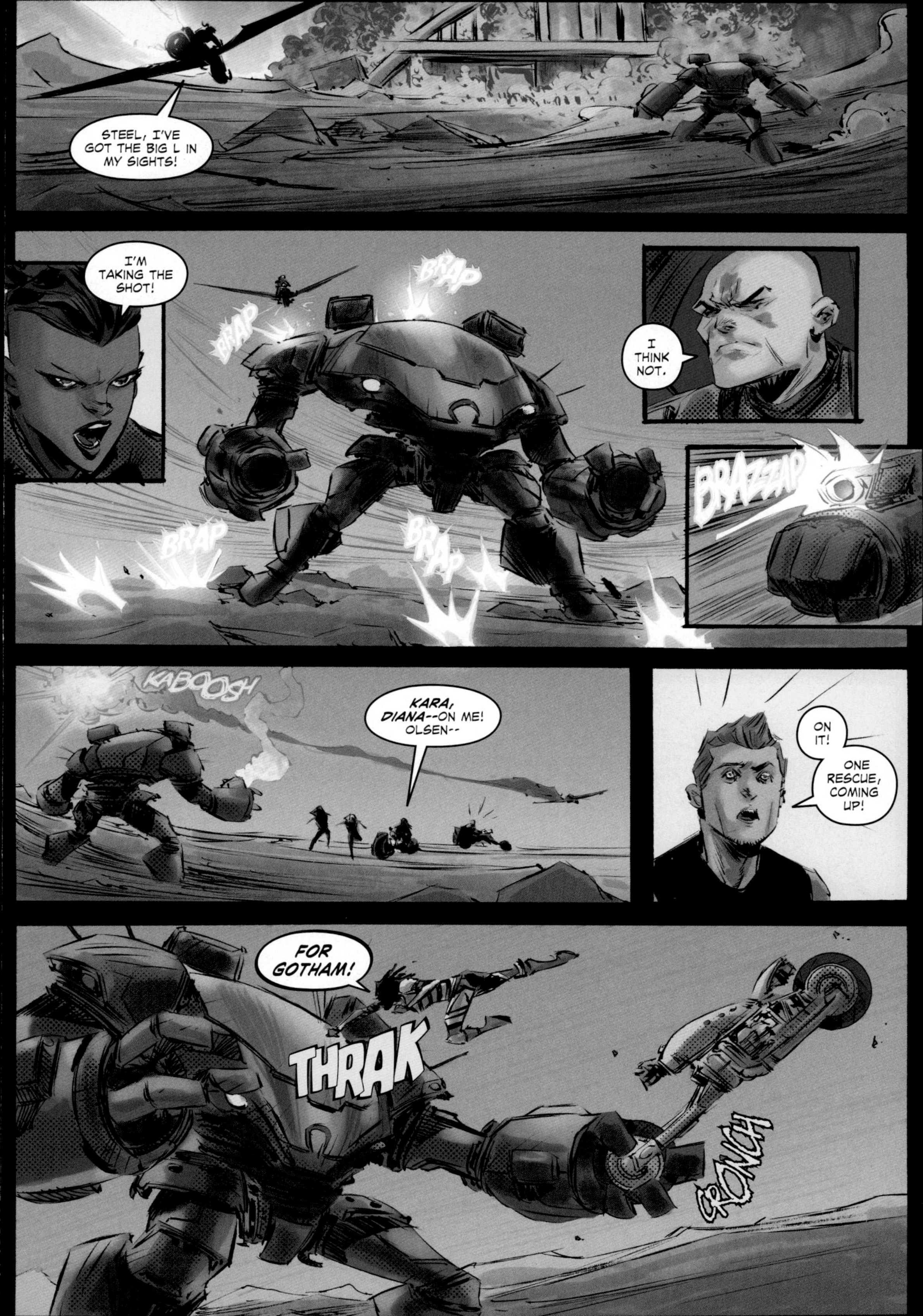
STEEL, I'VE GOT THE BIG L IN MY SIGHTS!
I'M TAKING THE SHOT!
BRAP
BRAP
I THINK NOT.
BRAP
BRAP
BRAZZAP
KABOOOSH
KARA, DIANA--ON ME! OLSEN--
ON IT!
ONE RESCUE, COMING UP!
FOR GOTHAM!
THRAK
CRUNCH

SO IT ALL COMES DOWN TO THIS. THIS MOMENT INGRAINED FOREVER IN MY MIND.

WE FIGHT, ALL OF US, LIKE WE'RE GOING TO WIN. LIKE WE'VE NEVER KNOWN DOUBT. LIKE WE'VE NEVER FELT ALONE.

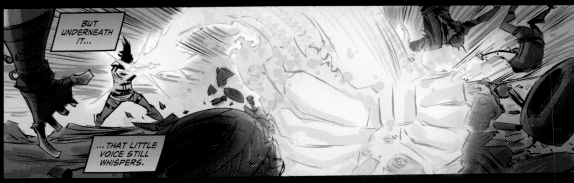

BUT UNDERNEATH IT...

...THAT LITTLE VOICE STILL WHISPERS.

TIME TO FACE THE *GOD KILLER!*

IF ONLY THAT WERE TRUE, *LITTLE AMAZON.*

KASH RAK

AND *YOU, LITTLE MECHANIC?*

I DON'T EVEN *KNOW YOUR NAME.*

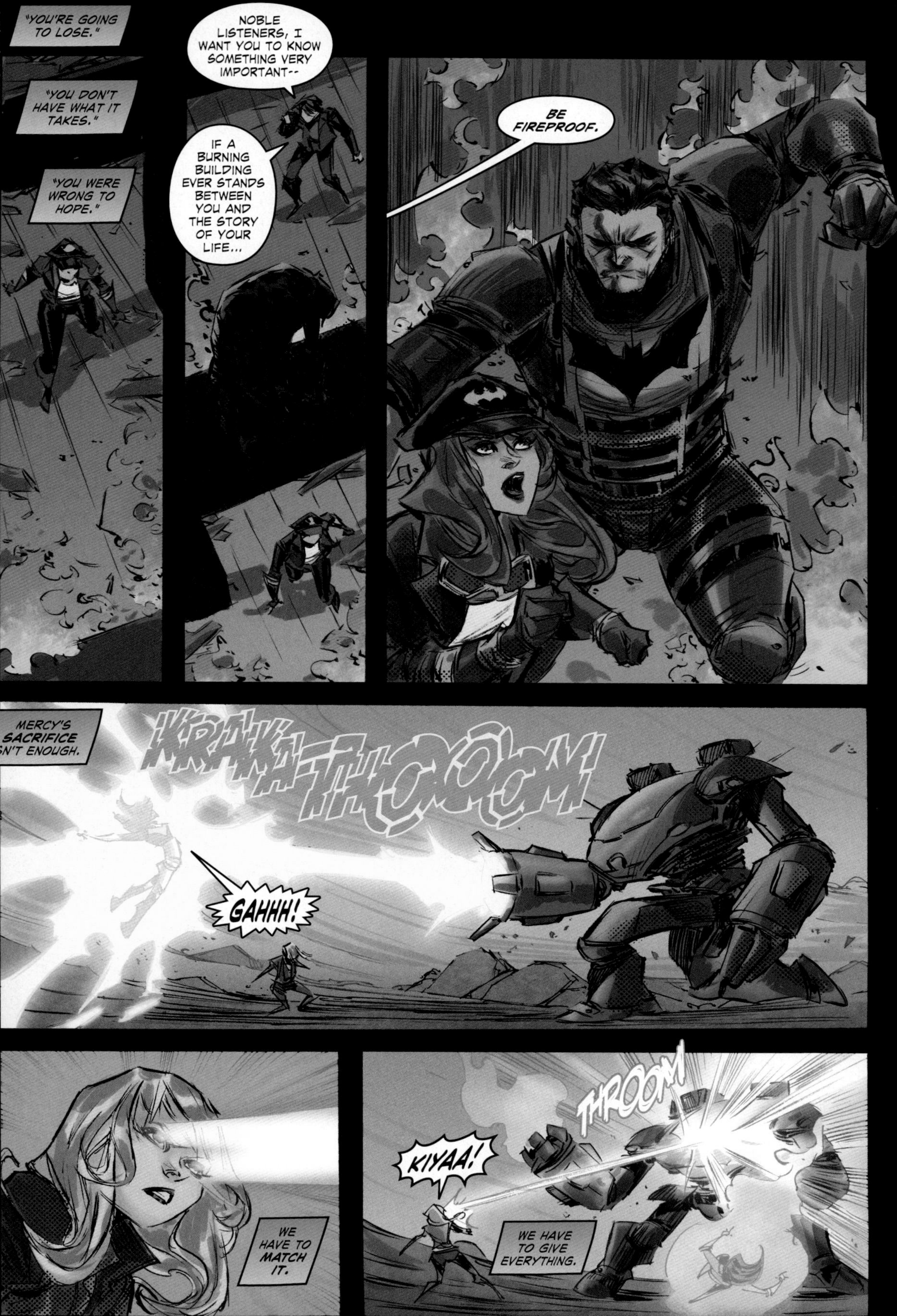
"YOU'RE GOING TO LOSE."
"YOU DON'T HAVE WHAT IT TAKES."
"YOU WERE WRONG TO HOPE."
NOBLE LISTENERS, I WANT YOU TO KNOW SOMETHING VERY IMPORTANT--
IF A BURNING BUILDING EVER STANDS BETWEEN YOU AND THE STORY OF YOUR LIFE...
BE FIREPROOF.
MERCY'S SACRIFICE ISN'T ENOUGH.
KRAKA-THOOOOM!
GAHHH!
WE HAVE TO MATCH IT.
THROOM
KIYAA!
WE HAVE TO GIVE EVERYTHING.

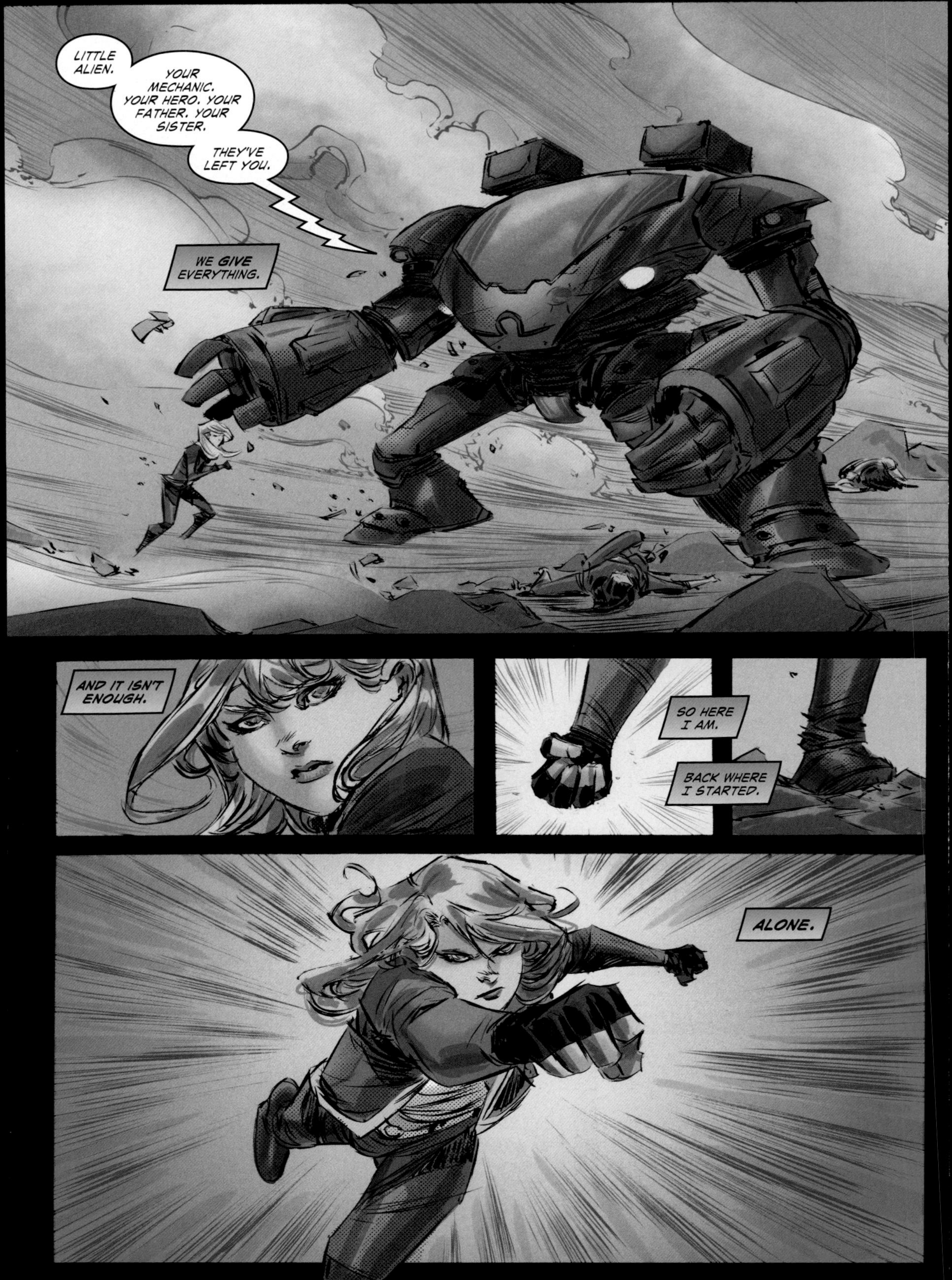
LITTLE ALIEN.
YOUR MECHANIC. YOUR HERO. YOUR FATHER. YOUR SISTER.
THEY'VE LEFT YOU.
WE GIVE EVERYTHING.
AND IT ISN'T ENOUGH.
SO HERE I AM.
BACK WHERE I STARTED.
ALONE.

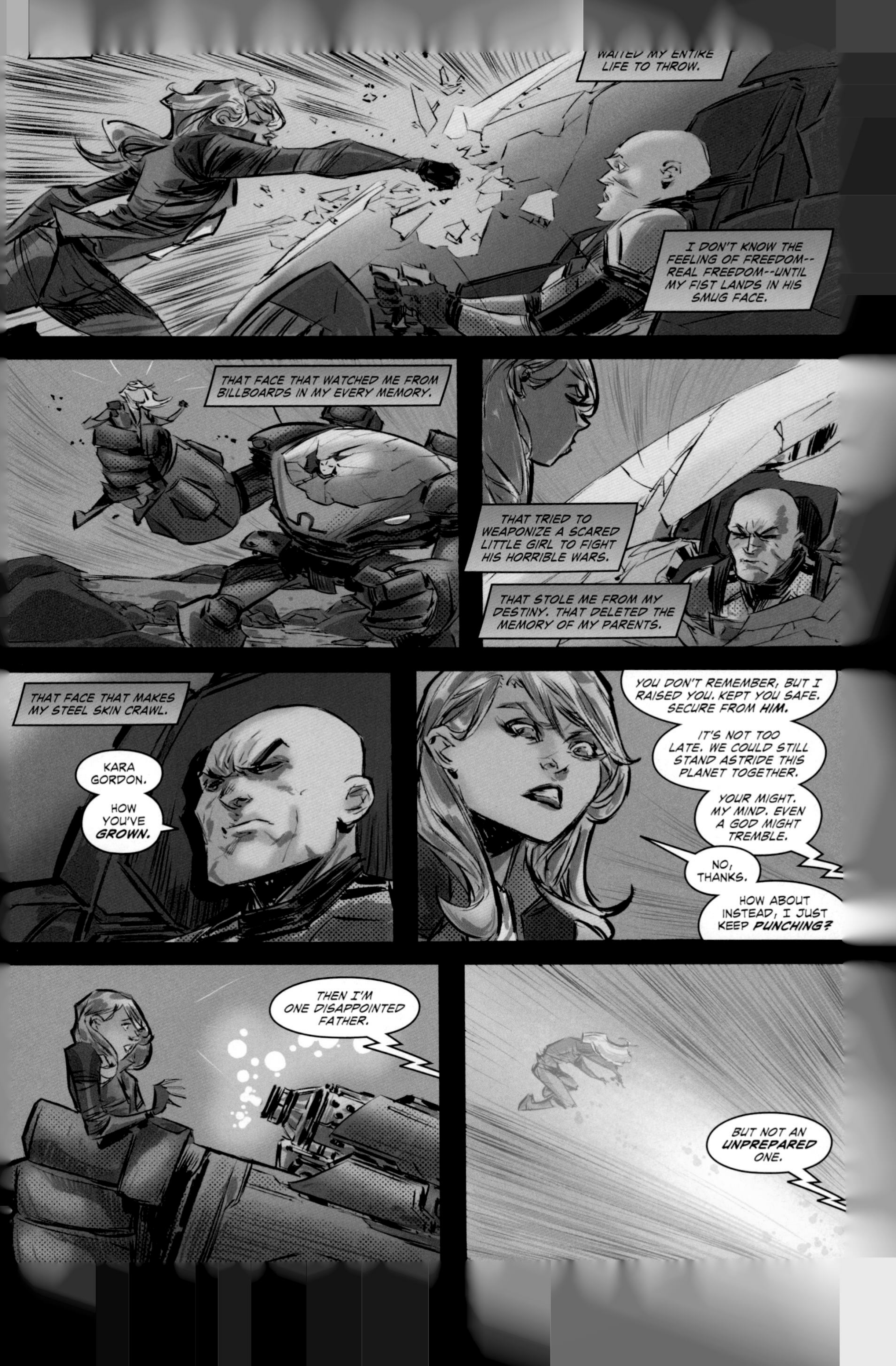
WAITED MY ENTIRE LIFE TO THROW.
I DON'T KNOW THE FEELING OF FREEDOM-- REAL FREEDOM--UNTIL MY FIST LANDS IN HIS SMUG FACE.
THAT FACE THAT WATCHED ME FROM BILLBOARDS IN MY EVERY MEMORY.
THAT TRIED TO WEAPONIZE A SCARED LITTLE GIRL TO FIGHT HIS HORRIBLE WARS.
THAT STOLE ME FROM MY DESTINY. THAT DELETED THE MEMORY OF MY PARENTS.
THAT FACE THAT MAKES MY STEEL SKIN CRAWL.
KARA GORDON.
HOW YOU'VE GROWN.
YOU DON'T REMEMBER, BUT I RAISED YOU. KEPT YOU SAFE. SECURE FROM HIM.
IT'S NOT TOO LATE. WE COULD STILL STAND ASTRIDE THIS PLANET TOGETHER.
YOUR MIGHT. MY MIND. EVEN A GOD MIGHT TREMBLE.
NO, THANKS.
HOW ABOUT INSTEAD, I JUST KEEP PUNCHING?
THEN I'M ONE DISAPPOINTED FATHER.
BUT NOT AN UNPREPARED ONE.

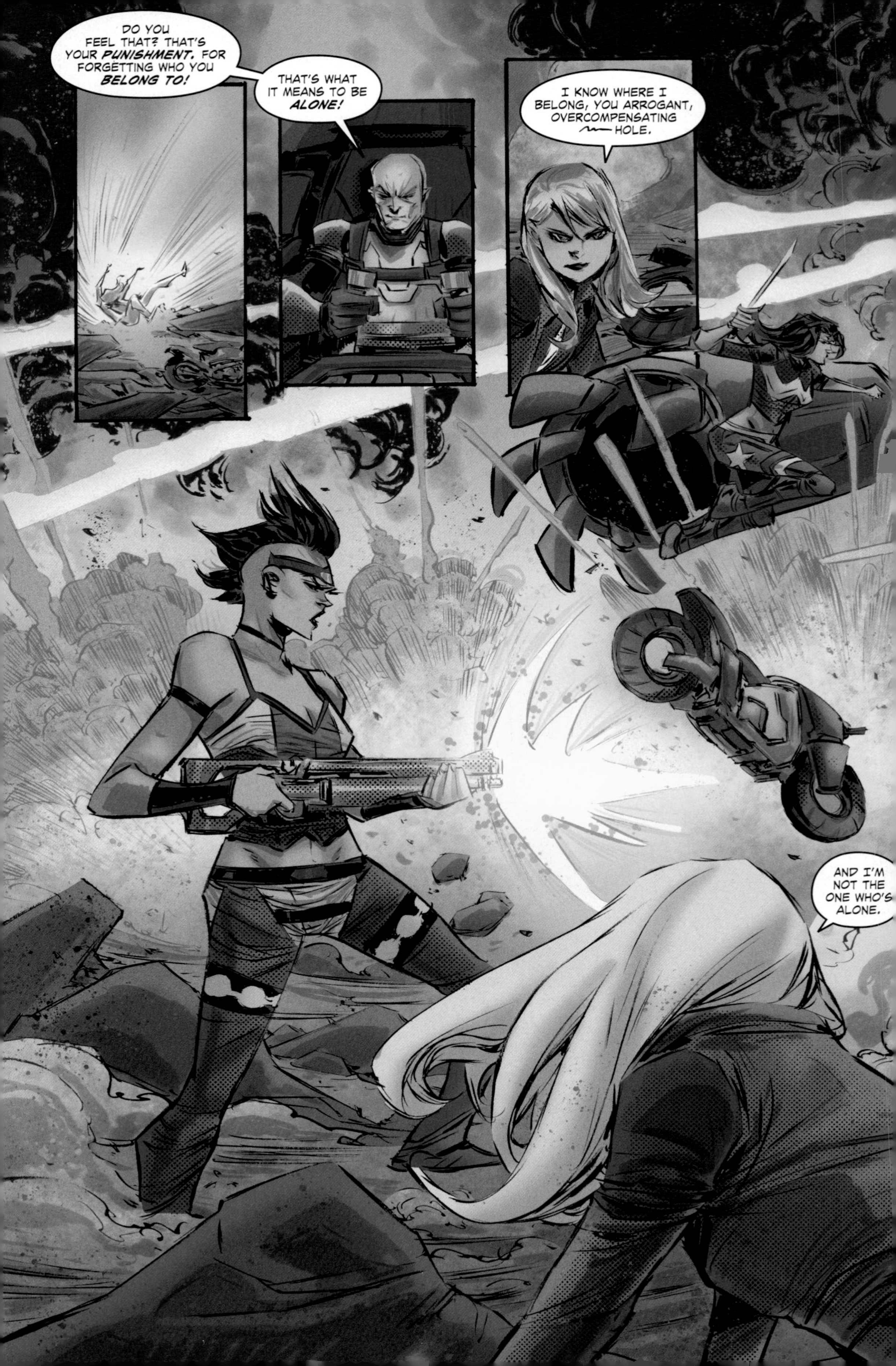
DO YOU FEEL THAT? THAT'S YOUR PUNISHMENT. FOR FORGETTING WHO YOU BELONG TO!
THAT'S WHAT IT MEANS TO BE ALONE!
I KNOW WHERE I BELONG, YOU ARROGANT, OVERCOMPENSATING HOLE.
AND I'M NOT THE ONE WHO'S ALONE.

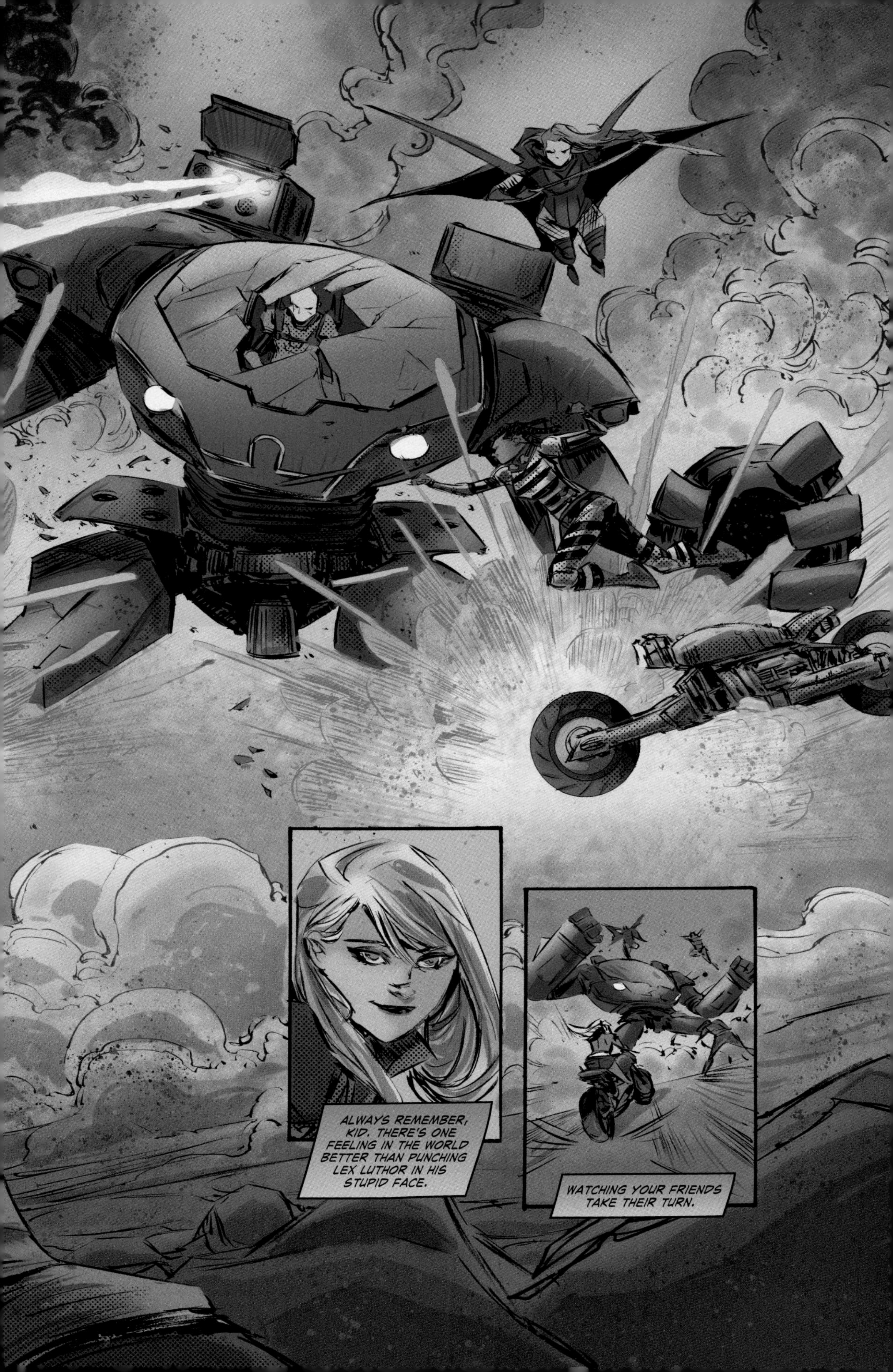
ALWAYS REMEMBER, KID. THERE'S ONE FEELING IN THE WORLD BETTER THAN PUNCHING LEX LUTHOR IN HIS STUPID FACE.
WATCHING YOUR FRIENDS TAKE THEIR TURN.

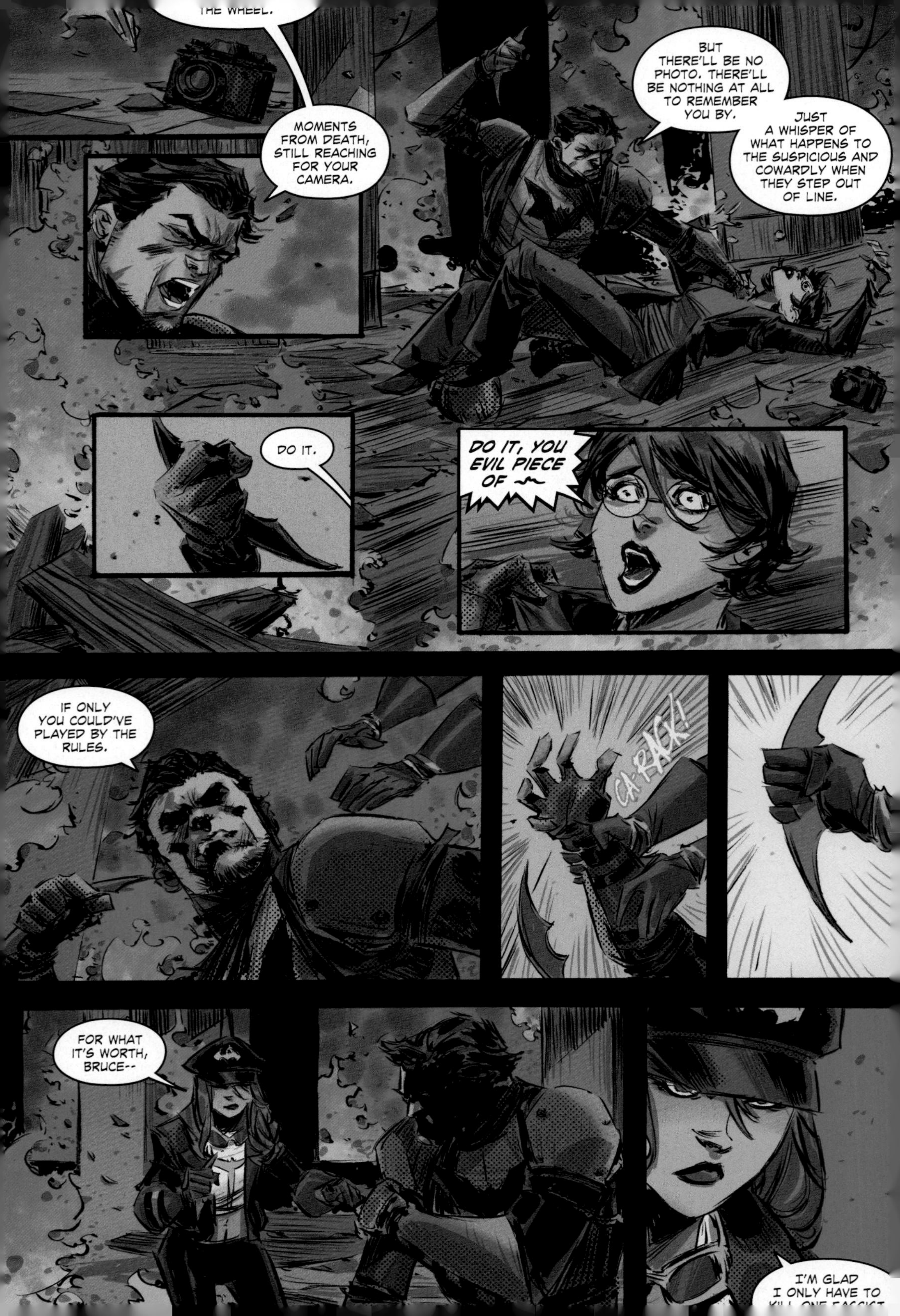
THE WHEEL.
MOMENTS FROM DEATH, STILL REACHING FOR YOUR CAMERA.
BUT THERE'LL BE NO PHOTO. THERE'LL BE NOTHING AT ALL TO REMEMBER YOU BY.
JUST A WHISPER OF WHAT HAPPENS TO THE SUSPICIOUS AND COWARDLY WHEN THEY STEP OUT OF LINE.
DO IT.
DO IT, YOU EVIL PIECE OF --
IF ONLY YOU COULD'VE PLAYED BY THE RULES.
CA-RACK!
FOR WHAT IT'S WORTH, BRUCE--
I'M GLAD I ONLY HAVE TO

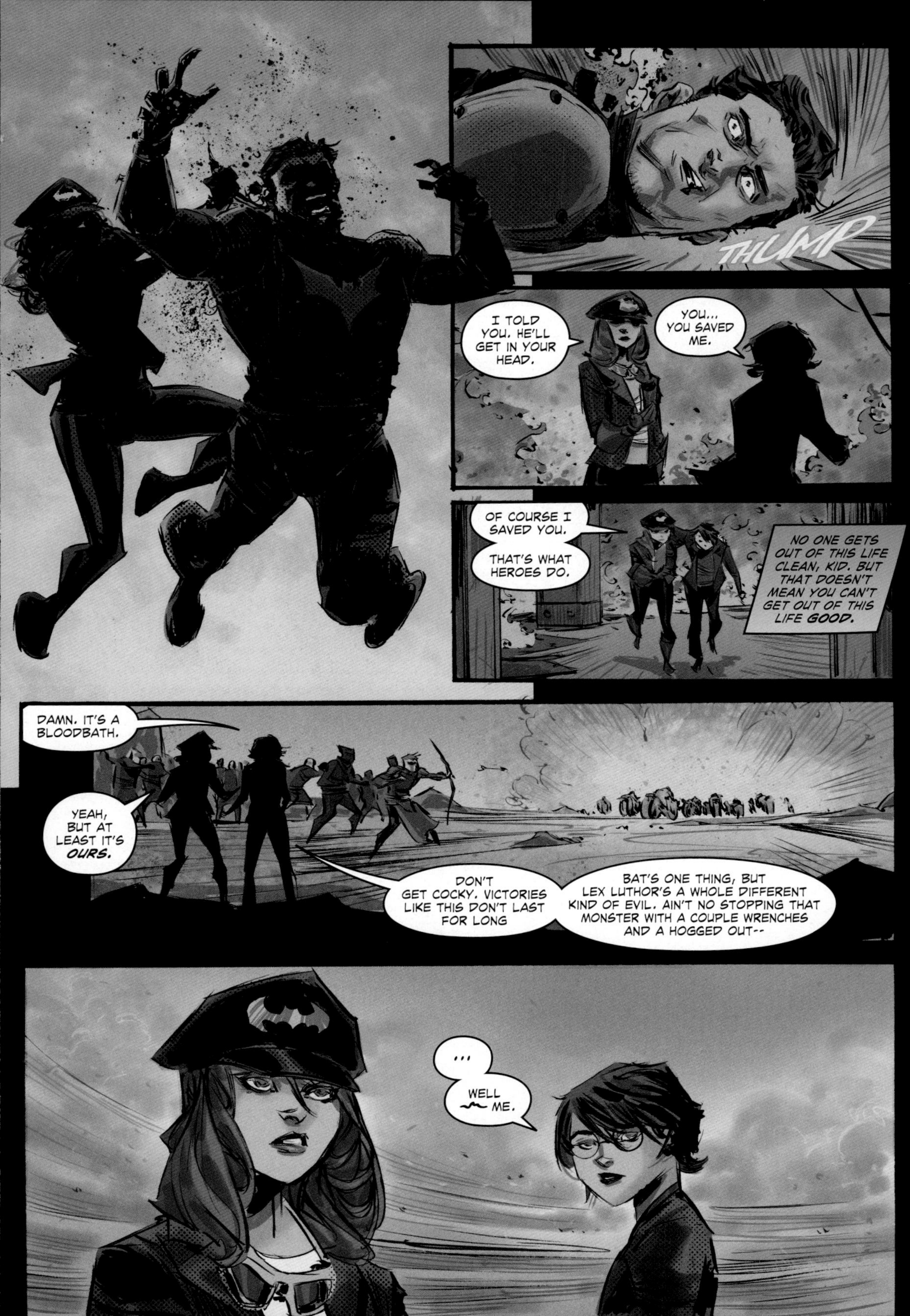
THUMP
I TOLD YOU. HE'LL GET IN YOUR HEAD.
YOU... YOU SAVED ME.
OF COURSE I SAVED YOU.
THAT'S WHAT HEROES DO.
NO ONE GETS OUT OF THIS LIFE CLEAN, KID. BUT THAT DOESN'T MEAN YOU CAN'T GET OUT OF THIS LIFE **GOOD.**
DAMN. IT'S A BLOODBATH.
YEAH, BUT AT LEAST IT'S ***OURS.***
DON'T GET COCKY. VICTORIES LIKE THIS DON'T LAST FOR LONG
BAT'S ONE THING, BUT LEX LUTHOR'S A WHOLE DIFFERENT KIND OF EVIL. AIN'T NO STOPPING THAT MONSTER WITH A COUPLE WRENCHES AND A HOGGED OUT--
...
WELL ~ ME.

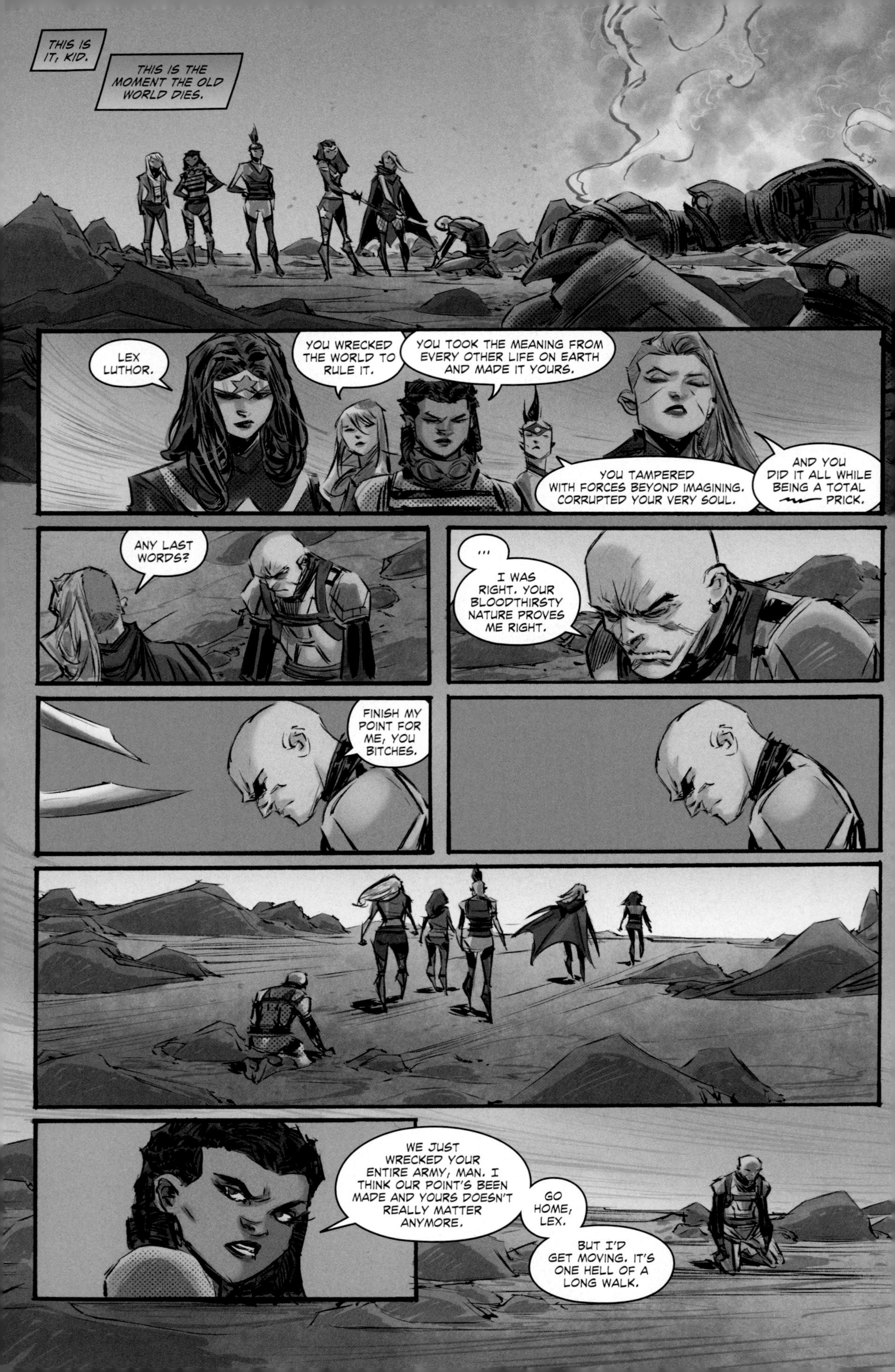
THIS IS IT, KID.
THIS IS THE MOMENT THE OLD WORLD DIES.
LEX LUTHOR.
YOU WRECKED THE WORLD TO RULE IT.
YOU TOOK THE MEANING FROM EVERY OTHER LIFE ON EARTH AND MADE IT YOURS.
YOU TAMPERED WITH FORCES BEYOND IMAGINING. CORRUPTED YOUR VERY SOUL.
AND YOU DID IT ALL WHILE BEING A TOTAL PRICK.
ANY LAST WORDS?
...
I WAS RIGHT. YOUR BLOODTHIRSTY NATURE PROVES ME RIGHT.
FINISH MY POINT FOR ME, YOU BITCHES.
WE JUST WRECKED YOUR ENTIRE ARMY, MAN. I THINK OUR POINT'S BEEN MADE AND YOURS DOESN'T REALLY MATTER ANYMORE.
GO HOME, LEX.
BUT I'D GET MOVING. IT'S ONE HELL OF A LONG WALK.

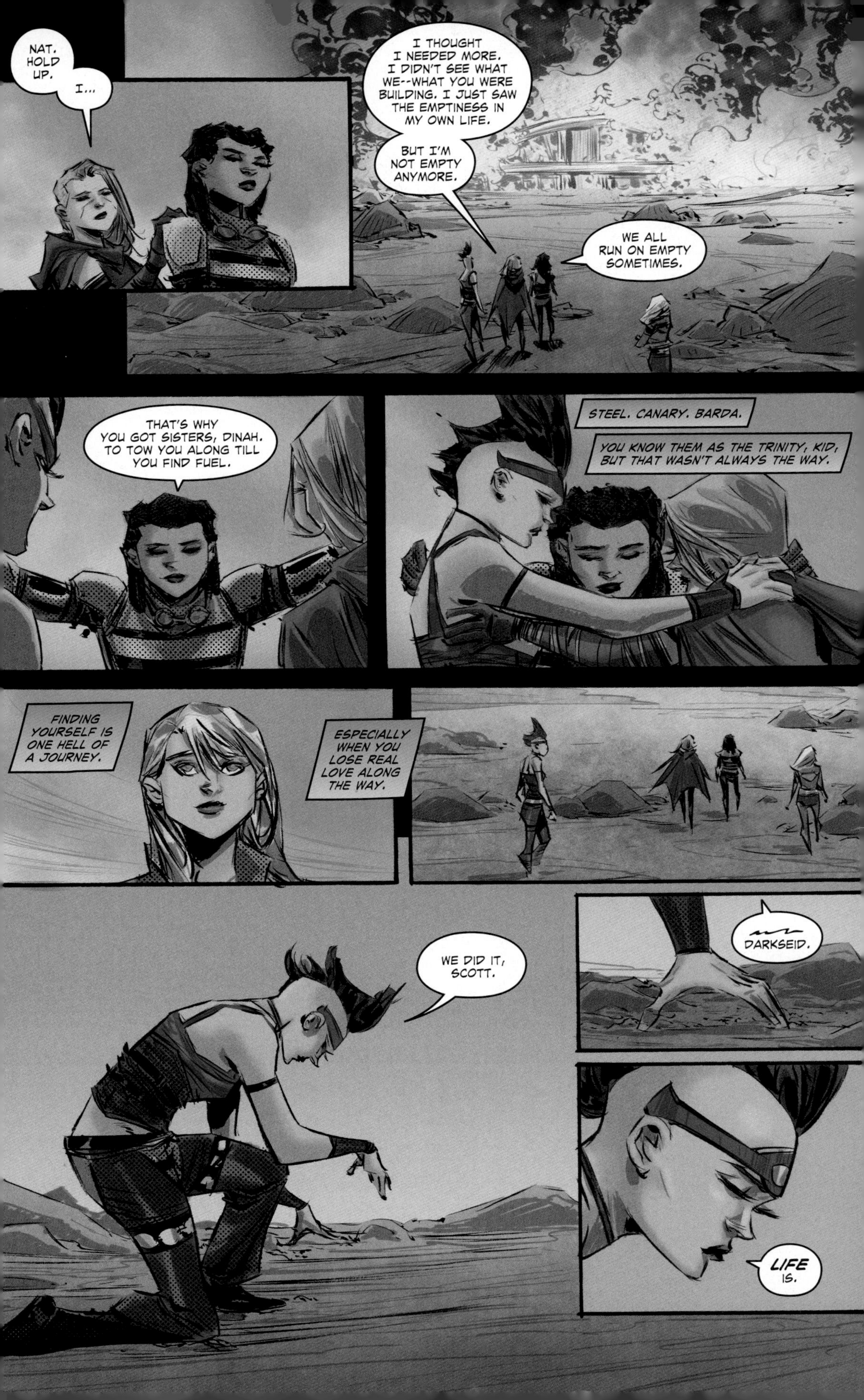
NAT. HOLD UP.
I...
I THOUGHT I NEEDED MORE. I DIDN'T SEE WHAT WE--WHAT YOU WERE BUILDING. I JUST SAW THE EMPTINESS IN MY OWN LIFE.
BUT I'M NOT EMPTY ANYMORE.
WE ALL RUN ON EMPTY SOMETIMES.
THAT'S WHY YOU GOT SISTERS, DINAH. TO TOW YOU ALONG TILL YOU FIND FUEL.
STEEL. CANARY. BARDA.
YOU KNOW THEM AS THE TRINITY, KID, BUT THAT WASN'T ALWAYS THE WAY.
FINDING YOURSELF IS ONE HELL OF A JOURNEY.
ESPECIALLY WHEN YOU LOSE REAL LOVE ALONG THE WAY.
WE DID IT, SCOTT.
DARKSEID.
LIFE IS.

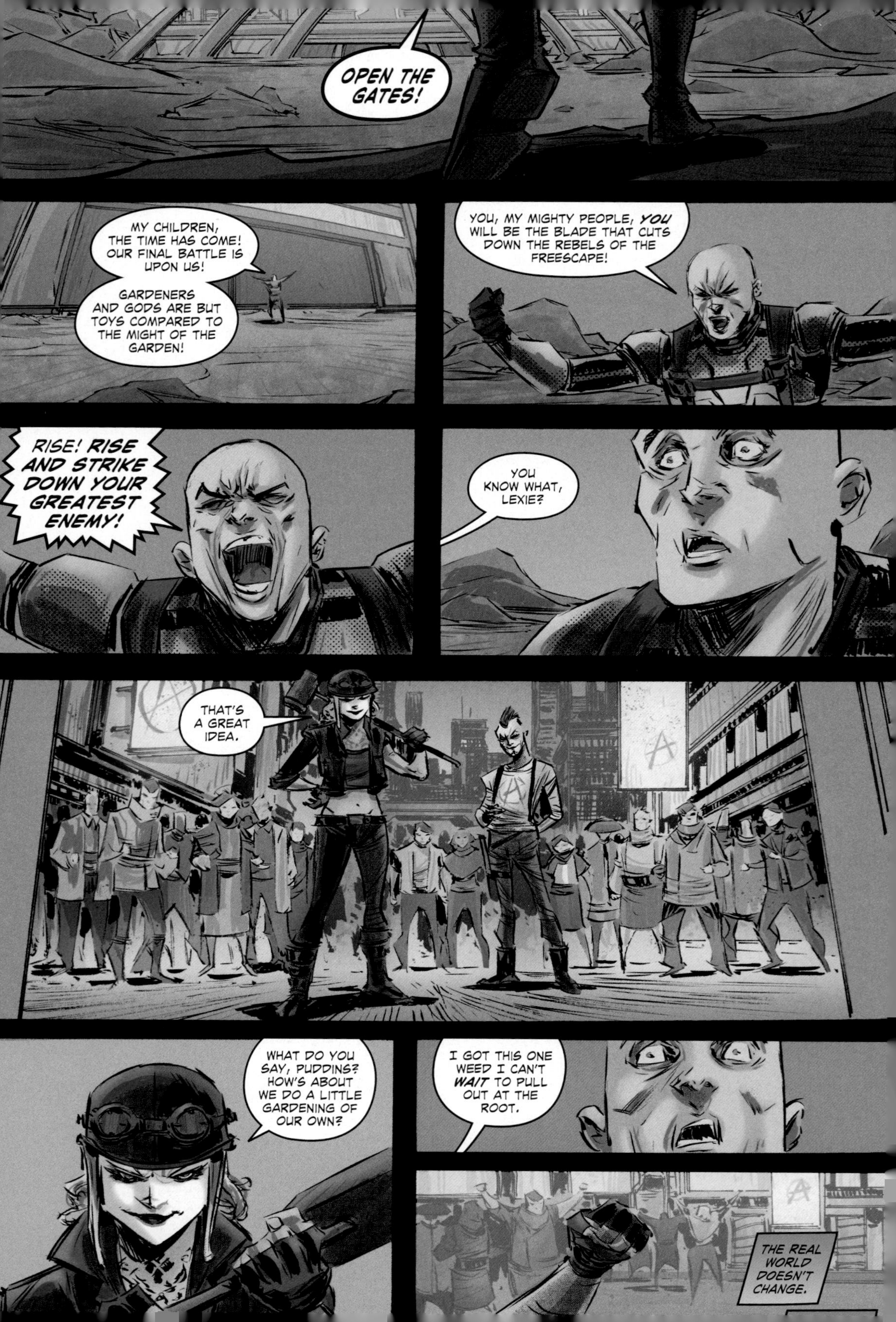

OPEN THE GATES!
MY CHILDREN, THE TIME HAS COME! OUR FINAL BATTLE IS UPON US!
GARDENERS AND GODS ARE BUT TOYS COMPARED TO THE MIGHT OF THE GARDEN!
YOU, MY MIGHTY PEOPLE, YOU WILL BE THE BLADE THAT CUTS DOWN THE REBELS OF THE FREESCAPE!
RISE! RISE AND STRIKE DOWN YOUR GREATEST ENEMY!
YOU KNOW WHAT, LEXIE?
THAT'S A GREAT IDEA.
WHAT DO YOU SAY, PUDDINS? HOW'S ABOUT WE DO A LITTLE GARDENING OF OUR OWN?
I GOT THIS ONE WEED I CAN'T WAIT TO PULL OUT AT THE ROOT.
THE REAL WORLD DOESN'T CHANGE.

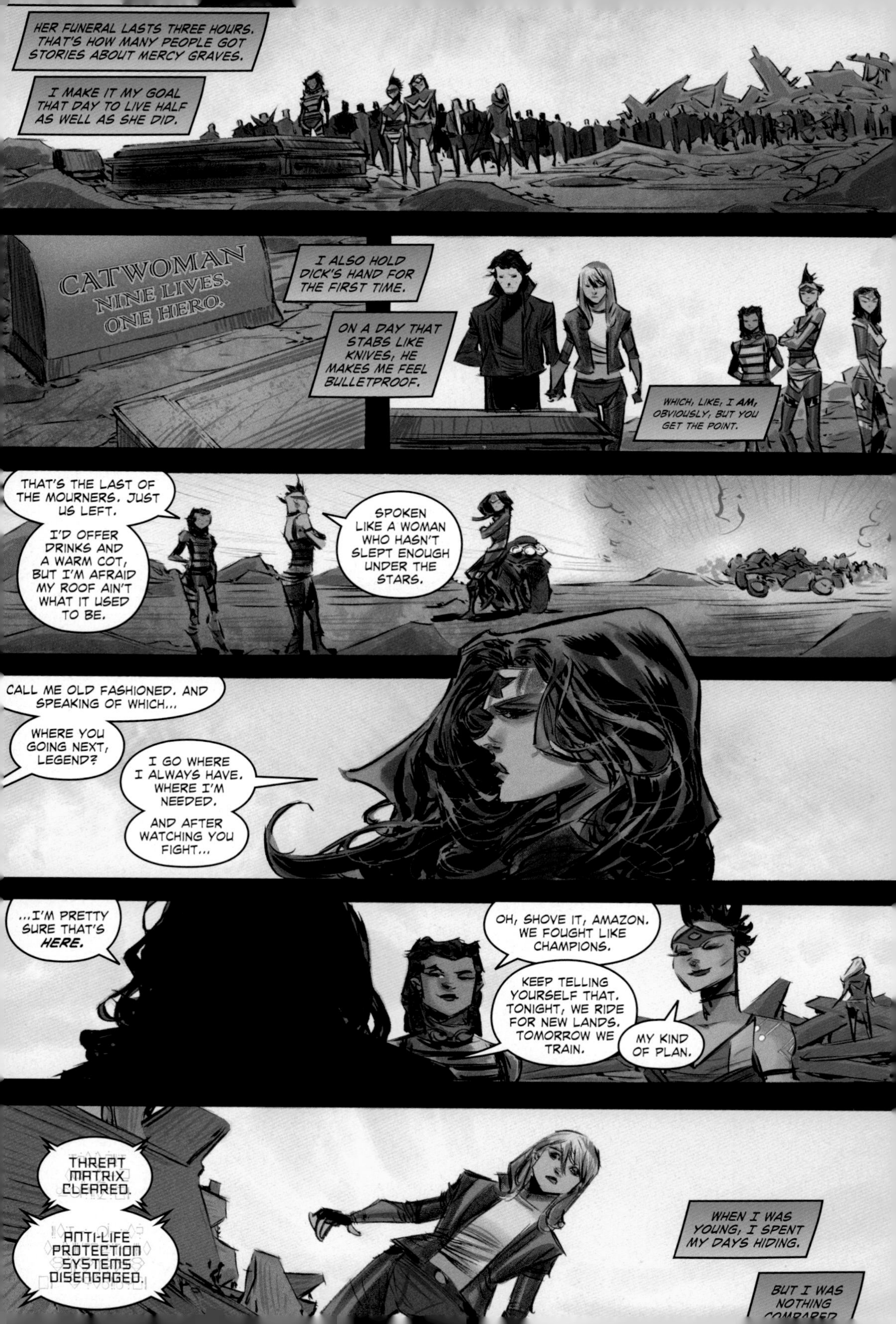

HER FUNERAL LASTS THREE HOURS. THAT'S HOW MANY PEOPLE GOT STORIES ABOUT MERCY GRAVES.
I MAKE IT MY GOAL THAT DAY TO LIVE HALF AS WELL AS SHE DID.
CATWOMAN NINE LIVES. ONE HERO.
I ALSO HOLD DICK'S HAND FOR THE FIRST TIME.
ON A DAY THAT STABS LIKE KNIVES, HE MAKES ME FEEL BULLETPROOF.
WHICH, LIKE, I AM, OBVIOUSLY, BUT YOU GET THE POINT.
THAT'S THE LAST OF THE MOURNERS. JUST US LEFT.
I'D OFFER DRINKS AND A WARM COT, BUT I'M AFRAID MY ROOF AIN'T WHAT IT USED TO BE.
SPOKEN LIKE A WOMAN WHO HASN'T SLEPT ENOUGH UNDER THE STARS.
CALL ME OLD FASHIONED. AND SPEAKING OF WHICH...
WHERE YOU GOING NEXT, LEGEND?
I GO WHERE I ALWAYS HAVE. WHERE I'M NEEDED.
AND AFTER WATCHING YOU FIGHT...
...I'M PRETTY SURE THAT'S HERE.
OH, SHOVE IT, AMAZON. WE FOUGHT LIKE CHAMPIONS.
KEEP TELLING YOURSELF THAT. TONIGHT, WE RIDE FOR NEW LANDS. TOMORROW WE TRAIN.
MY KIND OF PLAN.
THREAT MATRIX CLEARED.
ANTI-LIFE PROTECTION SYSTEMS DISENGAGED.
WHEN I WAS YOUNG, I SPENT MY DAYS HIDING.
BUT I WAS NOTHING

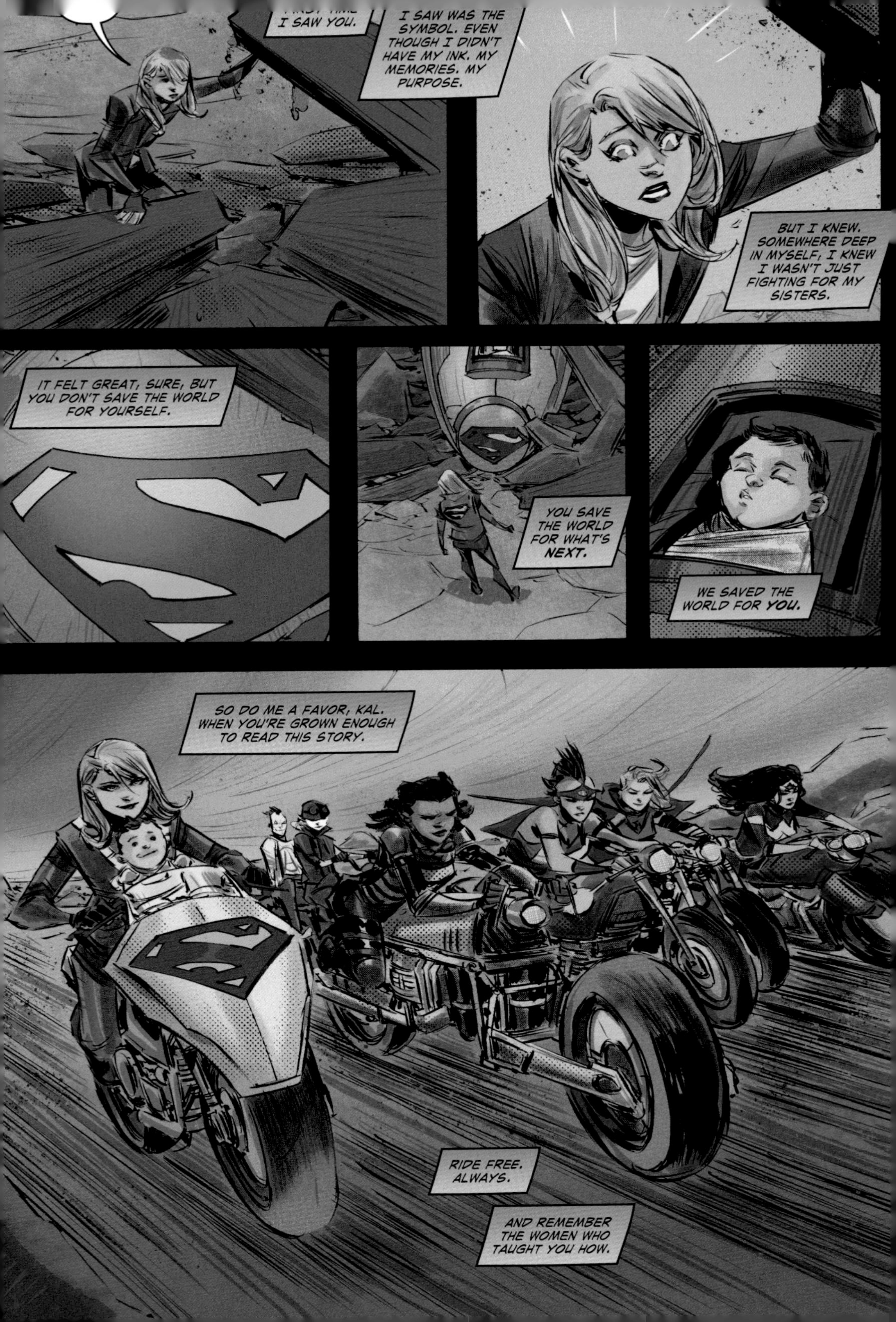
I SAW YOU.
I SAW WAS THE SYMBOL. EVEN THOUGH I DIDN'T HAVE MY INK. MY MEMORIES. MY PURPOSE.
BUT I KNEW. SOMEWHERE DEEP IN MYSELF, I KNEW I WASN'T JUST FIGHTING FOR MY SISTERS.
IT FELT GREAT, SURE, BUT YOU DON'T SAVE THE WORLD FOR YOURSELF.
YOU SAVE THE WORLD FOR WHAT'S NEXT.
WE SAVED THE WORLD FOR YOU.
SO DO ME A FAVOR, KAL. WHEN YOU'RE GROWN ENOUGH TO READ THIS STORY.
RIDE FREE. ALWAYS.
AND REMEMBER THE WOMEN WHO TAUGHT YOU HOW.

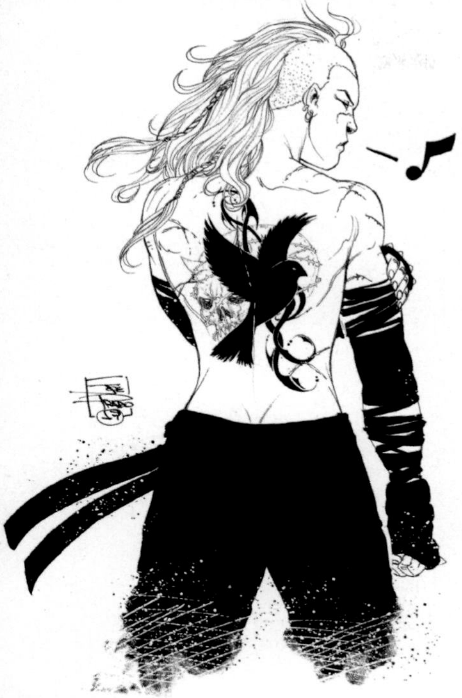

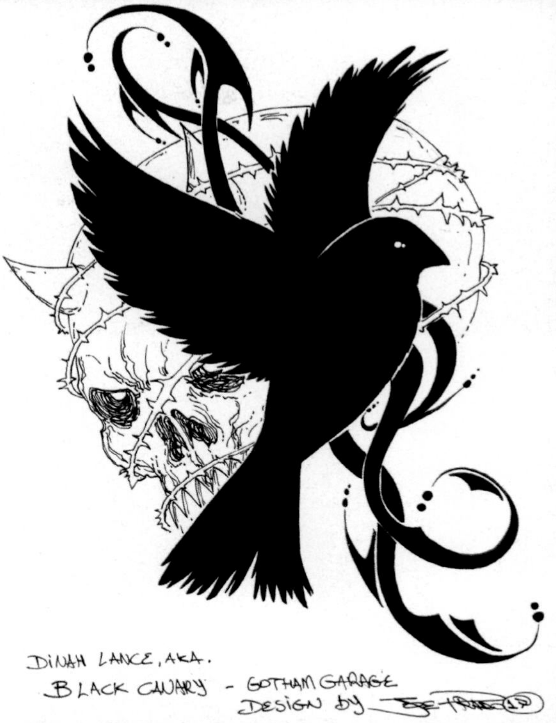
DINAH LANCE, AKA.
BLACK CANARY - GOTHAM GARAGE
DESIGN BY

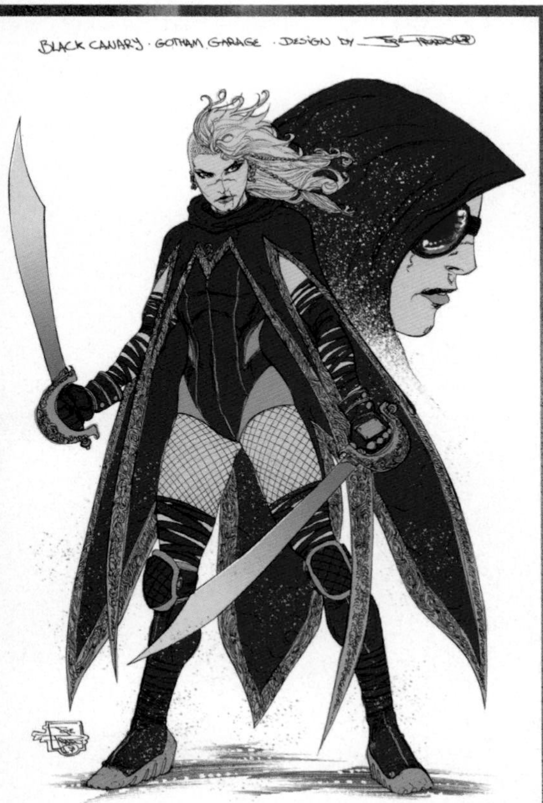
BLACK CANARY · GOTHAM GARAGE · DESIGN BY

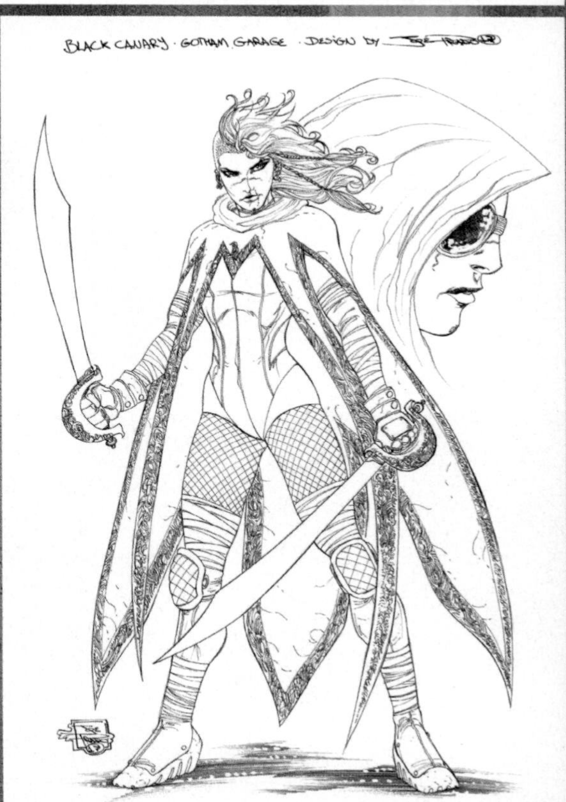
BLACK CANARY · GOTHAM GARAGE · DESIGN BY

FLASH concept sketches by BRIAN CHING

coolant line
gauges
y shaped leather straps to hold oxygen tank
oxygen tank
short term boost
coolant x2
thigh high boots
goggles
pressure release
molded leather pads
molded leather elbow pads
molded kneed pads
coolant line
pressure release
pressure gauge
GOTHAM CITY GARAGE
FLASH

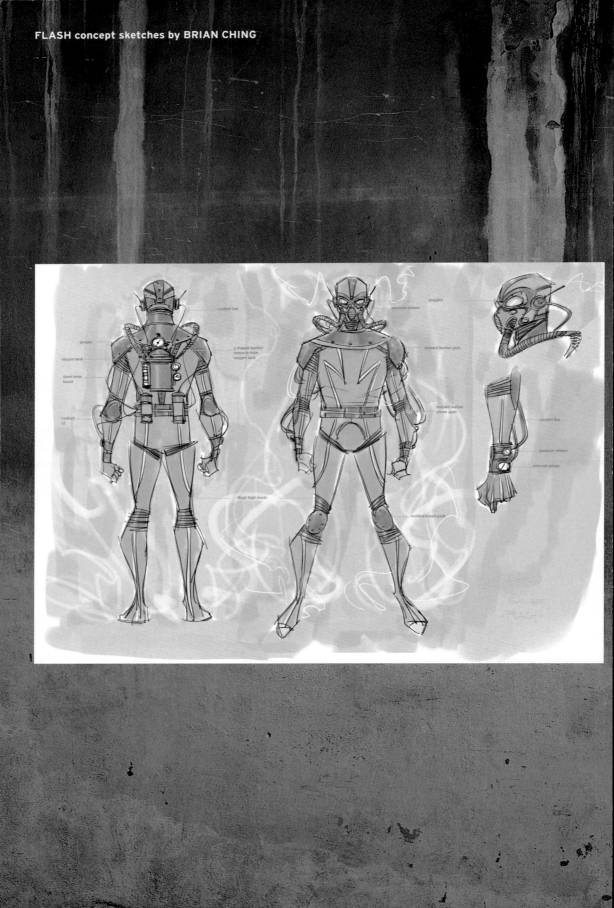

LOBO concept sketches by JIM FLETCHER

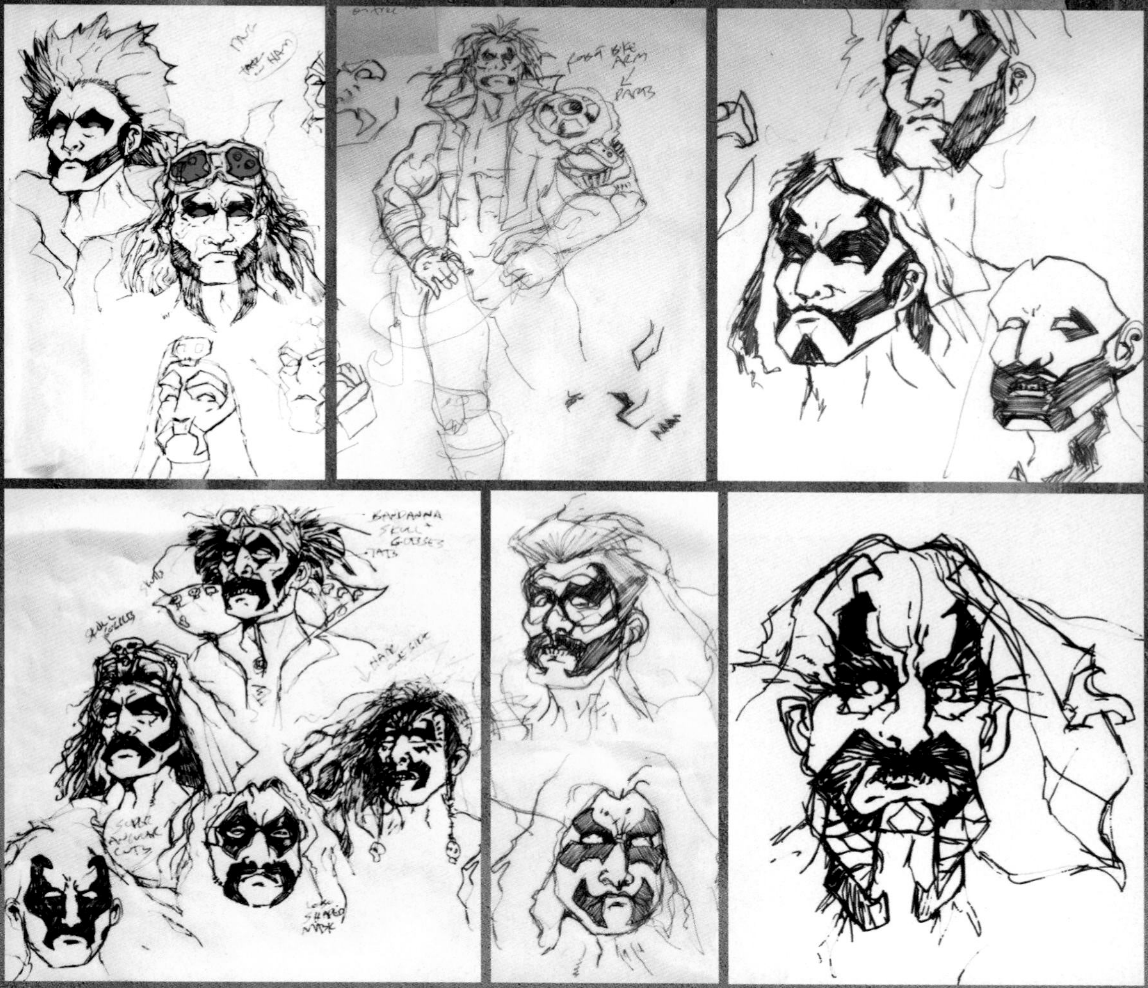

THE WEIRD GOES PRO

LUTHOR concept sketches by BRIAN CHING

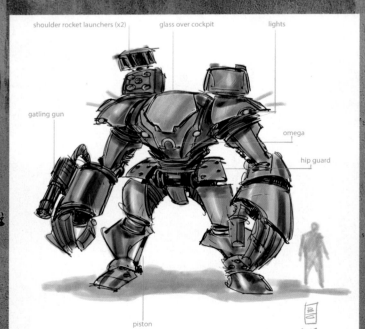

shoulder rocket launchers (x2) glass over cockpit lights

gatling gun

omega

hip guard

piston

2017

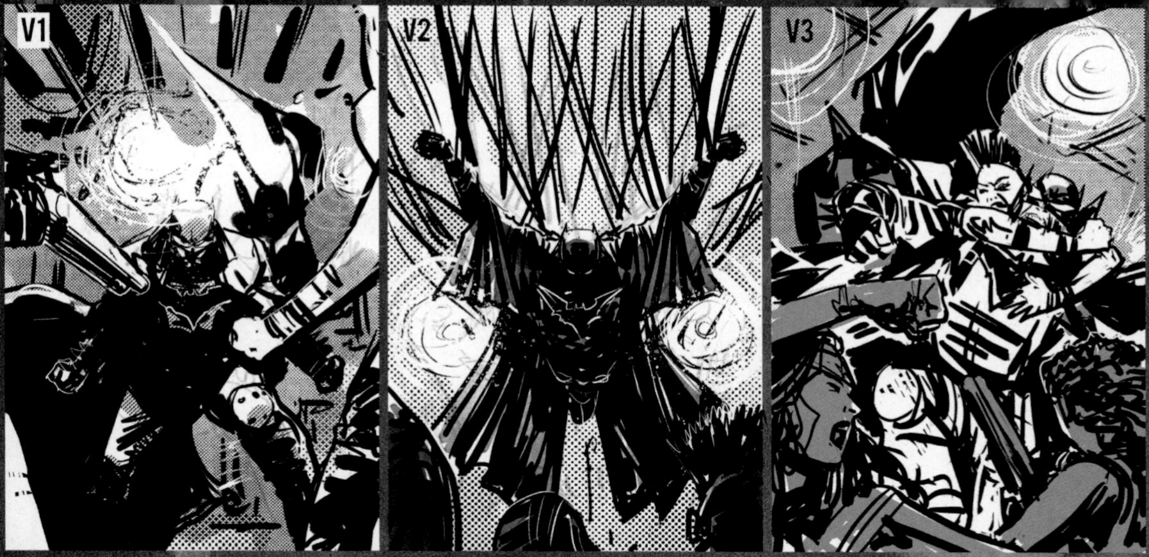
V1
V2
V3

GOTHAM CITY GARAGE #8 cover sketches by TULA LOTAY

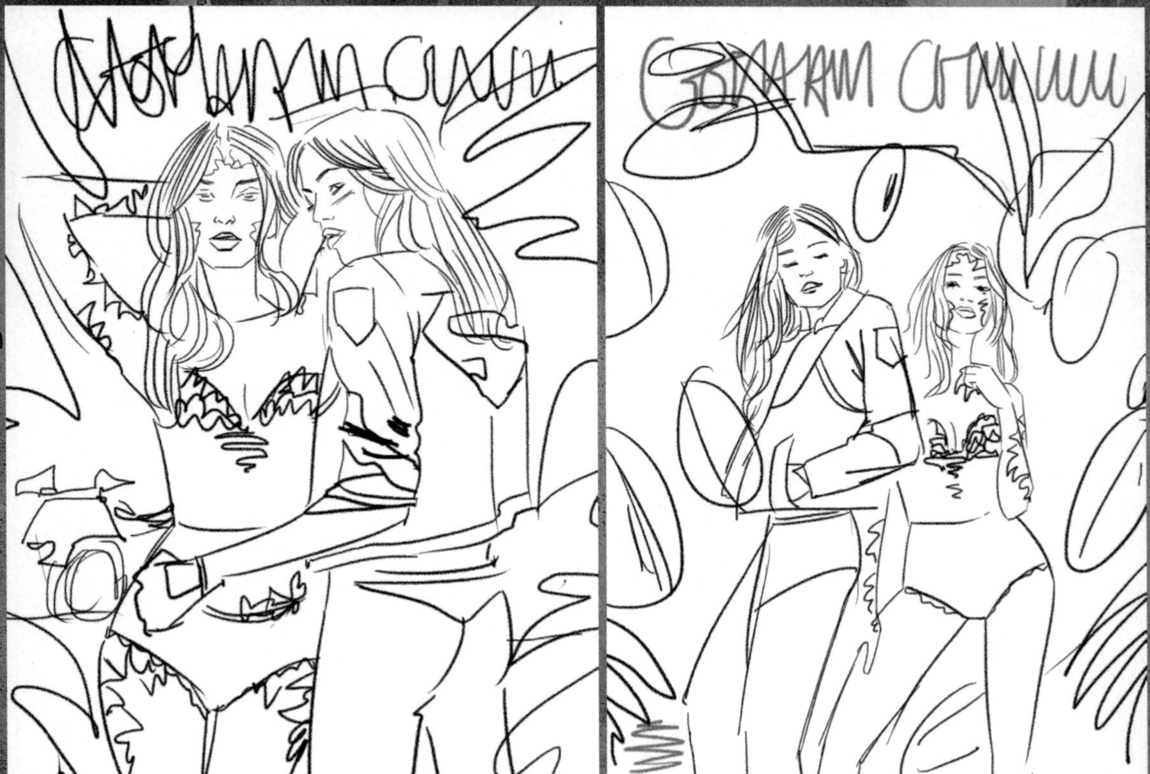

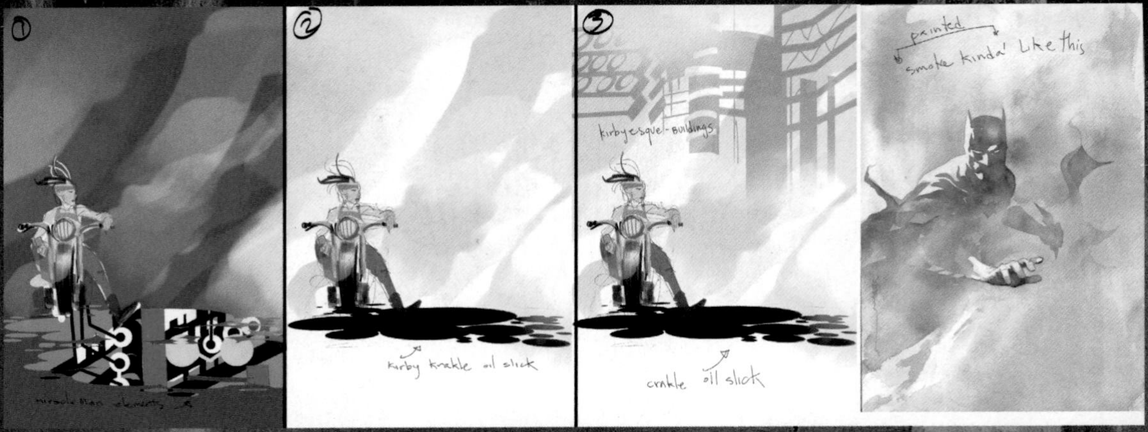
kirby knakle oil slick
kirbyesque - buildings
crnkle oil slick
painted
smoke kinda' like this

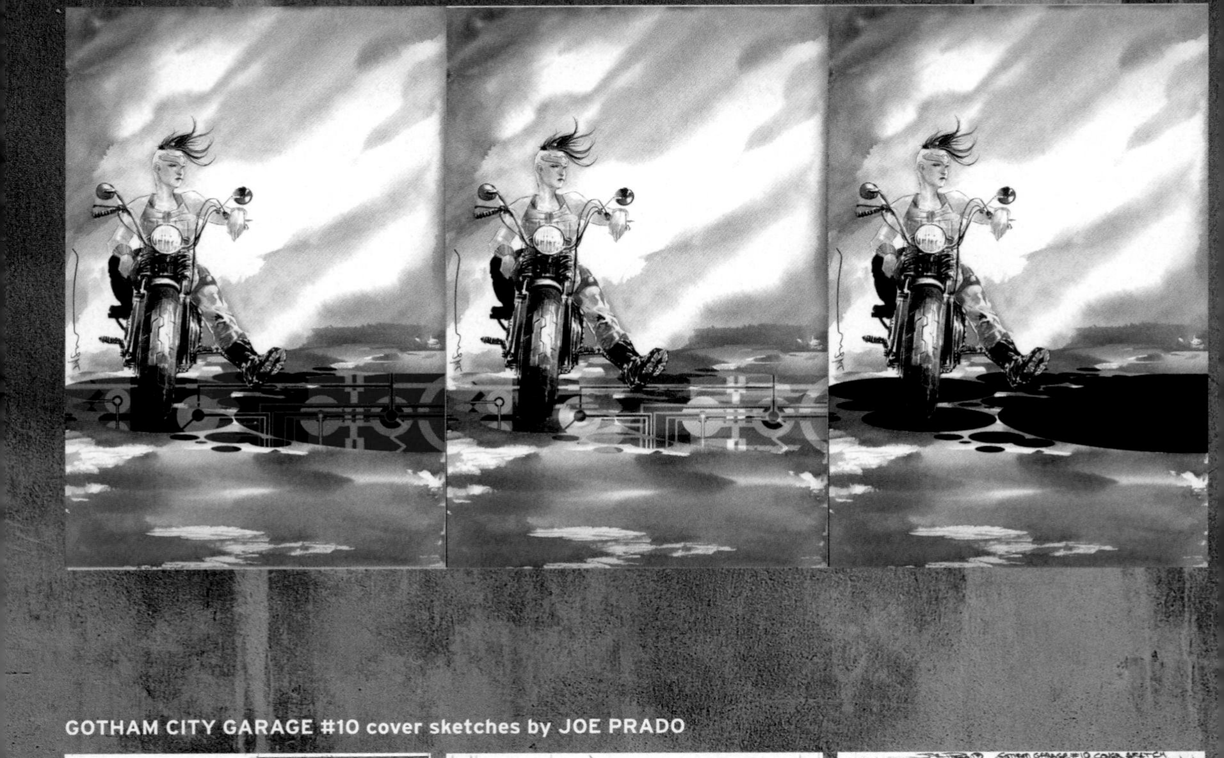

GOTHAM CITY GARAGE #10 cover sketches by JOE PRADO

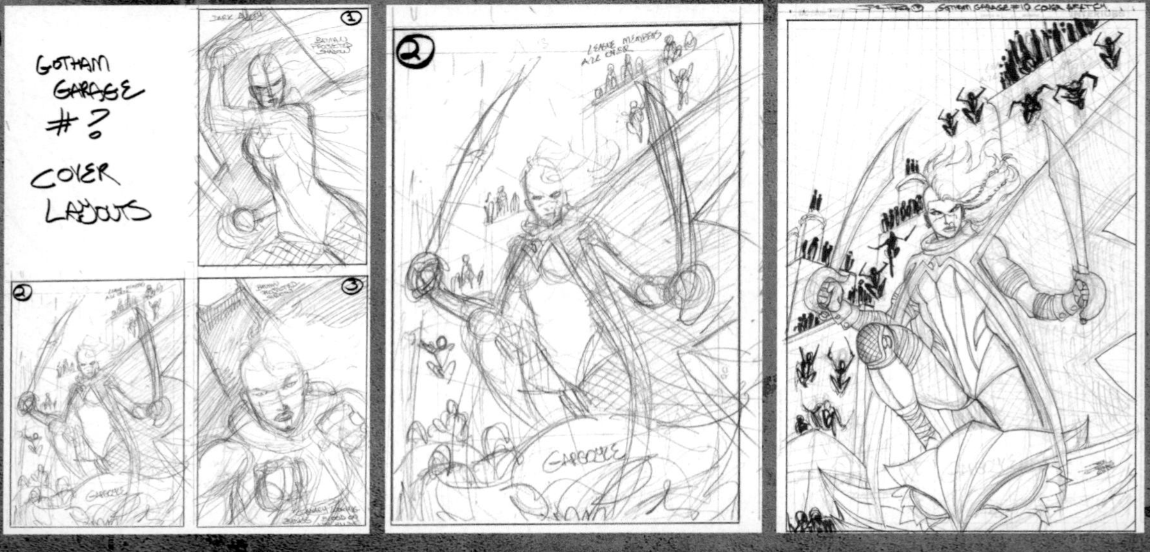
GOTHAM
GARAGE
#?
COVER
LAYOUTS
GARGOYLE

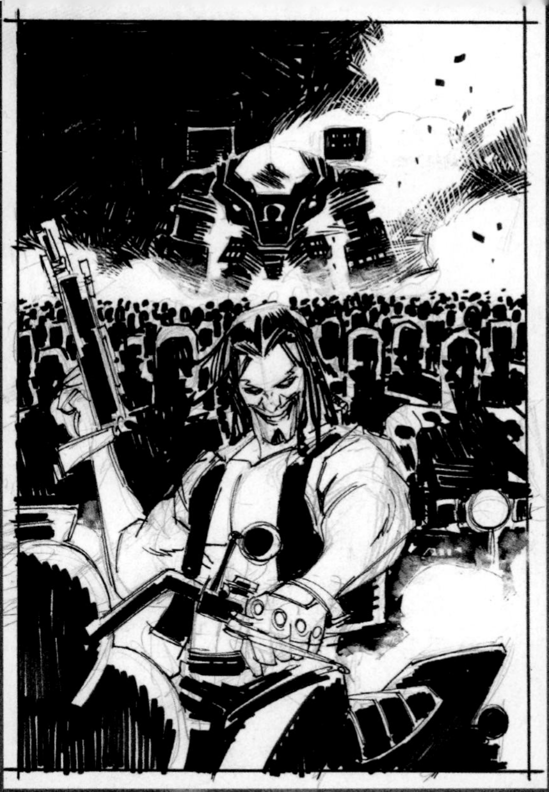

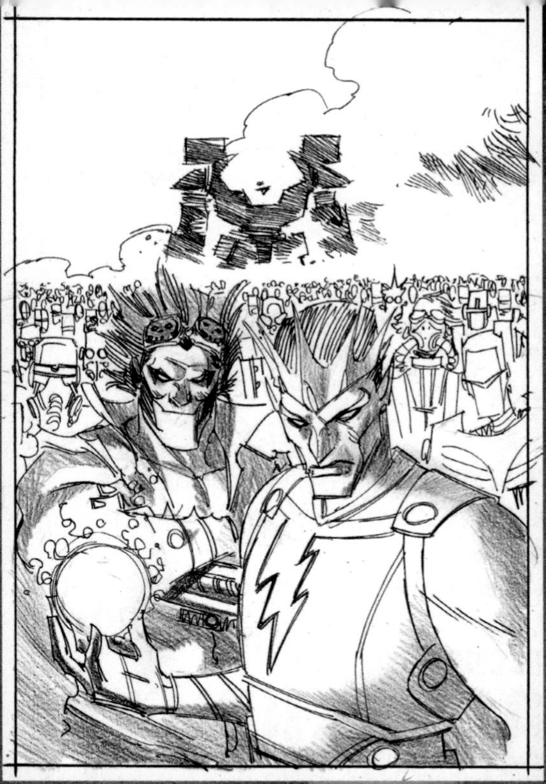

GOTHAM CITY GARAGE #12 cover sketch by DOUG MAHNKE

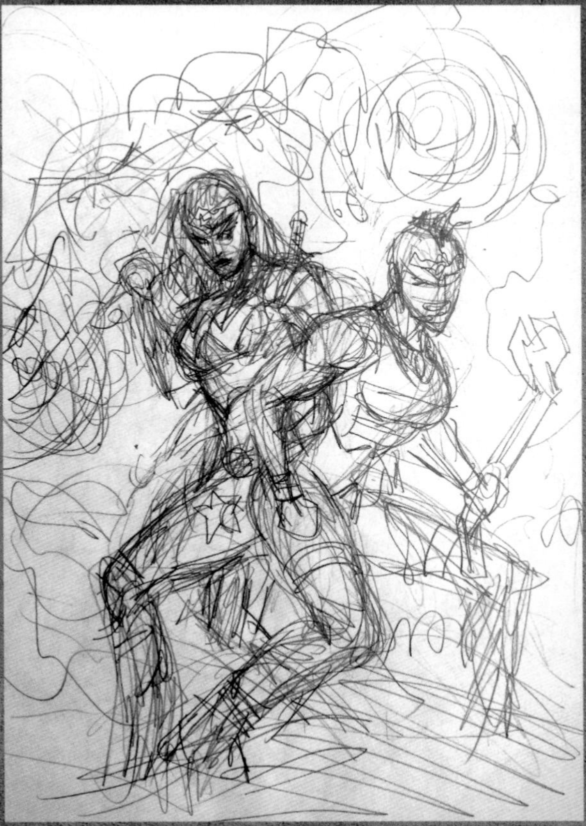

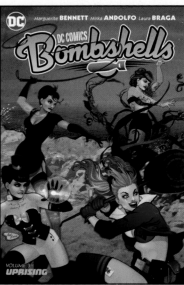